Shakespeare's Wordcraft

Shakespeare's Wordcraft

BY SCOTT KAISER

Limelight Editions
An Imprint of Hal Leonard Corporation
New York

Published in 2007 by
Limelight Editions (an imprint of Hal Leonard Corporation)
19 West 21st Street, New York, NY 10010

Printed in the United States of America

Book design by Kristina Rolander

Library of Congress Cataloging-in-Publication Data is available upon request.

ISBN 10: 0-87910-345-0

ISBN 13: 978-087910-345-3

www.limelighteditions.com

FOR RACHEL —

My life, my joy, my food, my all the world!   JN 3.4.104

Contents

Acknowledgments

First and foremost, I must thank my wife, Cathy, whose contributions to the book you now hold in your hands would be impossible to catalogue, except to say that without her, your hands, and my life, would be quite, quite empty.

I must express my deep gratitude to Barry Kraft, dramaturg, actor, and self-appointed gadfly, not only for his invaluable feedback on the manuscript, but also for sharing his googlesque knowledge of Shakespeare so generously with me — playing Heckle to my Jekyll through many years of spirited collaboration at the Oregon Shakespeare Festival.

I must convey my heartfelt appreciation to Kenneth Washington, director of company development at the Guthrie Theater, for unparalleled opportunities to teach "the best of the best" at *A Guthrie Experience for Actors in Training* — opportunities that have been vital to the development of my ideas on the training of young actors.

I must extend my sincere thanks to the many other beneficent individuals who gave their time and talents to this endeavor: John Sipes, theater director and movement coach extraordinaire, of Denison University, for his unwavering support, collaboration, and fellowship; the brilliant actress Elizabeth Norment, for her enthusiastic response to an early draft; Alan Armstrong, director of the Center for Shakespeare Studies at Southern Oregon University, for his insightful feedback on the manuscript; the team at Limelight Editions, namely, Carol Flannery, Gail Siragusa, Kristina Rolander, and Caroline Howell, for skillfully shepherding this book into print and into the marketplace; Stephany Evans of Imprint Agency, for her know-how, know-who, and know-why, as well as the tremendous pleasure it gives me whenever I utter the words "my agent"; Stevie Kallos for her understanding, advice, and inspiration; Nancy Lane, for introducing me to figures of speech at the University of Washington in Seattle; Paul Nicholson, executive director of the Oregon Shakespeare Festival, for his advocacy; Jenny Graham, staff photographer at the Oregon Shakespeare Festival, for making me look highly respectable in two dimensions; the actors at the Oregon Shakespeare Festival, past and present, for all they have taught me about the art of acting; and the students of the Guthrie Experience for Actors in Training, past and present, for all they have taught me about the art of teaching.

Finally, but certainly not least of all, I must humbly acknowledge the sizable debt I owe to the thinking and writing of the scholars and wordsmiths—both living and departed—upon whose shoulders I stand. Their names and works are extensively detailed in the bibliography of this book.

Key to Abbreviations

SHAKESPEARE'S PLAYS

All's Well That Ends Well	AWW	The Merry Wives of Windsor	WIV
Antony and Cleopatra	ANT	A Midsummer Night's Dream	MND
As You Like It	AYL	Much Ado About Nothing	ADO
The Comedy of Errors	ERR	Othello	OTH
Coriolanus	COR	Pericles	PER
Cymbeline	CYM	Romeo and Juliet	ROM
Hamlet	HAM	The Taming of the Shrew	SHR
Julius Caesar	JC	The Tempest	TMP
King Henry the Fourth, Part One	1H4	Timon of Athens	TIM
King Henry the Fourth, Part Two	2H4	Titus Andronicus	TIT
King Henry the Fifth	H5	Troilus and Cressida	TRO
King Henry the Sixth, Part One	1H6	Twelfth Night	TN
King Henry the Sixth, Part Two	2H6	The Two Gentlemen of Verona	TGV
King Henry the Sixth, Part Three	3H6	The Two Noble Kinsmen	TNK
King Henry the Eighth	H8	The Winter's Tale	WT
King John	JN		
King Lear	LR		
King Richard the Second	R2	**OTHER ABBREVIATIONS**	
King Richard the Third	R3		
Love's Labor's Lost	LLL	F = Folio	
Macbeth	MAC	Q = Quarto	
Measure for Measure	MM	pr = Prologue	
The Merchant of Venice	MV	ep = Epilogue	

A Note About Act, Scene, and Line Numbers

The letters and numbers that follow every Shakespearean example in this book are provided to guide you to the exact location of the quote in Shakespeare's canon. So, for example, the line below would be found in *King Lear* at act 5, scene 1, line 20:

> ALBANY: Our very loving sister, well bemet.   LR 5.1.20

And this line would be found in *Much Ado About Nothing* at act 4, scene 1, line 78:

> HERO: What kind of catechizing call you this?   ADO 4.1.78

These numbers are keyed to *The Riverside Shakespeare*, edited by G. Blakemore Evans, in both the first edition (1974) and second edition (1997). If you're using either of these editions, the act, scene, and line numbers will give you the precise longitude and latitude of the quote in your complete works.

Most other editions of Shakespeare, however, employ the same traditional system, and in the vast majority of cases the coordinates provided should get you within two or three lines of where you need to be.

At times these numbers may be followed by an (F) symbol, which means that the quote appears as printed in the First Folio of 1623, and may vary significantly in some editions, such as with this line:

> KING RICHARD: Cry woe, destruction, ruin, loss, decay:
> The worst is death, and death will have his day.   R2 3.2.102 (F)

Sometimes a (Q) symbol will follow, which means that the quote appears as printed in a quarto version of the play. This version of Lear's mournful cry over the dead Cordelia, for example, comes from the first quarto of *King Lear* (1608):

> LEAR: Howl, howl, howl, howl! O you are men of stones!   LR 5.3.258 (Q1)

The second quarto of *Hamlet* (1604/5) is the source of this version of Hamlet's graveside challenge to Laertes:

> HAMLET: 'Swounds, show me what thou't do.   HAM 5.1.274 (Q2)

The Shakespearean quotes themselves are based upon production scripts edited and performed at the Oregon Shakespeare Festival in Ashland over the last two decades, and represent the collective work of a large number of highly accomplished and superlatively talented actors, directors, dramaturges, and voice and text directors.

Prologue

"That's an epizeuxis," I said to a young actress one day in rehearsal.

"A what?" she sputtered, taken aback.

"An epizeuxis," I reiterated quietly.

"Gesundheit," she replied, deftly mocking me.

"No, seriously," I insisted. "It's an epizeuxis."

"Okay," she said, stiffening her spine in anticipation of a boring lecture. "So, what the hell's an epi-what-zis?"

"It's a repetition of a word with no other words in between," I explained. "So when Juliet says, 'Sweet, sweet, sweet nurse'—when she repeats the word 'sweet' three times—it's a figure of speech—an epizeuxis."

"Oh…that's cool," said the actress, clearly surprised that there was a name for such a thing. "Why didn't you just say so in the first place?"

That exchange stuck with me for quite some time. Why *didn't* I just say so in the first place?

Talking about language devices in Shakespeare's plays—which is what I do for a living—has become more and more challenging with every passing year, especially when talking with young people.

It should come as no great surprise to anyone interested in language, that, despite the increasing popularity of Shakespeare these days, it is the *image*, not the word, that now dominates our youth culture.

The generation that grew up huddled around the radio, listening to the speeches of FDR, the routines of Jack Benny, and the lyrics of Ira Gershwin, is slipping into twilight, and the generation now rising spends its time scrutinizing digital images displayed on iPods, Xboxes, cell-phones, Game Boys, laptops, digital cameras, and personal DVD players.

Because of this, the ability of young people to absorb and interpret complex *visual* information grows stronger with every new technological innovation, while their ability to read, write, hear, and speak complex language, like Shakespeare's, continues to atrophy.

No wonder, then, that the average teen can tell you with great ease what kind of shot a film director is using to tell a story—a close-up, a wide shot, a dolly shot, a zoom, a split screen—but is struck dumb when you ask about the verbal techniques Shakespeare uses to tell his stories—like Juliet's sweet epizeuxis.

One can hardly blame young people for this utter lack of sophistication about language devices. After all, the subject simply isn't being taught in their schools. True, students are commonly introduced to a few fundamental devices—like simile, metaphor, and antithesis. But, beyond that, the teaching of verbal techniques, including the hundreds of rhetorical figures used by Shakespeare, has become a rarity.

To make matters worse, when these devices are actually taught, as in, say, a graduate course in English, they are explained by scholars in a manner that is nearly impenetrable, using arcane Latin terms—like synathroesmus, bdelygma, and polyptoton—so difficult to remember, and so impossible to pronounce, that even experts flounder when grappling with them.

But the biggest reason that young people are "totally clueless" about these language devices has almost nothing to do with what goes on inside the classroom.

Rather, it is because—*outside* the classroom—young people are immersed in a culture so obsessed with the image, and so infatuated with image technology, that it no longer values these devices. In fact, it disdains them, disparages them, even *despises* them.

For we live in an era when a well-chosen word is met with suspicion, a well-crafted phrase is regarded with contempt, and a well-spoken person is slandered with pretentiousness and elitism.

We live in an era when the very word *rhetoric*—the art of using language to persuade or influence others—has become a toxic term, signifying speech that is empty, inflated, deceitful, insincere, artificial, and extravagant. And those who use rhetoric are eternally damned as fakes, cheats, liars, swindlers, scoundrels, imposters, hypocrites, and grandstanders.

Never mind that when Patrick Henry vowed, "Give me liberty or give me death," he was using rhetoric.

Never mind that when Abraham Lincoln pledged: "That government of the people, by the people, and for the people shall not perish from the earth," he was using rhetoric.

Never mind that when FDR warned, "The only thing we have to fear is fear itself," he was using rhetoric.

Never mind that when JFK urged, "Ask not what your country can do for you, ask what you can do for your country," he was using rhetoric.

Never mind that when MLK affirmed, "I have a dream today," he was using rhetoric.

Never mind that, for hundreds of years, the art of rhetoric has shaped the history of this country, creating from mere breath the irresistible force that moved America forward toward greater freedom and enlightenment.

Nowadays, rhetoric is bad, plain speech, good.

Compare this to what Shakespeare encountered as a young boy, sitting in a classroom in Stratford, wrestling with the figures of rhetoric.

For in Elizabethan England, every schoolboy learned by heart the ancient principles of rhetoric formulated by the Greek masters—by Plato and Aristotle—through endless repetition of the figures in Latin and English.

It was a time of great interest in the art of rhetoric—a "golden age" in which numerous books were published outlining the body of rules governing eloquent expression, including the great classic, Henry Peacham's *The Garden of Eloquence*.

It was time when the printed word was exploding, the spoken word was revered, the eloquent speaker was venerated, and the theater was a vital source of entertainment.

And because of this, Shakespeare, upon arriving in London as a young man, had the superb language skills he needed to begin his career as a playwright—not to mention the extreme good fortune to arrive at a time when conditions smiled upon his particular brand of genius.

The result: the creation of 38 plays, 154 sonnets, and 2 narrative poems so imaginative, so innovative, so brilliantly *crafted,* that even now, nearly four hundred years after the Bard laid down his quill, no one has been able to match his achievement.

That's why Shakespeare, like no other writer in the English language, has become a constant presence in our lives, surrounding us every day in the form of words, phrases, expressions, images, ideas, speeches, characters, so familiar to us, so ubiquitous, that we often take them for granted.

But here's the rub: even while we deify the man as an unsurpassed genius, we have ignored, or worse, *forgotten*—because of our cultural prejudices against language devices and wordplay—that a large portion of that genius was his masterful use of rhetoric.

We have forgotten that when Hamlet says, "I must be cruel only to be kind," he is using a figure of rhetoric.

We have forgotten that when King Richard cries, "A horse! A horse! My kingdom for a horse!" he is using a figure of rhetoric.

We have forgotten that when King Henry urges, "Once more unto the breach, dear friends, once more!" he is using a figure of rhetoric.

We have forgotten that when Antony pleads, "Friends, Romans, countrymen, lend me your ears!" he is using a figure of rhetoric.

We have forgotten that when the Othello muses, "Put out the light, and then put out the light," he is using a figure of rhetoric.

For we have lost our primal connection to these rhetorical devices in our daily lives, just as we have lost our primal connection to the stars in the night sky.

And this makes our perception of Shakespeare's words — the ability to read, speak, listen to, comprehend, and appreciate them — hazy.

It's as if we're in a big city, looking skyward, knowing that multitudes of stunningly beautiful constellations illuminate our world, yet we, poor fools, because our electric lights obscure the magnificence of the cosmos, can only pick out the Big Dipper and Orion's belt.

This, then, is the aim of the book you hold in your hands: to take the reader well away from the glaring lights of the city, to a hilltop, on a clear moonless night, where the stellar patterns of Shakespeare's language can be seen for their exquisite beauty, appreciated for their power to ignite the imagination, and revered for their ability to tell stories.

In making this excursion, every attempt will be made to "just say so in the first place." That is to say, you will not be asked to master arcane terminology, nor remember unpronounceable names, nor grapple with complex definitions.

Rather, you will be asked to see *patterns*, and to recognize that these patterns were not accidental or coincidental, but designed and crafted by a master of the word.

For a study of Shakespeare's wordcraft, like an appreciation of music, is not, ultimately, about definitions and terms. It's about *patterns* — audible, discernable, memorable patterns that enter the ear and mix in the brain, giving meaning to the sounds and pleasure to the listener.

For this reason, the book is organized around nine basic patterns that will help the reader make sense of the dizzying array of devices that Shakespeare liked to employ.

Each chapter explores one of these nine patterns in depth, beginning with a general explanation of the qualities of the pattern, then introducing, in a logical progression, the various devices that follow that particular pattern. Each of these devices is briefly explained — sometimes using modern quotations as models — then illuminated by many examples of Shakespeare's use of the device in context. At times, for the sake of clarity, the examples are further divided into sub-categories, such as prose and verse, or soliloquy and dialogue.

It's important to understand that, although every effort has been made to present "pure" examples of each device, the patterns often defy attempts to place them into neatly arranged boxes. For Shakespeare often blends them, weaves them together, in much the same way

Beethoven and Mozart weave musical figures together to make symphonies. Because of this, many examples will contain more devices than the one being explained.

It's also important to understand that, although there are thousands of examples presented in these pages, the book is by no means a complete and unabridged presentation of Shakespeare's use of these devices, but rather a carefully selected and ordered sampling of them.

But now, the city is miles away, the moon is down, the clouds have vanished, and the night sky is breathtakingly clear.

To our hilltop!

And whether you're a young actress grappling with Juliet's verse, a student, a teacher, a director, a coach, a lover of Shakespeare, or a lover of all English literature, chances are you'll be amazed at what you discover. For all these wonders are visible to the naked eye once you've learned to see the patterns. And once you see and understand the patterns, you'll be on your way to better writing, better speaking, better reading, and better listening.

Shakespeare's Wordcraft

CHAPTER I

Words

If words are the building blocks of language, most writers are content to arrange the blocks neatly into phrases and sentences to build books and plays. Not Shakespeare. Rather than play nicely with the set of blocks he's given, he *changes* the blocks themselves—gluing on bits, slicing off chunks, and nailing them together in clever and imaginative ways.

PREFIXES
An addition to the beginning of a word.

Our modern lives are filled with rapid innovation and change, and our words must evolve to keep up with the times. One of the most common ways an existing word can be transformed into something ultra-current, something mega-trendy, something thermo-fashionable, is by adding a prefix to the beginning of an ordinary workaday word. Here are some nouveau-millennial words that were formed in this manner:

bi-coastal	bio-diversity	cyber-porn
e-book	eco-terrorism	Euro-pop
Franken-food	heli-skiing	hyper-drive
info-mercial	Mc-Mansion	metro-sexual

mega-mall	micro-brewery	multi-task
nano-technology	out-source	post-feminism
pre-loaded	re-boot	spokes-model
super-size	techno-babble	tele-commute

Four hundred years ago, Shakespeare used the exact same method of adding a prefix to existing words to coin new words. Just how many neo-words did he invent in this manner? Though some scholars like to suggest numbers, it's impossible to know. What we *do* know is that Shakespeare had an insatiable appetite for new words, relentlessly devising them for specific characters, in specific situations, in specific plays—expressive words, delicious words, gnarly words, words that he used once and never used again. Most of these words, like the ones below, never caught on with the general public:

"BE-"

ALBANY: Our very loving sister, well **bemet**. LR 5.1.20

QUEEN MARGARET: The worm of conscience still **begnaw** thy soul. R3 1.3.221

BASTARD: Zounds! I was never so **bethump'd** with words
Since I first call'd my brother's father Dad. JN 2.1.466

PROSPERO: By whose aid,
Weak masters though ye be, I have **bedimm'd**
The noontide sun TMP 5.1.41

"DIS-"

ENOBARBUS: The pois'nous damp of night **disponge** upon me ANT 4.9.13

GLOUCESTER: The presence of a king engenders love
Amongst his subjects and his loyal friends,
As it **disanimates** his enemies. 1H6 3.1.182

GONERIL: Be then desir'd
By her, that else will take the thing she begs,
A little to **disquantity** your train

LR 1.4.249

ANTONY: All come to this? The hearts
That spaniel'd me at heels, to whom I gave
Their wishes, do **discandy**, melt their sweets
On blossoming Caesar

ANT 4.12.22

"EN-"

ULYSSES: That were to **enlard** his fat-already pride

TRO 2.3.195

LUCIO: I hold you as a thing **ensky'd** and sainted
By your renouncement

MM 1.4.34

TITANIA: The female ivy so
Enrings the barky fingers of the elm.

MND 4.1.44

IAGO: So will I turn her virtue into pitch,
And out of her own goodness make the net
That shall **enmesh** them all.

OTH 2.3.362

CASSIO: Hail to thee, lady! And the grace of heaven
Before, behind thee, and on every hand,
Enwheel thee round!

OTH 2.1.87

"IM-"

KING HENRY: And never yet did insurrection want
Such water-colors to **impaint** his cause

1H4 5.1.80

POINS: And, sirrah, I have cases of buckram for the nonce, to **immask**
our noted outward garments.

1H4 1.2.180

❧ ❧ ❧

CLEOPATRA: Say, good Caesar,
That I some lady trifles have reserv'd,
Immoment toys, things of such dignity
As we greet modern friends withal   ANT 5.2.166

KING HENRY: Ay, marry, uncle, for I always thought
It was both impious and unnatural
That such **immanity** and bloody strife
Should reign among professors of one faith.   1H6 5.1.13

"IN-"

EXETER: Suffolk first died; and York, all haggled over,
Comes to him, where in gore he lay **insteep'd**   H5 4.6.12

TROILUS: When I do tell thee there my hopes lie drown'd,
Reply not in how many fathoms deep
They lie **indrench'd**.   TRO 1.1.51

MACBETH: Will all great Neptune's ocean wash this blood
Clean from my hand? No, this my hand will rather
The multitudinous seas **incarnadine**,
Making the green one red.   MAC 2.2.59

MENENIUS: 'Tis Aufidius,
Who, hearing of our Martius' banishment,
Thrusts forth his horns again into the world,
Which were **inshell'd** when Martius stood for Rome,
And durst not once peep out.   COR 4.6.45

"MIS-"

SHYLOCK: You call me **misbeliever**, cutthroat dog   MV 1.3.111

ROMEO: Then "banishèd"
Is death **misterm'd**.   ROM 3.3.21

CLIFFORD: And, now I fall, thy tough commixture melts,
Impairing Henry, strength'ning **misproud** York.

3H6 2.6.7

CAPULET: This dagger hath mista'en, for lo, his house
Is empty on the back of Montague,
And it **mis-sheathèd** in my daughter's bosom!

ROM 5.3.205 (Q2)

KING HENRY: But thou dost in thy passages of life
Make me believe that thou art only mark'd
For the hot vengeance and the rod of heaven
To punish my **mistreadings**.

1H4 3.2.11

"O'ER-"

QUEEN: I doubt it is no other but the main,
His father's death and our **o'erhasty** marriage.

HAM 2.2.56 (F)

HAMLET: O, I die, Horatio!
The potent poison quite **o'ercrows** my spirit.

HAM 5.2.353

ARIEL: At last I left them
I' th' filthy-mantled pool beyond your cell,
There dancing up to the chins, that the foul lake
O'erstunk their feet.

TMP 4.1.184

"PRE-"

ARMADO: Arts-man, **preambulate**.

LLL 5.1.81

DUKE: He is your husband on a **pre-contract**

MM 4.1.71

LEONTES: That false villain
Whom I employ'd was **pre-employ'd** by him.

WT 2.1.49

MORTON: It was your **presurmise**
That in the dole of blows your son might drop.

2H4 1.1.168

BENEDICK: God keep your ladyship still in that mind! So some gentleman
or other shall scape a **predestinate** scratched face.

ADO 1.1.134

"RE-"

PERICLES: Will you deliver
How this dead queen **re-lives**?

PER 5.3.64

KING EDWARD: Once more we sit in England's royal throne
Repurchas'd with the blood of enemies.

3H6 5.7.2

WARWICK: I will revenge his wrongs to Lady Bona
And **replant** Henry in his former state.

3H6 3.3.198

COMINIUS: Then straight his doubled spirit
Requicken'd what in flesh was fatigate,
And to the battle came he

COR 2.2.117

OTHELLO: But once put out thy light,
Thou cunning'st pattern of excelling nature,
I know not where is that Promethean heat
That can thy light **relume**.

OTH 5.2.13

"UN-"

SEBASTIAN: I have no hope
That he's **undrown'd**.

TMP 2.1.239

POSTHUMUS: I thought her
As chaste as **unsunn'd** snow

CYM 2.5.13

GAUNT: Though Richard my life's counsel would not hear,
My death's sad tale may yet **undeaf** his ear.

R2 2.1.16

SCROOP: Again **uncurse** their souls. Their peace is made
With heads and not with hands.

R2 3.2.137

IRAS: Go to him, madam, speak to him.
He's **unqualitied** with very shame.

ANT 3.11.44

KING RICHARD: Let me **unkiss** the oath 'twixt thee and me —
And yet not so, for with a kiss 'twas made.

R2 5.1.74

KING HENRY: And some are yet **ungotten** and unborn
That shall have cause to curse the Dauphin's scorn.

H5 1.2.287

KING HENRY: Why, now thou hast **unwish'd** five thousand men,
Which likes me better than to wish us one.

H5 4.3.76

CLEOPATRA: Hence,
Horrible villain, or I'll spurn thine eyes
Like balls before me! I'll **unhair** thy head!

ANT 2.5.64

LADY MACBETH: Come, you spirits
That tend on mortal thoughts, **unsex** me here,
And fill me, from the crown to the toe, top-full
Of direst cruelty!

MAC 1.5.41

PERICLES: Till she be marry'd, madam,
By bright Diana, whom we honor, all
Unscissor'd shall this hair of mine remain,
Though I show ill in't.

PER 3.3.29

"UNDER-"

IACHIMO: The flame o' the taper
Bows toward her, and would **underpeep** her lids
To see th' enclosèd lights

CYM 2.2.20

AGAMEMNON: And you shall not sin
If you should say we think him overproud
And **underhonest**

TRO 2.3.124

❧ ❧ ❧

"UP-"

BRUTUS: But when he once attains the **upmost** round
He then unto the ladder turns his back

JC 2.1.24

FRIAR LAURENCE: Therefore thy earliness doth me assure
Thou art **uprous'd** with some distemperature

ROM 2.3.40

ARIEL: The King's son, Ferdinand,
With hair **upstaring** — then like reeds, not hair —
Was the first that leapt

TMP 1.2.213

LANCASTER: You have ta'en up,
Under the counterfeited zeal of God,
The subjects of his substitute, my father,
And both against the peace of heav'n and him,
Have here **upswarm'd** them.

2H4 4.2.30

SUFFIXES
An addition to the end of a word.

Another common way existing words can be transformed into new words in our change-aholic age is by adding a suffix to end of a familiar household word. Here are some words — voguified, tonyesque, fabulicious words — that were formed in this manner:

aquacise	Bushism	Californication
downsize	emoticon	factoid
Monicagate	paperless	profiling
Reaganomics	schlock-meister	shopaholic
sizeist	slacker	smiley
spammer	spyware	usability
waitron	youthism	

So too, in the Age of Elizabeth, Shakespeare added suffixes to words in precisely the same fashion, creating one-of-a-kind wordances for his characters to utter on the stage. This is witnessable in each of the examples below, where a suffixized word was used once, and only once, in a play by Shakespeare:

"-ABLE"

CORIN: Those that are good manners at the court are as ridiculous in the country as the behavior of the country is **mockable** at the court.

AYL 3.2.48

TIMON: You are not **oathable**,
Although I know you'll swear — terribly swear
Into strong shudders and to heavenly agues —
Th' immortal gods that hear you.

TIM 4.3.136

ANTONIO: She that from Naples
Can have no note, unless the sun were post —
The man i' th' moon's too slow — till new-born chins
Be rough and **razorable**

TMP 2.1.250

FRENCHMAN: It was much like an argument that fell out last night, where each of us fell in praise of our country mistresses, this gentleman at that time vouching — and upon warrant of bloody affirmation — his to be more fair, virtuous, wise, chaste, constant, qualified, and less **attemptable** than any the rarest of our ladies in France.

CYM 1.4.60

"-AGE"

HAMLET: Come on, you hear this fellow in the **cellarage**;
Consent to swear.

HAM 1.5.151 (Q2)

CHORUS: Follow, follow!
Grapple your minds to **sternage** of this navy;
And leave your England

H5 3.pr.18

EXETER: He'll call you to so hot an answer for it,
That caves and womby **vaultages** of France
Shall chide your trespass, and return your mock

H5 2.4.124

TROILUS: As true as steel, as **plantage** to the moon,
As sun to day, as turtle to her mate,
As iron to adamant, as earth to the center

TRO 3.2.177

"-AL"

HOLOFERNES: I abhor such **fanatical** phantasimes, such insociable and
point-device companions, such rackers of orthography

LLL 5.1.18

BEROWNE: Taffeta phrases, silken terms precise,
Three-piled hyperboles, spruce affectation,
Figures **pedantical** — these summer flies have blown me
Full of maggot ostentation.

LLL 5.2.408

"-ANCE"

OTHELLO: What needs this **iterance**, woman? I say thy husband.

OTH 5.2.150

JULIA: Come, answer not, but to it presently!
I am impatient of my **tarriance**.

TGV 2.7.90

PHOEBE: I marvel why I answer'd not again.
But that's all one; **omittance** is no quittance.

AYL 3.5.133

THIRD GENTLEMAN: Come, let's do so,
For every minute is expectancy
Of more **arrivance**.

OTH 2.1.42 (Q1)

ORSINO: But hear me this:
Since you to **non-regardance** cast my faith,
And that I partly know the instrument
That screws me from my true place in your favor,
Live you the marble-breasted tyrant still.

TN 5.1.121

"-ANT"

BASTARD: Here entered Pucelle and her **practisants**.   1H6 3.2.20

CLOTEN: The lines of my body are as well drawn as his; no less young, more strong, not beneath him in fortunes, beyond him in the advantage of the time, above him in birth, alike conversant in general services, and more remarkable in single oppositions. Yet this **imperceiverant** thing loves him in my despite.   CYM 4.1.14

"-ED"

CHORUS: Fire answers fire, and through their paly flames,
Each battle sees the other's **umbered** face.   H5 4.pr.9

BEROWNE: Love's feeling is more soft and sensible
Than are the tender horns of **cockled** snails.   LLL 4.3.335

KING: This ring was mine, and when I gave it Helen
I bade her, if her fortunes ever stood
Necessitied to help, that by this token
I would relieve her.   AWW 5.3.85

ULYSSES: Imagin'd worth
Holds in his blood such swoll'n and hot discourse
That twixt his mental and his active parts
Kingdom'd Achilles in commotion rages
And batters down himself.   TRO 2.3.175

"-ER"

FRIAR LAURENCE: But come, young **waverer**, come, go with me   ROM 2.3.89

IAGO: Come, you are too severe a **moraler**.   OTH 2.3.299

BLUNT: I was not born a **yielder**, thou proud Scot   1H4 5.3.11

SEBASTIAN: You have taken it **wiselier** than I meant you should.   TMP 2.1.21

MARTIUS: Let the first **budger** die the other's slave,
And the gods doom him after!   COR 1.8.5

BRUTUS: Go see this **rumorer** whipp'd. It cannot be
The Volsces dare break with us.   COR 4.6.48

PERICLES: Reverend **appearer**, no;
I threw her overboard with these very arms.   PER 5.3.18

DUKE: Hence we shall see,
If power change purpose, what our **seemers** be.   MM 1.3.54

BURGUNDY: Her vine, the merry **cheerer** of the heart,
Unprunèd dies   H5 5.2.41

"-EST"

WIDOW: But she is arm'd for him, and keeps her guard
In **honestest** defense.   AWW 3.5.74

EDMUND: I should have been that I am, had the **maidenliest** star in the
firmament twinkled on my bastardizing.   LR 1.2.132 (F)

FALSTAFF: Thou hast the most unsavory similes, and art indeed the most
comparative, **rascalliest**, sweet young prince.   1H4 1.2.80

"-IDITY"

ISABELLA: Ay, just; perpetual durance; a restraint,
Though all the world's **vastidity** you had,
To a determin'd scope.   MM 3.1.68

"-IFIED"

MERCUTIO: O, flesh, flesh, how art thou **fishified**!   ROM 2.4.38

"-ING"

BEROWNE: Tush, none but minstrels like of **sonneting**!   LLL 4.3.156

ORSINO: A **baubling** vessel was he captain of   TN 5.1.54

POET: I am thinking what I shall say I have provided for him. It must be a **personating** of himself, a satire against the softness of prosperity, with a discovery of the infinite flatteries that follow youth and opulency.   TIM 5.1.34

ULYSSES: For beauty, wit,
High birth, vigor of bone, desert in service,
Love, friendship, charity, are subjects all
To envious and **calumniating** Time.   TRO 3.3.174

"-ISH"

ANTIPHOLUS OF EPHESUS: My wife is **shrewish** when I keep not hours.   ERR 3.1.2

PAROLLES: That is an advertisement to a proper maid in Florence, one Diana, to take heed of the allurement of one Count Rossillion, a foolish idle boy, but for all that very **ruttish**.   AWW 4.3.216

ROSALIND: At which time would I, being but a **moonish** youth, grieve, be effeminate, changeable, longing and liking, proud, fantastical, apish, shallow, inconstant, full of tears, full of smiles   AYL 3.2.410

LAERTES: Now pile your dust upon the quick and dead,
Till of this flat a mountain you have made
T' o'ertop old Pelion or the **skyish** head
Of blue Olympus.   HAM 5.1.253

IAGO: As he shall smile, Othello shall go mad;
And his **unbookish** jealousy must conster
Poor Cassio's smiles, gestures, and light behaviors
Quite in the wrong.   OTH 4.1.101 (Q1)

QUEEN: In his lawless fit,
Behind the arras hearing something stir,
Whips out his rapier, cries "A rat, a rat,"
And in his **brainish** apprehension kills
The unseen good old man.   HAM 4.1.11 (F)

"-ISM"

PROTEUS: Why, Valentine, what **braggartism** is this?   TGV 2.4.164

"-IST"

MERCUTIO: One, two, and the third in your bosom. The very butcher of a
silk button, a **duellist**, a duellist   ROM 2.4.24

"-ITY"

CASSIO: If my offense be of such mortal kind
That nor my service past, nor present sorrows,
Nor purposed merit in **futurity**
Can ransom me into his love again,
But to know so must be my benefit   OTH 3.4.117

"-IVE"

AGAMEMNON: Why then, you princes,
Do you with cheeks abashed behold our works
And think them shames, which are indeed naught else

But the **protractive** trials of great Jove
To find **persistive** constancy in men?   TRO 1.3.20

"-IZE"

RICHARD: To **royalize** his blood I spilt mine own.   R3 1.3.124 (Q1)

ARMADO: Dost thou **infamonize** me among potentates? Thou shalt die.   LLL 5.2.678

KING RICHARD: Allowing him a breath, a little scene,
To **monarchize**, be fear'd, and kill with looks   R2 3.2.165

LAERTES: To cut his throat i' th' church.
KING: No place indeed should murder **sanctu'rize**.   HAM 4.7.127

"-LESS"

PETRUCHIO: A **combless** cock, so Kate will be my hen.   SHR 2.1.226

MACBETH: Avaunt, and quit my sight! Let the earth hide thee!
Thy bones are **marrowless**, thy blood is cold   MAC 3.4.93

PANDER: Search the market narrowly. Mytilene is full of gallants. We lost
too much money this mart by being too **wenchless**.   PER 4.2.5

CLAUDIO: To be imprison'd in the **viewless** winds
And blown with restless violence round about
The pendant world   MM 3.1.123

PROSPERO: And ye that on the sands with **printless** foot
Do chase the ebbing Neptune, and do fly him
When he comes back   TMP 5.1.34

GLOUCESTER: And had I twenty times so many foes,
And each of them had twenty times their power,

All these could not procure me any scathe,
So long as I am loyal, true, and **crimeless**.

2H6 2.4.63

LEAR: Return with her?
Why the hot-blooded France, that **dowerless** took
Our youngest born — I could as well be brought
To knee his throne and, squirelike, pension beg
To keep base life afoot.

LR 2.4.212

KING HENRY: Had I so lavish of my presence been,
So common-hackney'd in the eyes of men,
So stale and cheap to vulgar company,
Opinion, that did help me to the crown,
Had still kept loyal to possession
And left me in **reputeless** banishment

1H4 3.2.44

"-LY"

LEWIS: Let me wipe off this honorable dew
That **silverly** doth progress on thy cheeks.

JN 4.2.46

DUKE: Canst thou believe thy living is a life,
So **stinkingly** depending? Go mend, go mend.

MM 3.2.27

SECOND SERVINGMAN: And had he been **cannibally** given, he might
have boiled and eaten him too.

COR 4.5.188

THESEUS: It more imports me
Than all the actions that I have forgone,
Or **futurely** can cope.

TNK 1.1.174

SYLVIA: Ay, ay. You writ them sir, at my request,
But I will none of them: they are for you.
I would have had them writ more **movingly**.

TGV 2.1.128

"-MENT"

ARMADO: I wish you the peace of mind, most royal **couplement**!

LLL 5.2.532

OSWALD: And in the **fleshment** of this dread exploit
Drew on me here again.

LR 2.2.123

PRIEST: Yet here she is allow'd her virgin crants,
Her maiden **strewments**, and the bringing home
Of bell and burial.

HAM 5.1.233 (Q2)

WOLSEY: Let it be nois'd
That through our intercession this **revokement**
And pardon comes.

H8 1.2.106

CLOTEN: He on the ground, my speech of **insultment** ended on his dead
body, and when my lust hath dined — which, as I say, to vex her I will execute
in the clothes that she so praised — to the court I'll knock her back, foot her
home again.

CYM 3.5.140

OLIVER: When from the first to last betwixt us two
Tears our **recountments** had most kindly bath'd,
As how I came into that desert place,
In brief, he led me to the gentle Duke

AYL 4.3.140

EGEUS: Thou hast by moonlight at her window sung
With feigning voice verses of feigning love,
And stol'n the impression of her fantasy
With bracelets of thy hair, rings, gauds, conceits,
Knacks, trifles, nosegays, sweetmeats — messengers
Of strong **prevailment** in unhardened youth.

MND 1.1.35

"-NESS"

FIRST SOLDIER: What say you to his **expertness** in war?

AWW 4.3.265

TOUCHSTONE: Well praised be the gods for thy foulness! **Sluttishness**
may come hereafter.

AYL 3.3.41

CLAUDIO: And she will die if he woo her, rather than she will bate one
breath of her accustomed **crossness**.

ADO 2.3.177

POLIXENES: He makes a July's day short as December,
And with his varying **childness** cures in me
Thoughts that would thick my blood.

WT 1.2.170

"-OUS"

SIR TOBY: Am I not **consanguineous**? Am I not of her blood?

TN 2.3.77

ORSINO: Diana's lip
is not more smooth and **rubious**

TN 1.4.32

IMOGEN: Thou,
Conspir'd with that **irregulous** devil, Cloten,
Hath here cut off my lord.

CYM 4.2.315

"-RIST"

OSWALD: Some five or six and thirty of his knights,
Hot **questrists** after him, met him at gate

LR 3.7.17

"-RY"

FAIRY: Are not you he
That frights the maidens of the **villagery**?

MND 2.1.35

BANQUO: This guest of summer,
The temple-haunting martlet, does approve
By his lov'd **mansionry** that the heaven's breath
Smells wooingly here.

MAC 1.6.5

"-URE"

HORATIO: Have heav'n and earth together demonstrated
Unto our **climatures** and countrymen.

HAM 1.1.125 (Q2)

PORTIA: Yet I insisted, yet you answer'd not,
But with an angry **wafture** of your hand
Gave sign for me to leave you.

JC 2.1.246

TIMON: The earth's a thief,
That feeds and breeds by a **composture** stol'n
From gen'ral excrement.

TIM 4.3.441

"-Y"

ULYSSES: He is so **plaguy** proud that the death-tokens of it
Cry "No recovery."

TRO 2.3.177

HELENA: What wicked and dissembling glass of mine
Made me compare with Hermia's **sphery** eyne?

MND 2.2.99

LAFEW: No, no, no, your son was misled with a snipped-taffeta fellow there, whose villainous saffron would have made all the unbaked and **doughy** youth of a nation in his color.

AWW 4.5.3

KING HENRY: And other times to see
The **beachy** girdle of the ocean
Too wide for Neptune's hips

2H4 3.1.50

DUKE: A breath thou art,
Servile to all the **skyey** influences

That dost this habitation where thou keepst
Hourly inflict.   MM 3.1.9

FRONT CLIPPING
A subtraction from the beginning of a word.

Sometimes the beginning of a word is lost over time, like the way a "telephone" became a "phone," and a "hamburger" a "burger." Sometimes the beginning of a word is discarded for efficiency, like the way the word "internet" has become the "net," and a "weblog" has become a "blog." Sometimes the beginning of a word is clipped off just to sound cool, like when young people refer to their parents as "'rents," pizza as "'za," the suburbs as the "'burbs," an attitude as a "'tude," a magazine as a "'zine," and a neighborhood as a "'hood."

Shakespeare does all of these things with the words in his dialogue as well. Sometimes he lops off the tip of a word to be brief; sometimes he does it to make a character sound cool; but most often he does it to remove a clunky syllable—to keep the feet of the verse tripping nimbly on the dance floor of the tongue.

POSTHUMUS: **'Lack**, to what end?   CYM 5.3.59
    (alack)

SEBASTIAN: No marrying **'mong** his subjects?   TMP 2.1.166
    (among)

KING RICHARD: After our sentence, **plaining** comes too late.   R2 1.3.175
    (complaining)

CRESSIDA: A woeful Cressid **'mongst** the merry Greeks   TRO 4.4.56
    (amongst)

PORTIA: The quality of mercy is not **strain'd.**   MV 4.1.184
    (constrained)

PORTIA: That **'scuse** serves many men to save their gifts.   MV 4.1.444
    (excuse)

ACHILLES: You know my mind: I'll fight no more **'gainst** Troy.   TRO 3.3.56
    (against)

FLUTE: **'Tide** life, **'tide** death, I come without delay.   MND 5.1.203
    (betide)

TRANIO: Why, sir, what **'cerns** it you if I wear pearl and gold?   SHR 5.1.75
    (concerns)

GRUMIO: Nay, 'tis no matter, sir, what he **'leges** in Latin.   SHR 1.2.28
    (alleges)

HAMLET: O wonderful son that can so **'stonish** a mother!   HAM 3.2.328 (Q2)
    (astonish)

HAMLET: Use every man after his desert, and who should **'scape**
whipping?   HAM 2.2.530
    (escape)

ROSALIND: **'Od's** my little life,
I think she means to tangle my eyes too!   AYL 3.5.43
    (God's)

BOLINGBROKE: Come, lords, away,
To fight with Glendower and his **complices**.   R2 3.1.43
    (accomplices)

CHARLES: I would ne'er have fled,
But that they left me **'midst** my enemies.   1H6 1.2.24
    (amidst)

VIOLA: With the same **'havior** that your passion bears
Goes on my master's griefs.   TN 3.4.206
    (behavior)

MACBETH: If't be so,
For Banquo's issue have I **'filed** my mind   MAC 3.1.64
    (defiled)

MACBETH: I **'gin** to be aweary of the sun
And wish the estate of the world were now undone.   MAC 5.5.48
    (begin)

PROSPERO: And **'twixt** the green sea and the azur'd vault
Set roaring war   TMP 5.1.43
    (betwixt)

ADRIAN: His bold head
'Bove the contentious waves he kept   TMP 2.1.119
    (above)

VOLUMNIA: To his surname "Coriolanus" **'longs** more pride
Than pity to our prayers.   COR 5.3.170
    (belongs)

PUCK: And so far blameless proves my enterprise
That I have **'nointed** an Athenian's eyes   MND 3.2.351
    (anointed)

TITUS: Remaineth naught but to inter our brethren
And with loud **'larums** welcome them to Rome.   TIT 1.1.147
    (alarums)

ANNE: Upon the like devotion as yourselves,
To **'gratulate** the gentle princes there.   R3 4.1.10
    (congratulate)

CAMILLO: **'Shrew** my heart,
You never spoke what did become you less
Than this.   WT 1.2.281
    (beshrew)

OLIVIA: If you mean well,
Now go with me and with this holy man
Into the chantry **by**.   TN 4.3.24
    (nearby)

FIRST MURDERER: Now spurs the **'lated** traveler apace
To gain the timely inn, and near approaches
The subject of our watch.   MAC 3.3.6
    (belated)

PETRUCHIO: Thus in plain terms: your father hath consented
That you shall be my wife, your dowry **'greed** on;
And will you, nill you, I will marry you.

SHR 2.1.270

(agreed)

BAPTISTA: This is the **'pointed** day
That Katherine and Petruchio should be marry'd,
And yet we hear not of our son-in-law.

SHR 3.2.1

(appointed)

ANTIPHOLUS OF EPHESUS: Fear not man, I will not break away.
I'll give thee ere I leave thee so much money
To warrant thee as I am **'rested** for.

ERR 4.4.3

(arrested)

ANTONY: See
How I convey my shame out of thine eyes
By looking back what I have left behind
'Stroyed in dishonor.

ANT 3.11.54

(destroyed)

END CLIPPING
A subtraction from the end of a word.

In modern life — when time presses — even an extra syllable at the end of a word can become a burden that needs to be offloaded. Suss out these modern words that were created by trimming the tail of a longer word:

abs	butt	carbs
celeb	condo	conglom
decaf	def	dis
exam	fax	goth
grunge	gym	improv

klepto	lab	lit
neo-con	nuke	nympho
perp	perv	pre-nup
prof	psycho	quad
rad	retro	suss
typo	veg	

Shakespeare characters, too, will occasionally remod a word by dropping a syllab or two from the back end. Sometimes—as with Gratiano's "ope" and Ajax's "seld"—the characters hope to impress an attent ear with their verbal dexterity. But more often Shakespeare uses this device as a poetic pacemaker—to keep the heartbeat of the verse line pulsing properly.

JULIET: It was the lark, the herald of the **morn**,
No nightingale.   ROM 3.5.6
    (morning)

GRATIANO: I am Sir Oracle,
And when I **ope** my lips, let no dog bark!   MV 1.1.94
    (open)

PETRUCHIO: Good sooth, even thus; therefore **ha'** done with words;
To me she's married, not unto my clothes.   SHR 3.2.116
    (ha' for have)

KING RICHARD: No lord of thine, thou **haught** insulting man,
Nor no man's lord.   R2 4.1.254
    (haughty)

AJAX: If I might in entreaties find success,
As **seld** I have the chance, I would desire
My famous cousin to our Grecian tents.   TRO 4.5.150
    (seldom)

KENT: Thy youngest daughter does not love thee least
Nor are those empty-hearted whose low sounds
Reverb no hollowness.   LR 1.1.154 (F)
>   *(reverberate)*

POLONIUS: You shall do marv'lous wisely, good Reynaldo,
Before you visit him, to make **inquire**
Of his behavior.   HAM 2.1.4 (Q2)
>   *(inquiry)*

HAMLET: Season your admiration for a while
With an **attent** ear till I may deliver,
Upon the witness of these gentlemen,
This marvel to you.   HAM 1.2.193
>   *(attentive)*

COMPOUND WORDS
The addition of two or more words joined together to form a hyphenated compound.

Another way to describe new ideas, or to name new things, in our ever shifting world, is to form a *compound word*—a device that uses a simple hyphen to join two words together in verbal matrimony:

baby-boomer	bodice-ripper	body-piercing
channel-surfing	cherry-pick	dolphin-safe
drive-by	drop-dead	empty-nesters
full-figured	gender-neutral	high-five
hearing-impaired	hot-bunking	house-sitting
jet-ski	kick-start	morning-after
no-fly	oven-ready	physician-assisted

self-gift   spell-check   supply-side

three-strikes   twenty-something   user-friendly

Like a master chief in a gourmet kitchen, Shakespeare liked to cook up tasty *words-du-jour* by combining common ingredients—adjectives, nouns, and verbs— in unique ways. Although he used hundreds of hyphenated compounds in his writing, the *recipes* he used to create them were rather simple. Throw two adjectives into a pot and boil to make a crazy-fresh adjective. Put an adjective and a noun in a frying pan and simmer to get a super-noun. Place a noun and a verb in a baking pan and pepper-roast to get a hot new verb.

All of the word-dishes in the following examples were cooked up—but served only *once*—by Shakespeare in his plays.

ADJECTIVE COMPOUNDS

These hyphenated compounds join two or more words together to function as an *adjective*:

Adjective + Adjective

RICHARD: I am too **childish-foolish** for this world.   R3 1.3.141

BUCKINGHAM: You are too **senseless-obstinate,** my lord   R3 3.1.44

ROMEO: The time and my intents are **savage-wild**   ROM 5.3.37

ARTHUR: Are you more **stubborn-hard** than hammer'd iron?   JN 4.1.67

KING RICHARD: Urge the necessity and state of times,
And be not **peevish-fond** in great designs.   R3 4.4.417 (Q1)

MARSHALL: On pain of death, no person be so bold
Or **daring-hardy** as to touch the lists   R2 1.3.43

TROILUS: With venomous wights she stays
As tediously as hell, but flies the grasps of love
With wings more **momentary-swift** than thought.   TRO 4.2.14

CASSIUS: Now know you, Casca, I have mov'd already
Some certain of the **noblest-minded** Romans
To undergo with me an enterprise
Of **honorable-dangerous** consequence

JC 1.3.124

Noun + Adjective

JULIET: And therefore hath the **wind-swift** Cupid wings.

ROM 2.5.8

BIONDELLO: O, master, master, I have watch'd so long
That I am **dog-weary**

SHR 4.2.60

LADY MACBETH: Why, worthy Thane,
You do unbend your noble strength to think
So **brain-sickly** of things.

MAC 2.2.43

SHYLOCK: The patch is kind enough, but a huge feeder,
Snail-slow in profit, and he sleeps by day
More than the wildcat.

MV 2.5.47

ENOBARBUS: The silken tackle
Swell with the touches of those **flower-soft** hands
That yarely frame the office.

ANT 2.2.210

CHORUS: The poor condemnèd English,
Like sacrifices, by their watchful fires
Sit patiently and inly ruminate
The morning's danger; and their gesture sad,
Investing lank-lean cheeks and **war-worn** coats

H5 4.pr.26

OTHELLO: If after every tempest come such calms,
May the winds blow till they have waken'd death,
And let the laboring bark climb hills of seas,
Olympus-high, and duck again as low
As hell's from heaven!

OTH 2.1.188

❧ ❧ ❧

Adjective + Noun + "ed"

HOTSPUR: What a **frosty-spirited** rogue is this! 1H4 2.3.20

FALSTAFF: Good faith, this same young **sober-blooded** boy doth not love me 2H4 4.3.87

JAQUES: This is the **motley-minded** gentleman that I have so often met in the forest. AYL 5.4.41

JULIET: Gallop apace, you **fiery-footed** steeds,
Towards Phoebus' lodging! ROM 3.2.1

CLEOPATRA: Fulvia perchance is angry, or who knows
If the **scarce-bearded** Caesar have not sent
His powerful mandate to you ANT 1.1.21

QUEEN MARGARET: Now 'tis the spring, and weeds are **shallow-rooted**;
Suffer them now, and they'll o'ergrow the garden
And choke the herbs for want of husbandry. 2H6 3.1.31

Adjective + Verb + "ing"

JULIET: O God, I have an **ill-divining** soul! ROM 3.5.54

KING RICHARD: **High-reaching** Buckingham grows circumspect. R3 4.2.31

YORK: Yea, even my foes will shed **fast-falling** tears
And say, "Alas it was a piteous deed." 3H6 1.4.162

KING RICHARD: That hand shall burn in **never-quenching** fire
That staggers thus my person. R2 5.5.108

Adjective + Verb + "ed"

CHIRON: Come, mistress, now perforce we will enjoy
That **nice-preservèd** honesty of yours. TIT 2.3.135

QUEEN: This way the King will come. This is the way
To Julius Caesar's **ill-erected** tower

R2 5.1.2

FALSTAFF: The brain of this **foolish-compounded** clay, man, is not able
to invent anything that tends to laughter more than I invent or is invented
on me.

2H4 1.2.7

MORTON: But these mine eyes saw him in bloody state
Rend'ring faint quittance, weary'd and outbreath'd,
To Harry Monmouth, whose swift wrath beat down
The **never-daunted** Percy to the earth

2H4 1.1.110

Noun + Verb + "ing"

KING RICHARD: **Tear-falling** pity dwells not in this eye.

R3 4.2.65

VALENTINE: **Home-keeping** youths have ever homely wits.

TGV 1.1.2

CAPULET: At my poor house, look to behold this night
Earth-treading stars that make dark heaven light.

ROM 1.2.25

ROMEO: Do thou but close our hands with holy words,
Then **love-devouring** death do what he dare

ROM 2.6.7

HELENA: Poor lord, is't I
That chase thee from thy country, and expose
Those tender limbs of thine to the event
Of the **none-sparing** war?

AWW 3.2.105

Noun + Verb + "ed"

YORK: Great Duke of Lancaster, I come to thee
From **plume-pluck'd** Richard

R2 4.1.108

IMOGEN: That **drug-damn'd** Italy hath out-craftied him,
And he's at some hard point.   CYM 3.4.15

CHORUS: From forth the fatal loins of these two foes,
A pair of **star-cross'd** lovers take their life   ROM pr.6 (Q2)

BUCKINGHAM: A **care-craz'd** mother to a many sons,
A beauty-waning and distressèd widow   R3 3.7.184 (F)

PRIEST: We should profane the service of the dead
To sing a requiem and such rest to her
As to **peace-parted** souls.   HAM 5.1.238 (Q2)

ROMEO: O here
Will I set up my everlasting rest
And shake the yoke of inauspicious stars
From this **world-wearied** flesh.   ROM 5.3.112

Three-Word Adjectives

The adjectives in these lines were created by joining *three* words together with a hyphen:

PRINCESS: A time methinks too short
To make a **world-without-end** bargain in.   LLL 5.2.788

EGEON: A league from Epidamnum had we sail'd
Before the **always-wind-obeying** deep
Gave any tragic instance of our harm.   ERR 1.1.63

POMPEY: But let us rear
The higher our opinion, that our stirring
Can from the lap of Egypt's widow pluck
The **ne'er-lust-wearied** Antony.   ANT 2.1.38

Four-Word Adjectives

These adjectives were constructed by hyphenating *four* words.

MOWBRAY: A jewel in a **ten-times-barr'd-up** chest
Is a bold spirit in a loyal breast.   R2 1.1.180

TRINCULO: A fish; he smells like a fish; a very ancient and fishlike smell; a kind of **not-of-the-newest** Poor John.   TMP 2.2.27

GONERIL: Your insolent retinue
Do hourly carp and quarrel, breaking forth
In rank and **not-to-be-endurèd** riots.   LR 1.4.204

Five-Word Adjectives
And these, *five* words:

ACHILLES: Tell him I humbly desire the valiant Ajax to invite the most valorous Hector to come unarmed to my tent, and to procure safe-conduct for his person of the magnanimous and most illustrious **six-or-seven-times-honored** Captain-General of the Grecian army, Agamemnon, etcetera.   TRO 3.3.277

NOUN COMPOUNDS
These hyphenated compounds join two or more words together to function as a *noun*.

Noun + Noun

QUEEN MARGARET: Murder is thy **alms-deed**.   3H6 5.5.79

PROSPERO: Sit still, and hear the last of our **sea-sorrow**.   TMP 1.2.170

THERSITES: He's grown a very **land-fish**, languageless, a monster!   TRO 3.3.263

HAMLET: But my **uncle-father** and **aunt-mother** are deceived.   HAM 2.2.376

PORTER: But this place is too cold for hell. I'll **devil-porter** it no further.   MAC 2.3.17

LUCIO: Upon his place,
And with full line of his authority,
Governs Lord Angelo, a man whose blood
Is very **snow-broth**   MM 1.4.58

Adjective + Noun

BEROWNE: Saint George's **half-cheek** in a brooch.   LLL 5.2.616

RODERIGO: What a full fortune does the **thick-lips** owe
If he can carry't thus!   OTH 1.1.66 (Q1)

BORACHIO: Seest thou not, I say, what a deformed thief this fashion is,
how giddily he turns about all the **hot-bloods** between fourteen and five
and thirty   ADO 3.3.132

Verb + Noun

GAUNT: To be a **make-peace** shall become my age.   R2 1.1.160

PUCK: Pretty soul, she durst not lie
Near this **lack-love**, this **kill-courtesy**.   MND 2.2.77

ROSALIND: If you break one jot of your promise, or come one minute
behind your hour, I will think you the most pathetical **break-promise** AYL 4.1.192

Verb + ing + Noun

TOUCHSTONE: I'll rhyme you so eight years together, dinners and suppers
and **sleeping-hours** excepted.   AYL 3.2.97

DEMETRIUS: Why, boy, although our mother, unadvis'd,
Gave you a **dancing-rapier** by your side,
Are you so desperate grown to threat your friends?   TIT 2.1.39

PRINCE HENRY: The life of all his blood
Is touch'd corruptibly, and his pure brain,
Which some suppose the soul's frail **dwelling-house**,
Doth by the idle comments that it makes
Foretell the ending of mortality.   JN 5.7.3

Noun + Verb + "er"

BENEDICK: Well, you are a rare **parrot-teacher**.   ADO 1.1.138
ROSALINE: Thou art an old **love-monger**, and speakest skillfully.   LLL 2.1.254

LEAR: I do not bid the **thunder-bearer** shoot,
Nor tell tales of thee to high-judging Jove.   LR 2.4.227

SALISBURY: O, it grieves my soul
That I must draw this metal from my side
To be a **widow-maker**!   JN 5.2.17

CALIBAN: Do that good mischief which may make this island
Thine own forever, and I, thy Caliban,
For aye thy **foot-licker**.   TMP 4.1.219

Three-Word Nouns
These nouns were fashioned by joining *three* words with a hyphen:

NURSE: Why, lamb, why, lady! Fie, you **slug-a-bed**!   ROM 4.5.2

PRINCE: This sanguine coward, this bed-presser, this **horse-back-breaker**, this huge hill of flesh—   1H4 2.4.241

FALSTAFF: I pressed me none but such **toasts-and-butter**, with hearts in their bellies no bigger than pins' heads, and they have bought out their services.   1H4 4.2.21

OBERON: It fell upon a little western flower,
Before milk-white, now purple with love's wound,
And maidens call it **love-in-idleness**.   MND 2.1.168

VERB COMPOUNDS
These hyphenated compounds join two or more words together to function as a *verb*.

Adjective + Verb

BEROWNE: By heaven, all **dry-beaten** with pure scoff!   LLL 5.2.263

FALSTAFF: Pistol, I will **double-charge** thee with dignities.   2H4 5.3.124

ANTONY: She, Eros, has
Pack'd cards with Caesar, and **false-play'd** my glory
Unto an enemy's triumph.   ANT 4.14.19

DAUPHIN: Our madams mock at us and plainly say
Our mettle is bred out, and they will give
Their bodies to the lust of English youth
To **new-store** France with bastard warriors.   H5 3.5.31

Noun + Verb

ANTIGONUS: Would I knew the villain;
I would **land-damn** him.   WT 2.1.143

FLAVIUS: Ah, when the means is gone that buys this praise
The breath is gone whereof this praise is made.
Feast-won, **fast-lost**.   TIM 2.2.171

ARIEL: Confin'd together
In the same fashion as you gave in charge,
Just as you left them; all pris'ners, sir,
In the lime grove which **weather-fends** your cell.   TMP 5.1.10

HINKY-PINKIES

Shakespeare also employed a few compounds where two words are joined together that rhyme, or nearly rhyme. Usually one or both of the words forming the compound isn't even a word, but pure nonsense. We still hear compounds like this today in terms like "herky-jerky," "hanky-panky," and "loosey-goosey." Each of these hinky-pinkies appear in his plays only once:

SECOND WITCH: When the **hurly-burly**'s done,
When the battle's lost and won.   MAC 1.1.3

HOTSPUR: And such a deal of **skimble-skamble** stuff
As puts me from my faith.   1H4 3.1.152

PAROLLES: He wears his honor in a box unseen,
That hugs his **kicky-wicky** here at home   AWW 2.3.280
    (meaning, a woman)

FESTE: Malvolio, Malvolio, thy wits the heavens restore. Endeavor thyself
to sleep, and leave thy vain **bibble-babble**.   TN 4.2.96

LEAR: See how yond justice rails upon yond simple thief. Hark in thine ear:
change places and, **handy-dandy**, which is the justice, which is the thief?   LR 4.6.153 (F)

FLUELLEN: If you would take the pains but to examine the wars of Pompey
the Great, you shall find, I warrant you, that there is no **tiddle-taddle** nor
pibble-pabble in Pompey's camp.   H5 4.1.70

KING: The people muddy'd,
Thick, and unwholesome in their thoughts and whispers
For good Polonius' death, and we have done but greenly
In **hugger-mugger** to inter him.   HAM 4.5.84 (F)
    (meaning, with haste and in secrecy)

PISTOL: Sir John, I am thy Pistol and thy friend,
And **helter-skelter** have I rode to thee,
And tidings do I bring, and lucky joys,
And golden times, and happy news of price.   2H4 5.3.94
    (meaning, in disordered haste)

CHAPTER 2

Additions

Shakespeare's characters often don't know when to quit. Rather than say something concise and to the point, they sometimes ramble, adding one more thought, one more image, one more description, one more explanation, one more insult, one more curse.

ADDED CONNECTING WORDS
The addition of unnecessary conjunctions and prepositions.

Think of *connecting words*—conjunctions such as *and*, *or*, and *but*, and prepositions such as *of*, *by*, and *with*—as the glue that holds ideas together in a speech. By applying too much glue—that is, by adding unnecessary connecting words—a character often reveals that he is improvising, and that the speech was not complete in the mind of the speaker when he began to speak, but is being formed on the fly, from breath to breath, or thought to thought, or phrase to phrase, with little premeditation, or none at all, of what to say, or how to say it.

"AND"

In Verse

> SEBASTIAN: My kind Antonio,
> I can no other answer make but thanks,
> **And** thanks, **and** ever thanks   TN 3.3.13

PORTIA: How all the other passions fleet to air,
As doubtful thoughts, **and** rash-embrac'd despair,
And shudd'ring fear, **and** green-eyed jealousy.   MV 3.2.108

HAMLET: I do not know
Why yet I live to say "This thing's to do,"
Since I have cause, **and** will, **and** strength, **and** means
To do't.   HAM 4.4.43 (Q2)

MACBETH: Tomorrow **and** tomorrow **and** tomorrow
Creeps in this petty pace from day to day
To the last syllable of recorded time,
And all our yesterdays have lighted fools
The way to dusty death.   MAC 5.5.19

ADRIANA: Wouldst thou not spit at me, **and** spurn at me,
And hurl the name of husband in my face,
And tear the stain'd skin off my harlot brow,
And from my false hand cut the wedding ring,
And break it with a deep-divorcing vow?   ERR 2.2.134

AARON: Go pack with him, **and** give the mother gold,
And tell them both the circumstance of all,
And how by this their child shall be advanc'd,
And be receivèd for the emperor's heir,
And substituted in the place of mine,
To calm this tempest whirling in the court,
And let the emperor dandle him for his own.   TIT 4.2.155

ROSALINE: That same Berowne I'll torture ere I'll go.
O that I knew he were but in by th' week!
How I would make him fawn, **and** beg, **and** seek,
And wait the season, **and** observe the times,
And spend his prodigal wits in bootless rhymes,
And shape his service wholly to my hests,
And make him proud to make me proud that jests!   LLL 5.2.60

DON PEDRO: I know we shall have reveling tonight;
I will assume thy part in some disguise,
And tell fair Hero I am Claudio,
And in her bosom I'll unclasp my heart,
And take her hearing pris'ner with the force
And strong encounter of my am'rous tale.
Then after to her father will I break
And the conclusion is, she shall be thine.   ADO 1.1.320

PORTIA: I'll hold thee any wager,
When we are both accouter'd like young men,
I'll prove the prettier fellow of the two,
And wear my dagger with the braver grace,
And speak between the change of man and boy
With a reed voice, **and** turn two mincing steps
Into a manly stride, **and** speak of frays
Like a fine bragging youth, **and** tell quaint lies
How honorable ladies sought my love,
Which I denying, they fell sick and died —
I could not do withal!   MV 3.4.62

In Prose

DOGBERRY: I am a wise fellow, **and** which is more, an officer, **and** which is more, a householder, **and** which is more, as pretty a piece of flesh as any is in Messina   ADO 4.2.80

NURSE: Your love says, like an honest gentleman, **and** a courteous, **and** a kind, **and** a handsome, **and**, I warrant, a virtuous — Where is your mother?   ROM 2.5.55

FLUELLEN: The Duke of Exeter is as magnanimous as Agamemnon, **and** a man that I love and honor with my soul, **and** my heart, **and** my duty, **and** my life, **and** my living, **and** my uttermost power.   H5 3.6.6

HOSTESS QUICKLY: A hundred mark is a long one for a poor lone woman to bear, **and** I have borne, **and** borne, **and** borne, **and** have been fubb'd off, **and** fubb'd off, **and** fubb'd off, from this day to that day, that it is a shame to be thought on.

2H4 2.1.32

PRINCE: Unless hours were cups of sack, **and** minutes capons, **and** clocks the tongues of bawds, **and** dials the signs of leaping-houses, **and** the blessed sun himself a fair hot wench in flame-colored taffeta, I see no reason why thou shouldst be so superfluous to demand the time of day.

1H4 1.2.7

"OR"

BENVOLIO: Either withdraw unto some private place,
Or reason coldly of your grievances,
Or else depart. Here all eyes gaze on us.

ROM 3.1.51

OTHELLO: If there be cords, **or** knives,
Poison, **or** fire, **or** suffocating streams,
I'll not endure it.

OTH 3.3.388

KING RICHARD: O that I were as great
As is my grief, **or** lesser than my name,
Or that I could forget what I have been,
Or not remember what I must be now.

R2 3.3.136

CALIBAN: Why, as I told thee, 'tis a custom with him
I' th' afternoon to sleep. There thou may'st brain him,
Having first seiz'd his books; **or** with a log
Batter his skull, **or** paunch him with a stake,
Or cut his weasand with thy knife.

TMP 3.2.87

DESDEMONA: Why this is not a boon.
'Tis as I should entreat you wear your gloves,
Or feed on nourishing dishes, **or** keep you warm,
Or sue to you to do a peculiar profit
To your own person.

OTH 3.3.76

BEROWNE: For wisdom's sake, a word that all men love,
Or for love's sake, a word that loves all men,
Or for men's sake, the authors of these women,
Or women's sake, by whom we men are men,
Let us once lose our oaths to find ourselves,
Or else we lose ourselves to keep our oaths.   LLL 4.3.354

APEMANTUS: Grant I may never prove so fond
To trust a man on his oath or bond,
Or a harlot for her weeping,
Or a dog that seems a-sleeping,
Or a keeper with my freedom,
Or my friends, if I should need 'em.
Amen.   TIM 1.2.64

MOWBRAY: The language I have learn'd these forty years,
My native English, now I must forgo,
And now my tongue's use is to me no more
Than an unstringèd viol **or** a harp,
Or like a cunning instrument cas'd up,
Or, being open, put into his hands
That knows no touch to tune the harmony.   R2 1.3.159

"NOR"

In Verse

TROILUS: I cannot sing
Nor heel the high lavolt, **nor** sweeten talk,
Nor play at subtle games — fair virtues all
To which the Grecians are most prompt and pregnant.   TRO 4.4.85

YORK: How long shall I be patient? Oh, how long
Shall tender duty make me suffer wrong?
Not Gloucester's death, **nor** Hereford's banishment,
Nor Gaunt's rebukes, **nor** England's private wrongs,

Have ever made me sour my patient cheek,
Or bend one wrinkle on my sov'reign's face.   R2 2.1.163

HAMLET: 'Tis not alone my inky cloak, good mother,
Nor customary suits of solemn black,
Nor windy suspiration of forc'd breath,
No, **nor** the fruitful river in the eye,
Nor the dejected 'havior of the visage,
Together with all forms, moods, shows of grief,
That can denote me truly.   HAM 1.2.77 (F)

KING RICHARD: You never shall, so help you truth and God,
Embrace each other's love in banishment,
Nor never look upon each other's face,
Nor never write, regreet, **nor** reconcile
This low'ring tempest of our home-bred hate,
Nor never by advisèd purpose meet
To plot, contrive, or complot any ill
'Gainst us, our state, our subjects, or our land.   R2 1.3.183

In Prose

FESTE: Well held out, i' faith! No, I do not know you, **nor** I am not sent to
you by my lady to bid you come speak with her, **nor** your name is not
Master Cesario, **nor** this is not my nose neither. Nothing that is so is so.   TN 4.1.5

"BY"

MARTIUS: I do beseech you
By all the battles wherein we have fought,
By th' blood we've shed together,
By th' vows we've made
To endure friends, that you directly set me
Against Aufidius and his Antiates   COR 1.6.55

❧ ❧ ❧

HERMIA: My good Lysander,
I swear to thee **by** Cupid's strongest bow,
By his best arrow with the golden head,
By the simplicity of Venus' doves,
By that which knitteth souls and prospers loves,
And **by** that fire which burn'd the Carthage queen
When the false Trojan under sail was seen,
By all the vows that ever men have broke
(In number more than ever women spoke)
In that same place thou hast appointed me,
Tomorrow truly will I meet with thee.   MND 1.1.168

"OF"

LADY PERCY: And thou hast talk'd
Of sallies and retires, **of** trenches, tents,
Of palisadoes, frontiers, parapets,
Of basilisks, **of** cannon, culverin,
Of pris'ners' ransom, and **of** soldiers slain,
And all the currents of a heady fight.   1H4 2.3.50

OTHELLO: Wherein I spoke **of** most disastrous chances,
Of moving accidents by flood and field,
Of hair-breadth 'scapes i' th' imminent deadly breach,
Of being taken by the insolent foe
And sold to slavery, **of** my redemption thence   OTH 1.3.134

"THAT"

MARTIUS: They said they were an-hungry, sigh'd forth proverbs —
That hunger broke stone walls, **that** dogs must eat,
That meat was made for mouths, **that** the gods sent not
Corn for the rich men only.   COR 1.1.205

BOTTOM: O, wherefore, Nature didst thou lions frame,
Since lion vile hath here deflower'd my dear,

Which is — no, no — which was the fairest dame
That liv'd, **that** lov'd, **that** lik'd, **that** look'd with cheer?   MND 5.1.291

"WITH"

VALENTINE: I have done penance for contemning Love,
Whose high imperious thoughts have punish'd me
With bitter fasts, **with** penitential groans,
With nightly tears, and daily heartsore sighs   TGV 2.4.129

PETRUCHIO: And now, my honey love,
We will return unto thy father's house,
And revel it as bravely as the best,
With silken coats and caps and golden rings,
With ruffs and cuffs and farthingales and things,
With scarves and fans and double change of brav'ry,
With amber bracelets, beads, and all this knav'ry.   SHR 4.3.52

"BUT"

In Verse

ISABELLA: There is a vice that most I do abhor,
And most desire should meet the blow of justice;
For which I would not plead, **but** that I must,
For which I must not plead, **but** that I am
At war 'twixt will and will not.   MM 2.2.29

In Prose

FALSTAFF: For, Harry, now I do not speak to thee in drink, **but** in tears;
not in pleasure, **but** in passion; not in words only, **but** in woes also.   1H4 2.4.414

❧ ❧ ❧

"YET"

ARMADO: Love is a familiar; Love is a devil; there is no evil angel but Love. **Yet**, was Samson so tempted, and he had an excellent strength; **yet** was Solomon so seduced, and he had a very good wit.

LLL 1.2.172

LAUNCE: I am but a fool, look you, and **yet** I have the wit to think my master is a kind of knave. But that's all one, if he be but one knave. He lives not now that knows me to be in love, **yet** I am in love. But a team of horse shall not pluck that from me, nor who 'tis I love. And **yet** 'tis a woman. But what woman I will not tell myself. And **yet** 'tis a milkmaid. **Yet** 'tis not a maid, for she hath had gossips. **Yet** 'tis a maid, for she is her master's maid, and serves for wages.

TGV 3.1.263

"THOUGH"

MACBETH: I conjure you, by that which you profess,
Howe'er you come to know it, answer me:
Though you untie the winds and let them fight
Against the churches; **though** the yeasty waves
Confound and swallow navigation up;
Though bladed corn be lodg'd, and trees blown down;
Though castles topple on their warders' heads;
Though palaces and pyramids do slope
Their heads to their foundations; **though** the treasure
Of nature's germens tumble all together,
Even till destruction sicken; answer me
To what I ask you.

MAC 4.1.50

REPHRASING
Saying essentially the same thing in different ways.

Shakespeare's characters often say the same thing in many different ways, attempting to find the precise set of words that will express, convey, vocalize, articulate, communicate their thoughts and feelings on the matter at hand. It's as if they're shooting arrows repeatedly at the same target, trying to hit a bull's-eye.

IN VERSE

MACBETH: But now I am cabin'd, cribb'd, confin'd, bound in
To saucy doubts and fears.   MAC 3.4.23

HAMLET: How weary, stale, flat, and unprofitable
Seem to me all the uses of this world.   HAM 1.2.133 (Q2)

CONSTANCE: Shall Lewis have Blanche, and Blanche those provinces?
It is not so; thou hast misspoke, misheard;
Be well advis'd, tell o'er thy tale again.
It cannot be; thou dost but say 'tis so.
I trust I may not trust thee; for thy word
Is but the vain breath of a common man.
Believe me, I do not believe thee man;
I have a king's oath to the contrary.   JN 3.1.3

SALISBURY: Therefore, to be possess'd with double pomp,
To guard a title that was rich before,
To gild refinèd gold, to paint the lily,
To throw a perfume on the violet,
To smooth the ice, or add another hue
Unto the rainbow, or with taperlight
To seek the beauteous eye of heav'n to garnish,
Is wasteful and ridiculous excess.   JN 4.2.9

BASTARD: That hand which had the strength, even at your door,
To cudgel you and make you take the hatch,
To dive like buckets in concealèd wells,
To couch in litter of your stable planks,
To lie like pawns lock'd up in chests and trunks,
To hug with swine, to seek sweet safety out
In vaults and prisons, and to thrill and shake,
Even at the crying of your nation's crow,
Thinking his voice an armèd Englishman:
Shall that victorious hand be feebl'd here,
That in your chambers gave you chastisment?   JN 5.2.137

IN PROSE

EVANS: I do despise a liar as I do despise one that is false, or as I despise one that is not true.

WIV 1.1.68

SHALLOW: I will not excuse you, you shall not be excused, excuses shall not be admitted, there is no excuse shall serve, you shall not be excused.

2H4 5.1.4

QUINCE: But, masters, here are your parts. And I am to entreat you, request you, and desire you to con them by tomorrow night

MND 1.2.98

ARMADO: By my sweet soul, I mean setting thee at liberty, enfreedoming thy person. Thou wert immured, restrained, captivated, bound.

LLL 3.1.123

BOTTOM: Nay, you must name his name, and half his face must be seen through the lion's neck, and he himself must speak through, saying thus, or to the same defect: "Ladies," or "Fair ladies, I would wish you," or "I would request you," or "I would entreat you not to fear, not to tremble!"

MND 3.1.36

HOLOFERNES: This is a gift that I have, simple, simple — a foolish extravagant spirit, full of forms, figures, shapes, objects, ideas, apprehensions, motions, revolutions. These are begot in the ventricle of memory, nourished in the womb of pia mater, and delivered upon the mellowing of occasion.

LLL 4.2.65

TOUCHSTONE: Therefore you clown, abandon — which is in the vulgar leave — the society — which in the boorish is company — of this female — which in the common is woman; which together is, abandon the society of this female, or clown thou perishest; or to thy better understanding, diest; or, to wit, I kill thee, make thee away, translate thy life into death, thy liberty into bondage.

AYL 5.1.47

MACMORRIS: It is no time to discourse, so Christ save me: the day is hot, and the weather, and the wars, and the King, and the Dukes: it is no time to discourse. The town is besieged. If the trumpet call us to the breach, and we talk, and by Christ do nothing, 'tis shame for us all, so God save me; 'tis shame to stand still; it is shame, by my hand: and there is throats

to be cut, and works to be done; and there is nothing done, so Christ save
me, la.

H5 3.2.105

SUPERFLUOUS WORDS
The addition of unneeded words to state what is clear without them.

Sometimes Shakespeare's characters will say much more than is necessary, making elaborate speeches to state the obvious. The device is used for laughs, as when Bottom demonstrates his dramatic flair; for character development, as when Polonius delivers an oration explaining his intention to be brief; or for plot, as when Iachimo utters a "feigned" soliloquy to gain the trust of Imogen. The device is usually spiced with additional ingredients, such as pounding rhythms, heavy couplets, duplicated ideas, bombastic phrasing, tortured sentences, and numerous references to classical mythology. The Player King in *Hamlet*—the epitome of this device—uses *all* of these elements.

IN VERSE

BOTTOM: O grim look'd night! O night with hue so black!
O night, which ever art when day is not!
O night! O night! Alack, alack, alack!

MND 5.1.170

PLAYER KING: Full thirty times hath Phoebus' cart gone round
Neptune's salt wash and Tellus' orbèd ground,
And thirty dozen moons with borrow'd sheen
About the world have times twelve thirties been,
Since love our hearts, and Hymen did our hands,
Unite commutual in most sacred bands.

HAM 3.2.155

POLONIUS: My liege, and madam, to expostulate
What majesty should be, what duty is,
Why day is day, night night, and time is time,
Were nothing but to waste night, day, and time.
Therefore, since brevity is the soul of wit,

And tediousness the limbs and outward flourishes,
I will be brief. Your noble son is mad.

HAM 2.2.86 (F)

IACHIMO: Thanks, fairest lady.
What, are men mad? Hath nature giv'n them eyes
To see this vaulted arch, and the rich crop
Of sea and land, which can distinguish 'twixt
The fiery orbs above, and the twinn'd stones
Upon the number'd beach? And can we not
Partition make with spectacles so precious
'Twixt fair and foul?

CYM 1.6.31

PRIEST: A contract of eternal bond of love,
Confirm'd by mutual joinder of your hands,
Attested by the holy close of lips,
Strengthen'd by interchangement of your rings,
And all the ceremony of this compact
Seal'd in my function, by your testimony;
Since when, my watch hath told me, toward my grave
I've travel'd but two hours.

TN 5.1.156

PETRUCHIO: Think you a little din can daunt mine ears?
Have I not in my time heard lions roar?
Have I not heard the sea, puff'd up with winds,
Rage like an angry boar chafèd with sweat?
Have I not heard great ordnance in the field
And heaven's artillery thunder in the skies?
Have I not in a pitchèd battle heard
Loud 'larums, neighing steeds, and trumpets' clang?
And do you tell me of a woman's tongue,
That gives not half so great a blow to hear
As will a chestnut in a farmer's fire?
Tush, tush! Fear boys with bugs.

SHR 1.2.199

❧ ❧ ❧

IN PROSE

ARMADO: A child of our grandmother Eve, a female; or for thy more sweet understanding, a woman.

LLL 1.1.264

ARMADO: Sir, it is the King's most sweet pleasure and affection to congratulate the Princess at her pavilion in the posteriors of this day, which the rude multitude call the afternoon.

LLL 5.1.87

FLUELLEN: Hold, there is twelvepence for you, and I pray you to serve God, and keep you out of brawls and brabbles, and quarrels and dissensions, and I warrant you it is the better for you.

H5 4.8.63

HAMLET: For the satirical rogue says here that old men have grey beards that their faces are wrinkled, their eyes purging amber or plum-tree gum, and that they have a plentiful lack of wit, together with most weak hams

HAM 2.2.196 (Q2)

LAUNCELOT: Talk not of Master Launcelot, father, for the young gentleman, according to the Fates and Destinies and such odd sayings, the Sisters Three, and other such branches of learning, is indeed deceased, or as you would say in plain terms, gone to heaven.

MV 2.2.61

DOGBERRY: I leave an arrant knave with your worship, which I beseech your worship to correct yourself, for the example of others. God keep your worship! I wish your worship well. God restore you to health! I humbly give you leave to depart; and if a merry meeting may be wished, God prohibit it! Come, neighbor.

ADO 5.1.321

OSRIC: Sir, here is newly come to court Laertes — believe me, an absolute gentleman, full of most excellent differences, of very soft society, and great showing. Indeed, to speak feelingly of him, he is the card or calendar of gentry, for you shall find in him in the continent of what part a gentlemen would see.

HAM 5.2.106 (Q2)

FLUELLEN: By your patience, Ancient Pistol, Fortune is painted blind, with a muffler afore her eyes, to signify to you that Fortune is blind; and she is painted also with a wheel, to signify to you, which is the moral of it, that she is turning, and inconstant, and mutability, and variation: and her foot, look you, is fixed upon a spherical stone, which rolls, and rolls and rolls.

H5 3.6.30

POLONIUS: The best actors in the world, either for tragedy, comedy, history, pastoral, pastoral-comical, historical-pastoral, tragical-historical, tragical-comical-historical-pastoral, scene individable, or poem unlimited. Seneca cannot be too heavy, nor Plautus too light. For the law of writ, and the liberty, these are the only men.

HAM 2.2.396 (F)

AUTOLYCUS: He has a son, who shall be flayed alive; then 'nointed over with honey, set on the head of a wasps' nest; then stand till he be three-quarters and a dram dead; then recovered again with aqua vitae, or some other hot infusion; then, raw as he is, and in the hottest day prognostication proclaims, shall he be set against a brick-wall, the sun looking with a southward eye upon him, where he is to behold him, with flies blown to death.

WT 4.4.783

FLUELLEN: So! In the name of Jesu Christ speak lower. It is the greatest admiration in the universal world, when the true and ancient prerogatives and laws of the wars is not kept. If you would take the pains but to examine the wars of Pompey the Great, you shall find, I warrant you, that there is no tiddle-taddle nor pibble-pabble in Pompey's camp. I warrant you, you shall find the ceremonies of the wars, and the cares of it, and the forms of it, and the sobriety of it, and the modesty of it, to be otherwise.

H5 4.1.65

AMPLIFICATION
The addition of various definitions, no one of which declares the pith of the matter, but which amplify the thing defined.

Shakespeare's characters often list various definitions of a thing, attempting to make sense of their situation, or trying to get others to see things as they do. This device is quite similar to rephrasing, but is more specific in that a *noun* is clearly stated in the text as the object to be repeatedly defined. Macbeth, for example, having said the word "sleep," proceeds to punish himself with an attempt to define sleep. Hamlet does the same with the word "man," listing superlatives to define man's essence.

The device is hardest to recognize — and for an audience to hear — when the noun, the thing being defined, comes late in the speech, as it does with the word "England" in Gaunt's speech, or the word "Commodity" in the Bastard's speech.

❧ ❧ ❧

IN VERSE

DEMETRIUS: O Helen, goddess, nymph, perfect, divine!   MND 3.2.137

CONSTANCE: O Lord! my boy, my Arthur, my fair son!
My life, my joy, my food, my all the world!
My widow-comfort, and my sorrows' cure!   JN 3.4.103

MACBETH: Sleep that knits up the ravel'd sleave of care,
The death of each day's life, sore labor's bath,
Balm of hurt minds, great nature's second course,
Chief nourisher in life's feast.   MAC 2.2.34

PETRUCHIO: Nay, look not big, nor stamp, nor stare, nor fret;
I will be master of what is mine own.
She is my goods, my chattels; she is my house,
My household stuff, my field, my barn,
My horse, my ox, my ass, my anything!   SHR 3.2.228

BEROWNE: Some carry-tale, some please-man, some slight zany,
Some mumble-news, some trencher-knight, some Dick,
That smiles his cheek in years, and knows the trick
To make my lady laugh when she's dispos'd,
Told our intents before   LLL 5.2.463

BASTARD: With that same purpose-changer, that sly devil,
That broker that still breaks the pate of faith,
That daily break-vow, he that wins of all,
Of kings, of beggars, old men, young men, maids —
Who, having no external thing to lose
But the word "maid," cheats the poor maid of that —
That smooth-fac'd gentleman, tickling Commodity,
This bawd, this broker, this all-changing word   JN 2.1.567

BEROWNE: This wimpled, whining, purblind, wayward boy,
This senior-junior, giant-dwarf, Dan Cupid,
Regent of love rhymes, lord of folded arms,
Th' anointed sovereign of sighs and groans,

Liege of all loiterers and malcontents,
Dread prince of plackets, king of codpieces,
Sole imperator and great general
Of trotting paritors — O my little heart!   LLL 3.1.179

GAUNT: This royal throne of kings, this scepter'd isle
This earth of majesty, this seat of Mars,
This other Eden, demi-paradise,
This fortress built by Nature for herself
Against infection and the hand of war,
This happy breed of men, this little world,
This precious stone set in the silver sea...
Which serves it in the office of a wall,
Or as a moat defensive to a house
Against the envy of less happier lands;
This blessèd plot, this earth, this realm, this England   R2 2.1.40

QUEEN MARGARET: I called thee then vain flourish of my fortune;
I called thee then poor shadow, painted queen,
The presentation of but what I was,
The flatt'ring index of a direful pageant,
One heav'd a-high to be hurl'd down below,
A mother only mock'd with two fair babes,
A dream of what thou wast, a garish flag
To be the aim of every dang'rous shot,
A sign of dignity, a breath, a bubble,
A queen in jest, only to fill the scene.   R3 4.4.82 (F)

IN PROSE

HAMLET: What a piece of work is a man, how noble in reason, how infinite
in faculties, in form and moving how express and admirable, in action how
like an angel, in apprehension how like a god: the beauty of the world, the
paragon of animals — and yet to me, what is this quintessence of dust?   HAM 2.2.303

IN DIALOGUE

In dialogue, amplification is often used as a tactic, where the speaker, given an opportunity by the listener, repeatedly defines a thing in order to score points: such as Hamlet, who shames his mother; Malvolio, who belittles Cesario; Antony, who ridicules Lepidus; and Silvius, who woos Phoebe—all thru *amplification*:

QUEEN: Have you forgot me?
HAMLET: No, by the rood, not so.
You are the Queen, your husband's brother's wife,
And (would it were not so) you are my mother.   HAM 3.4.14 (Q2)

OLIVIA: Of what personage and years is he?
MALVOLIO: Not yet old enough for a man, nor young enough for a boy —
as a squash is before 'tis a peascod, or a codling when 'tis almost an apple.
'Tis with him in standing water, between boy and man. He is very well-
favored, and he speaks very shrewishly. One would think his mother's milk
were scarce out of him.   TN 1.5.155

LEPIDUS: What manner o' thing is your crocodile?
ANTONY: It is shaped, sir, like itself, and it is as broad as it hath breadth.
It is just so high as it is, and moves with its own organs. It lives by that
which nourisheth it, and the elements once out of it, it transmigrates.
LEPIDUS: What color is it of?
ANTONY: Of its own color, too.
LEPIDUS: 'Tis a strange serpent.
ANTONY: 'Tis so. And the tears of it are wet.   ANT 2.7.41

PHOEBE: Good shepherd, tell this youth what 'tis to love.
SILVIUS: It is to be all made of sighs and tears;
And so am I for Phoebe.
PHOEBE: And I for Ganymede.
ORLANDO: And I for Rosalind.
ROSALIND: And I for no woman.
SILVIUS: It is to be all made of faith and service;
And so am I for Phoebe.
PHOEBE: And I for Ganymede.
ORLANDO: And I for Rosalind.
ROSALIND: And I for no woman.

SILVIUS: It is to be all made of fantasy,
All made of passion and all made of wishes,
All adoration, duty and observance,
All humbleness, all patience and impatience,
All purity, all trial, all observance;
And so am I for Phoebe.
PHOEBE: And I for Ganymede.
ORLANDO: And I for Rosalind.
ROSALIND: And I for no woman.

AYL 5.2.83

CORRECTIONS
A correction of what one has uttered.

Shakespeare's characters will sometimes stop themselves—or rather, *correct* themselves—in mid-sentence, hoping to erase—or rather, to *emend*—the words that slipped from their tongues—no, not their tongues, but their *lips*—only a moment before. This device brilliantly imitates the human vices of speaking before thinking, as with Launce; of changing one's mind like the moon, as with Petruchio; or of thinking too precisely on an event, as with Hamlet.

In addition, as Freud will tell you, these self-corrections usually reveal some inner-conflict: between reason and desire, between a thought and a deed, between the truth and deceit, between love and hate, between respect and disdain, between control and surrender.

IN VERSE

HAMLET: That it should come to this!
But two months dead, nay, not so much, not two.

HAM 1.2.137

OTHELLO: If she come in, she'll sure speak to my wife.
My wife, my wife! What wife? I have no wife.

OTH 5.2.96

ISABELLA: Justice, O royal Duke! Vail your regard
Upon a wrong'd — I would fain have said, a maid.

MM 5.1.20

SEBASTIAN: Whiles we stood here securing your repose,
Ev'n now we heard a hollow burst of bellowing,
Like bulls, or rather lions. Did't not wake you?   TMP 2.1.310

TROILUS: At Priam's royal table do I sit,
And when fair Cressid comes into my thoughts —
So, traitor! "When she comes!" When is she thence?   TRO 1.1.29

KING HENRY: From Scotland am I stol'n, ev'n of pure love,
To greet mine own land with my wishful sight.
No, Harry, Harry, 'tis no land of thine;
Thy place is fill'd   3H6 3.1.13

OLIVIA: Get you to your lord,
I cannot love him. Let him send no more —
Unless perchance you come to me again
To tell me how he takes it.   TN 1.5.279

PORTIA: Beshrew your eyes,
They have o'erlook'd me and divided me!
One half of me is yours, the other half yours —
Mine own, I would say; but if mine, then yours,
And so all yours.   MV 3.2.14

LADY MACDUFF: Whither should I fly?
I've done no harm. But I remember now
I'm in this earthly world, where to do harm
Is often laudable, to do good sometime
Accounted dang'rous folly.   MAC 4.2.73

LEAR: But yet thou art my flesh, my blood, my daughter,
Or rather a disease that's in my flesh,
Which I must needs call mine. Thou art a boil,
A plague-sore, or embossèd carbuncle
In my corrupted blood.   LR 2.4.221 (F)

AARON: Away with slavish weeds and servile thoughts!
I will be bright, and shine in pearl and gold

To wait upon this new-made empress.
To wait, said I? To wanton with this queen,
This goddess, this Semiramis, this nymph

TIT 2.1.18

ADAM: Your brother — no, no brother; yet the son —
Yet not the son, I will not call him son
Of him I was about to call his father —
Hath heard your praises, and this night he means
To burn the lodgings where you use to lie,
And you within it.

AYL 2.3.19

PAULINA: Now, good my liege,
Sir, royal sir, forgive a foolish woman.
The love I bore your queen — lo, fool again!
I'll speak of her no more, nor of your children;
I'll not remember you of my own lord
(Who is lost too). Take your patience to you,
And I'll say nothing.

WT 3.2.226

PHOEBE: 'Tis but a peevish boy — yet he talks well —
But what care I for words? Yet words do well
When he that speaks them pleases those that hear.
It is a pretty youth — not very pretty —
But sure he's proud — and yet his pride becomes him.
He'll make a proper man.

AYL 3.5.110

IN PROSE

KING HENRY: A good heart, Kate, is the sun and the moon, or rather the
sun and not the moon; for it shines bright and never changes, but keeps
his course truly.

H5 5.2.162

LAUNCE: I am the dog. No, the dog is himself, and I am the dog — O, the
dog is me, and I am myself.

TGV 2.3.22

LAUNCE: Nay, I'll show you the manner of it. This shoe is my father. No, this left shoe is my father. No, no, this left shoe is my mother. Nay, that cannot be neither. Yes, it is so, it is so — it hath the worser sole. This shoe with the hole in it is my mother, and this my father.

TGV 2.3.14

LAUNCELOT: Well, my conscience hanging about the neck of my heart says very wisely to me, "My honest friend Launcelot, being an honest man's son" — or rather an honest woman's son, for indeed my father did something smack, something grow to, he had a kind of taste

MV 2.2.13

FALSTAFF: I was as virtuously given as a gentleman need to be, virtuous enough: swore little, diced not above seven times — a week, went to a bawdy house not above once in a quarter — of an hour, paid money that I borrowed — three or four times, lived well and in good compass

1H4 3.3.14

ABUSE

The piling on of language that condemns or vilifies another person or persons.

Abuse in Shakespeare, more often than not, is a verbal assault with malice aforethought — an opportunity for a character to stand to toe-to-toe with another, with intent to insult, disparage, and vent spleen in his direction. But abuse has other uses. Abuse can be a strategem, as when Coriolanus abuses his soldiers to motivate them. Abuse can be a smoke screen, as when Benedick rants about Beatrice to hide his true feelings. Abuse can also be a bluff, as when the Bastard threatens the French without the forces to back up his words.

IN VERSE

MURELLUS: You blocks, you stones, you worse than senseless things!

JC 1.1.35

PETRUCHIO: A whoreson, beetle-headed, flap-ear'd knave!

SHR 4.1.157

SYLVIA: Thou subtle, perjur'd, false, disloyal man!

TGV 4.2.95

ANTONIO: Boys, apes, braggarts, Jacks, milksops!

ADO 5.1.91

EMILIA: O gull, O dolt,
As ignorant as dirt!

OTH 5.2.163

HERMIA: O me! You juggler, you cankerblossom,
You thief of love!   MND 3.2.282

LYSANDER: Hang off, thou cat, thou burr! Vile thing, let loose,
Or I will shake thee from me like a serpent.   MND 3.2.260

LYSANDER: Thy love? Out, tawny Tartar, out!
Out, loathèd medicine! O, hated potion, hence!   MND 3.2.263

LYSANDER: Get you gone, you dwarf,
You minimus of hind'ring knotgrass made,
You bead, you acorn —   MND 3.2.328

CORIOLANUS: You common cry of curs, whose breath I hate
As reek o' th' rotten fens, whose loves I prize
As the dead carcasses of unbury'd men
That do corrupt my air: I banish you!   COR 3.3.120

PETRUCHIO: Thou liest, thou thread, thou thimble,
Thou yard, three-quarters, half-yard, quarter, nail!
Thou flea, thou nit, thou winter-cricket thou!
Brav'd in mine own house with a skein of thread?
Away, thou rag, thou quantity, thou remnant   SHR 4.3.107

KING HENRY: I know thee not old man. Fall to thy prayers.
How ill white hairs become a fool and jester!
I have long dream'd of such a kind of man,
So surfeit-swell'd, so old, and so profane,
But being awak'd, I do despise my dream.   2H4 5.5.47

YORK: O tiger's heart wrapp'd in a womans' hide!
How couldst thou drain the lifeblood of the child,
To bid the father wipe his eyes withal,
And yet be seen to bear a woman's face?
Women are soft, mild, pitiful, and flexible;
Thou stern, obdurate, flinty, rough, remorseless.   3H6 1.4.137

GLOUCESTER: No, Prelate, such is thy audacious wickedness,
Thy lewd, pestiferous, and dissentious pranks,

That even infants prattle of thy pride.
Thou art a most pernicious usurer,
Froward by nature, enemy to peace,
Lascivious, wanton, more than well beseems
A man of thy profession and degree.   1H6 3.1.14

CONSTANCE: O Austria! Thou dost shame
That bloody spoil. Thou slave, thou wretch, thou coward!
Thou little valiant, great in villainy!
Thou ever strong upon the stronger side!
Thou Fortune's champion, that dost never fight
But when her hum'rous ladyship is by
To teach thee safety! Thou art perjur'd too,
And sooth'st up greatness. What a fool thou art,
A ramping fool, to brag and stamp and swear
Upon my party!   JN 3.1.114

BASTARD: Now hear our English King,
For thus his royalty doth speak in me:
He is prepar'd — and reason too he should —
This apish and unmannerly approach,
This harness'd masque and unadvisèd revel,
This unhair'd sauciness and boyish troops,
The King doth smile at; and is well prepar'd
To whip this dwarfish war, these pygmy arms,
From out the circle of his territories.   JN 5.2.128

ISABELLA: O, you beast!
O, faithless coward! O, dishonest wretch!
Wilt thou be made a man out of my vice?
Is't not a kind of incest to take life
From thine own sister's shame? What should I think?
Heav'n shield my mother play'd my father fair,
For such a warpèd slip of wilderness
Ne'er issu'd from his blood. Take my defiance,
Die, perish!   MM 3.1.135

CORIOLANUS: All the contagion of the south light on you,
You shames of Rome! You herd of — Boils and plagues
Plaster you o'er, that you may be abhorr'd
Farther than seen, and one infect another
Against the wind a mile! You souls of geese
That bear the shapes of men, how have you run
From slaves that apes would beat! Pluto and hell:
All hurt behind! Backs red and faces pale
With flight and agu'd fear! Mend and charge home,
Or, by the fires of heav'n, I'll leave the foe
And make my wars on you.   COR 1.4.30

IN PROSE

PISTOL: Pish for thee, Iceland dog! Thou prick-eared cur of Iceland!   H5 2.1.42

PANDARUS: Asses, fools, dolts! Chaff and bran, chaff and bran! Porridge
after meat!   TRO 1.2.241

SIR TOBY: Will you help? An ass-head, and a coxcomb, and a knave, a
thin-faced knave, a hgull?   TN 5.1.206

DOLL: I scorn you, scurvy companion! What? you poor, base, rascally,
cheating, lack-linen mate! Away, you mouldy rogue, away!   2H4 2.4.123

FLUELLEN: If the enemy is an ass, and a fool, and a prating coxcomb, is
it meet, think you, that we should also be an ass, and a fool, and a prating
coxcomb, in your conscience, now?   H5 4.1.77

FALSTAFF: 'Sblood, you starveling, you eel-skin, you dried neat's tongue,
you bull's pizzle, you stockfish! O, for breath to utter what is like thee! You
tailor's yard, you sheathe, you bow-case, you vile standing tuck   1H4 2.4.244

PRINCE: Why dost thou converse with that trunk of humors, that bolting-
hutch of beastliness, that swollen parcel of dropsies, that huge bombard of

sack, that stuffed cloak-bag of guts, that roasted Manningtree ox with the pudding in his belly, that reverend vice, that grey iniquity, that father ruffian, that vanity in years?   1H4 2.4.449

KENT: A knave, a rascal, an eater of broken meats; a base, proud, shallow, beggarly, three-suited, hundred-pound, filthy worsted-stocking knave; a lily-livered, action-taking, whoreson, glass-gazing, superservicable, finical rogue; one-trunk-inheriting slave; one that wouldst be a bawd in way of good service, and art nothing but the composition of a knave, beggar, coward, pandar, and the son and heir of a mongrel bitch; one whom I will beat into clamorous whining if thou deny'st the least syllable of thy addition.   LR 2.2.15 (F)

BENEDICK: O, she misused me past the endurance of a block! An oak but with one green leaf on it would have answered her. My very visor began to assume life and scold with her. She told me — not thinking I had been myself — that I was the Prince's jester, that I was duller than a great thaw, huddling jest upon jest with such impossible conveyance upon me, that I stood like a man at a mark, with a whole army shooting at me. She speaks poniards, and every word stabs. If her breath were as terrible as her terminations, there were no living near her, she would infect to the North Star. I would not marry her though she were endowed with all that Adam had left him before he transgressed. She would have made Hercules have turned spit, yea, and have cleft his club to make the fire, too. Come, talk not of her. You shall find her the infernal Ate in good apparel. I would to God some scholar would conjure her, for certainly, while she is here, a man may live as quiet in hell as in a sanctuary, and people sin upon purpose because they would go thither; so indeed all disquiet, horror, and perturbation follows her.   ADO 2.1.239

IN DIALOGUE

Why do Shakespeare's characters just stand there and take such abuse? Sometimes they don't. These are streams of abuse that are cut off by a scene partner.

QUEEN MARGARET: Thou elvish-mark'd, abortive, rooting hog,
Thou that wast seal'd in thy nativity
The slave of nature, and the son of hell;
Thou slander of thy mother's heavy womb,
Thou loathèd issue of thy father's loins,

Thou rag of honor, thou detested —
RICHARD: Margaret.   R3 1.3.227 (F)

KING HENRY: The owl shriek'd at thy birth, an evil sign;
The night-crow cry'd, aboding luckless time;
Dogs howl'd, and hideous tempest shook down trees.
The raven rook'd her on the chimney's top,
And chatt'ring pies in dismal discords sung.
Thy mother felt more than a mother's pain,
And yet brought forth less than a mother's hope,
To wit, an indigested and deform'd lump,
Not like the fruit of such a goodly tree.
Teeth hadst thou in thy head when thou wast born,
To signify thou cam'st to bite the world;
And, if the rest be true which I have heard,
Thou cam'st —
RICHARD: I'll hear no more. Die, prophet, in thy speech.
[*Stabs him.*]
For this, amongst the rest, was I ordain'd.   3H6 5.6.44

CURSES

A prayer or invocation for harm or injury to come upon another person or persons.

The highest order of abuse is the curse — the utterance of a wish or a spell with the aim of bringing damage and destruction to someone else. The harm that is wished upon the victim is usually requested from a higher power — from God, from Nature, from the sun, from disease, from death itself. Inanimate objects can be cursed too, of course, as with the wall in *Pyramus and Thisby*. And curses can unwittingly be brought upon oneself, as with Lady Anne.

IN VERSE

IMOGEN: Pisanio,
All curses madded Hecuba gave the Greeks
And mine to boot, be darted on thee!   CYM 4.2.312

CALIBAN: You taught me language, and my profit on't
Is, I know how to curse. The red-plague rid you
For learning me your language!   TMP 1.2.363

BOTTOM: But what see I? No Thisby do I see.
O wicked wall through whom I see no bliss,
Curs'd be thy stones for thus deceiving me!   MND 5.1.179

PUCELLE: Then lead me hence, with whom I leave my curse:
May never glorious sun reflex his beams
Upon the country where you make abode;
But darkness and the gloomy shade of death
Environ you, till mischief and despair
Drive you to break your necks, or hang yourselves.   1H6 5.4.86

TIMON: Live loath'd and long,
Most smiling, smooth, detested parasites,
Courteous destroyers, affable wolves, meek bears,
You fools of fortune, trencher-friends, time's flies,
Cap-and-knee slaves, vapors, and minute-jacks!
Of man and beast, the infinite malady
Crust you quite o'er!   TIM 3.6.93

LEAR: Hear Nature, hear dear Goddess, hear:
Suspend thy purpose, if thou dost intend
To make this creature fruitful.
Into her womb convey sterility,
Dry up the organs of increase,
And from her derogate body never spring
A babe to honor her. If she must teem,
Create her child of spleen, that it may live
And be a thwart disnatur'd torment to her.
Let it stamp wrinkles in her brow of youth,
With cadent tears fret channels in her cheeks,
Turn all her mother's pains and benefits
To laughter and contempt, that she may feel
How sharper than a serpent's tooth it is
To have a thankless child.   LR 1.4.275

ANNE: O, cursèd be the hand that made these holes!
Cursèd the heart that had the heart to do it!
Cursèd the blood that let this blood from hence!
More direful hap betide that hated wretch
That makes us wretched by the death of thee
Than I can wish to wolves, to spiders, toads,
Or any creeping venom'd thing that lives.
If ever he have child, abortive be it,
Prodigious, and untimely brought to light,
Whose ugly and unnatural aspect
May fright the hopeful mother at the view,
And that be heir to his unhappiness.
If ever he have wife, let her be made
More miserable by the life of him
Than I am made by my young lord, and thee.   R3 1.2.14

IN PROSE

THERSITES: The plague of Greece upon thee, thou mongrel, beef-witted
lord!   TRO 2.1.12

SHYLOCK: I would my daughter were dead at my foot, and the jewels in
her ear! Would she were hearsed at my foot, and the ducats in her coffin!   MV 3.1.87

HAMLET: If thou dost marry, I'll give thee this plague for thy dowry: be thou
as chaste as ice, as pure as snow, thou shalt not escape calumny.   HAM 3.1.134 (Q2)

CHAPTER 3

Repetitions

Humans are wired to take pleasure in hearing repetition—from the soothing sound of a mother's voice saying "ma-ma," to the absurd verses of *Green Eggs and Ham*, to the slap-clap of a game of *Patty Cake*, to the jump-rope rhymes of *"A" My Name Is Alice*, to the bubble-gum lyrics of the pop singer, to the verbal poly-rhythms of the rapper.

But don't forget to add Shakespeare to the list. For he's the all-time Master of Repetition, as we'll see in the next three chapters, which cover the enormous number of ways Shakespeare uses repetition in the language of his plays.

REPEATED CONSONANTS
The repetition of the same consonant sound in a series of neighboring words.

Shakespeare is very fond of repeating consonant sounds in his lines, a device that is commonly called *alliteration*. Most often these repeated consonants appear in the *initial* position—that is, in the first sound in a word—in phrases such as "**b**rave **b**rood" and "**h**appy **h**orse." But sometimes Shakespeare will repeat a consonant in the *medial* position—such as the *f* sound in "**f**it**f**ul." Or in the *final* position—such as the *d* in "**d**ea**d**."

Repeating an *initial* consonant often creates comic effects, as in Woody Allen's 1977 film *Annie Hall,* when Alvy Singer says: "Honey, there's a spider in your **b**athroom the size of a **B**uick" (Allen 1982, 70). A spider the size of a Toyota isn't nearly so funny.

The same is true with Bottom's rendition of Pyramus, where excessive alliteration in phrases like "**g**racious, **g**olden, **g**littering **g**leams" makes his overblown performance sound all the more ridiculous.

But Shakespeare also uses repeated consonants for *dramatic* effect as well—such as Edgar catching his breath through a series of initial *h* sounds, or Beatrice spitting out her bitterness in a series of initial *t* sounds.

Remember that *spelling* will sometimes disguise a repeated consonant sound—such as the repeated *k* sound in the word "**cate**ch**izing."

P SOUNDS

PEMBROKE: O death, made **p**roud with **p**ure and **p**rincely beauty! JN 4.3.35

HOLOFERNES: The **p**reyful **P**rincess **p**ierc'd and **p**rick'd a **p**retty **p**leasing **p**ricket LLL 4.2.56

BRUTUS: We do here **p**ronounce,
U**p**on the **p**art o' the **p**eople, in whose **p**ower
We were elected theirs, Martius is worthy of
Present death. COR 3.1.208

B SOUNDS

QUINCE: Whereat, with **b**lade, with **b**loody **b**lameful **b**lade,
He **b**ravely **b**roach'd his **b**oiling **b**loody **b**reast MND 5.1.146

CALIBAN: She will **b**ecome thy **b**ed, I warrant,
And **b**ring thee forth **b**rave **b**rood. TMP 3.2.104

PERICLES: Now mild **b**e thy life!
For a more **b**lusterous **b**irth had never **b**abe. PER 3.1.28

❧ ❧ ❧

T SOUNDS

BEATRICE: And men are only **t**urned in**t**o **t**ongue, and **t**rim ones **t**oo.   ADO 4.1.320

ARCITE: He has a **t**ongue will **t**ame
Tempests, and make the wild rocks wan**t**on.   TNK 2.3.16

D SOUNDS

LADY MACBETH: 'Tis safer to be that which we **d**estroy,
Than by **d**estruction **d**well in **d**oubtful joy.   MAC 3.2.6

KENT: All's cheerless, **d**ark and **d**eadly;
Your el**d**est **d**aughters have fore**d**one themselves,
And **d**esperately are **d**ea**d**.   LR 5.3.291

K SOUNDS

HERO: What **k**ind of **c**ate**ch**izing **c**all you this?   ADO 4.1.78

QUEEN MARGARET: For **q**ueen, a very **c**aitiff **c**rown'd with **c**are   R3 4.4.101

IMOGEN: I hope I dream;
For so I thought I was a **c**ave-**k**eeper
And **c**ook to honest **c**reatures.   CYM 4.2.297

BOTTOM: O Fates, **c**ome, **c**ome,
Cut thread and thrum,
Quail, **c**rush, **c**onclude, and **q**uell!   MND 5.1.285

G SOUNDS

PISTOL: Why then, let **g**rievous, **g**hastly, **g**aping wounds
Untwine the Sisters Three.   2H4 2.4.198

BOTTOM: I thank thee moon for shining now so bright,
For by thy **g**racious, **g**olden, **g**littering **g**leams,
I trust to take of truest Thisby's sight.   MND 5.1.273

F SOUNDS

IAGO: She's **f**ram'd as **f**ruitful
As the **f**ree elements.   OTH 2.3.341

THESEUS: **F**or you, **f**air Hermia, look you arm yoursel**f**
To **f**it your **f**ancies to your **f**ather's will   MND 1.1.117

MACBETH: Duncan is in his grave.
A**f**ter life's **f**it**f**ul **f**ever he sleeps well.   MAC 3.2.22

KING: Arm you, I pray you, to this speedy voyage,
For we will **f**etters put upon this **f**ear,
Which now goes too **f**ree-**f**ooted.   HAM 3.3.24 (F)

V SOUNDS

DUCHESS: Ah, that deceit should steal such gentle shape
And with a **v**irtuous **v**isor hide deep **v**ice.   R3 2.2.27 (F)

S SOUNDS

DON JOHN: O plague right well prevented! **S**o will you **s**ay when you have
seen the **s**equel.   ADO 3.2.133

KING HENRY: And I have built
Two chantries, where the **s**ad and **s**olemn prie**st**s
Sing **st**ill for Richard's **s**oul.   H5 4.1.300

SALISBURY: Away with me, all you whose **s**ouls abhor
Th' uncleanly **s**avors of a **s**laughterhouse,
For I am **st**ifled with thi**s s**mell of **s**in.   JN 4.3.111

H SOUNDS

CLEOPATRA: O **h**appy **h**orse, to bear the weight of Antony!   ANT 1.5.21

FALSTAFF: What **h**ole in **h**ell were **h**ot enough for **h**im?   1H4 1.2.107

NORTHUMBERLAND: Richard not far from **h**ence **h**ath **h**id **h**is **h**ead.   R2 3.3.6

EDGAR: I **h**eard myself proclaim'd,
And by the **h**appy **h**ollow of a tree   LR 2.3.2
Escap'd the **h**unt.

HELENA: For ere Demetrius look'd on **H**ermia's eyne,
He **h**ail'd down oaths that **h**e was only mine;
But when this **h**ail some **h**eat from **H**ermia felt,
So **h**e dissolv'd, and show'rs of oaths did melt.   MND 1.1.244

CH SOUNDS

GLOUCESTER: Virtue is **ch**ok'd with foul ambition,
And **ch**arity **ch**as'd hence by rancor's hand   2H6 3.1.143

J SOUNDS

MOWBRAY: As **g**entle and as **j**ocund as to **j**est
Go I to fight. Truth hath a quiet breast.   R2 1.3.95

SH SOUNDS

FALSTAFF: I had been drowned, but that the **sh**ore was **sh**elvy and
shallow   WIV 3.5.14

M SOUNDS

FABIAN: **M**ore **m**atter for a **M**ay **m**orning.   TN 3.4.142

DOCTOR: **M**y **m**ind she has **m**ated and a**m**az'd **m**y sight.

MAC 5.1.78

DON JOHN: I wonder that thou, being, as thou sayst thou art, born under Saturn, goest about to apply a **m**oral **m**edicine to a **m**ortifying **m**ischief.

ADO 1.3.12

L SOUNDS

LUCIO: A **l**ittle more **l**enity to **l**echery would do no harm in him.

MM 3.2.97

ERPINGHAM: No so, my **l**iege. This **l**odging **l**ikes me better, Since I may say, "Now **l**ie **l** **l**ike a king."

H5 4.1.16

BOTTOM: The fairest dame That **l**iv'd, that **l**ov'd, that **l**ik'd, that **l**ook'd with cheer.

MND 5.1.294

W SOUNDS

HORATIO: These are but **w**ild and **w**hirling **w**ords, my lord.

HAM 1.5.133 (Q2)

FLUELLEN: All the **w**ater in **W**ye cannot **w**ash your Majesty's **W**elsh blood out of your body, I can tell you that!

H5 4.7.106

LADY MACBETH: O, these flaws and starts, Imposters to true fear, **w**ould **w**ell become A **w**oman's story at a **w**inter's fire Authoriz'd by her grandam.

MAC 3.4.62

R SOUNDS

GLOUCESTER: And if you**r** grace mark every ci**r**cumstance, You have great **r**eason to do **R**ichard **r**ight.

1H6 3.1.152

SNUG: May now pe**r**chance both quake and t**r**emble here When lion **r**ough in wildest **r**age doth **r**oar.

MND 5.1.221

ULYSSES: For**c**e should be **r**ight: or **r**ather, **r**ight and **wr**ong,
Between whose endless ja**r** justice **r**esides

TRO 1.3.116

COMBINATIONS

Shakespeare often creates *combinations* of consonants by repeating several different sounds in the same line. These combinations blend in the listener's ear to create a soundscape—an aural environment evoked by the distinct tonal qualities of the consonants.

Sometimes Shakespeare orchestrates these combinations to suggest the sound of the thing being spoken of—the buzzing of insects, the ticking of a clock, a sword hitting a rival's helmet, the pounding of a kettledrum, an axe chopping off a head.

KING RICHARD: O **v**illains, **v**ipers, **d**amn'**d** without re**d**emption!
  (v, d)

R2 3.2.129

SUFFOLK: There be more wa**sp**s that bu**zz** about his no**s**e
Will make this **s**ting the **s**ooner.
  (s, z)

H8 3.2.55

DUKE SENIOR: And **ch**urlish **ch**iding of the **w**inter's **w**ind
Which **w**hen it **b**ites and **b**lows upon my **b**ody
  (ch, w, b)

AYL 2.1.7

IAGO: But O, what damnèd minu**tes** tell**s** he o'er
Who do**tes**, yet doub**ts**; **s**uspe**cts**, yet **s**trongly love**s**!
  (s, z, ts)

OTH 3.3.169 (Q1)

DUKE SENIOR: And this our life, exempt from public haunt,
Finds **t**ongues in **t**rees, **b**ooks in the running **b**rooks,
Sermons in **s**tones, and good in everything.
  (t, b, s)

AYL 2.1.15

CHORUS: The hum of either army stilly sounds
That the fi**x**'d **s**entinels almo**s**t re**c**eive
The **s**ecret **w**hisper**s** of each other'**s** **w**atch.
  (s, z, w)

H5 4.pr.5

GAUNT: **B**e swift **l**ike **l**ightning in the execution,
And **l**et thy **b**lows, **d**oubly re**d**oublè**d**,
Fall **l**ike amazing thun**d**er on the casque
Of thy pernicious a**d**verse enemy.   R2 1.3.79
    (b, d, l)

VIOLA: Ma**k**e me a **w**illow **c**abin at your gate
And **c**all upon my **s**oul **w**ithin the house;
Write **l**oyal **c**antons of **c**ontemnè**d** **l**ove
And **s**ing them **l**oud even in the dead of night   TN 1.5.268
    (w, k, l, s)

HAMLET: The **K**ing **d**oth wa**k**e **t**onigh**t**, and **t**akes his **r**ouse,
Keeps wassail, and the swagg'ring upspring **r**eels;
And, as he **d**rains his **d**raughts of **R**henish **d**own,
The **k**ettle**d**rum and **t**rumpet thus bray ou**t**
The **t**riumph of his pledge.   HAM 1.4.8
    (d, t, k, r)

ISABELLA: Yet hath he in him such a min**d** of honor
That ha**d** he **t**wenty heads to **t**ender **d**own
On **t**wenty **b**loo**d**y **b**locks, he'**d** yield them up,
Before his sister shoul**d** her **b**ody stoop
To such abhorr'**d** pollution.   MM 2.4.179
    (t, d, b)

REPEATED VOWELS
The repetition of the same vowel sound in a series of neighboring words.

As with consonants, Shakespeare often repeats the same *vowel* sound in a phrase or line—a common poetic device that is sometimes called *assonance*.

In verse, a great deal of the musicality of any given line resides in the vowels. Like notes on a piano—which can be rendered high or low, loud or soft, long or short—the vowel sounds can express an infinite variety of moods, colors, and emotions through pitch, duration, and volume.

Differences in spelling can sometimes make repeated vowels harder to spot. The repeated vowel sounds in the words "girdle" and "earth" are easily overlooked, for example, as well as the similar vowels in "doth" and "summon." The surest way to recognize these repetitions, of course, is to say the line aloud.

OW SOUNDS

RICHARD: N**ow** are **our** br**ow**s b**ou**nd with victorious wreaths

R3 1.1.5

THESEUS: N**ow**, fair Hippolyta, **ou**r nuptial h**our**
Draws on apace.

MND 1.1.1

OH SOUNDS

THESEUS: But **O**, methinks how sl**ow**
This **o**ld moon wanes!

MND 1.1.3

HAMLET: **O** all you h**o**st of heaven! **O** earth! What else?
And shall I couple hell? **O** fie! H**o**ld, h**o**ld my heart,
And you, my sinews, gr**ow** not instant **o**ld,
But bear me stiffly up. Remember thee?
Ay, thou poor gh**o**st, whiles mem'ry h**o**lds a seat
In this distracted gl**o**be.

HAM 1.5.92

ER SOUNDS

PUCK: I'll put a g**ir**dle round about the **ear**th
In forty minutes.

MND 2.1.175

RICHARD: I do beseech your Grace to pardon me,
Who, **ear**nest in the s**er**vice of my God,
Def**er**red the visitation of my friends.

R3 3.7.105 (F)

❧ ❧ ❧

OO SOUNDS

MERCUTIO: Come, come, thou art as hot a jack in thy m**oo**d as any in Italy, and as s**oo**n m**o**ved to be m**oo**dy, and as s**oo**n m**oo**dy to be m**o**ved.　　　ROM 3.1.11

YOO SOUNDS

OBERON: We will, fair queen, up to the mountain's top
And mark the m**u**sical conf**u**sion
Of hounds and echo in conjunction.　　　MND 4.1.109

IH SOUNDS

ROMEO: Beauty's ens**i**gn yet
Is crimson **i**n thy l**i**ps and **i**n thy cheeks　　　ROM 5.3.94

EE SOUNDS

BASTARD: O, I am scalded in my violent motion
And spl**ee**n of sp**ee**d to s**ee** your Majesty!　　　JN 5.7.50

OBERON: B**e** as thou wast wont to b**e**;
S**ee** as thou wast wont to s**ee**.　　　MND 4.1.71

AW SOUNDS

MONTAGUE: His f**au**lt concludes but what the l**a**w should end,
The life of Tybalt.　　　ROM 3.1.185

AH SOUNDS

LUCENTIO: **A**h, Tr**a**nio, what a cruel f**a**ther's he!　　　SHR 1.1.185

AA SOUNDS

SHYLOCK: There I h**a**ve another b**a**d m**a**tch.   MV 3.1.44

HORATIO: So sh**a**ll you hear
Of carnal, bloody, and unn**a**t'ral **a**cts,
Of **a**ccidental judgements, c**a**sual slaughters   HAM 5.2.380

KING JOHN: These fl**a**gs of Fr**a**nce that are adv**a**ncèd here
Before the eye and prospect of your town
H**a**ve hither marched to your end**a**magement.   KJ 2.1.207

AI SOUNDS

KING RICHARD: All souls that will be safe, fl**y** from my s**i**de,
For t**i**me hath set a blot upon my pr**i**de.   R2 3.2.80

RICHARD: Wh**y**, **I**, in this weak p**i**ping t**i**me of peace
Have no del**i**ght to pass away the t**i**me
Unless to sp**y** m**y** shadow in the sun   R3 1.1.24 (Q1)

ANTONY: Our separation so ab**i**des and fl**i**es
That thou, res**i**ding here, goes yet with me,
And **I**, hence fleeting, here remain with thee.   ANT 1.3.102

EI SOUNDS

KING RICHARD: R**a**ge must be withstood.
Give me his g**a**ge. Lions make leopards t**a**me.
MOWBRAY: Y**ea**, but not ch**a**nge his spots. T**a**ke but my sh**a**me,
And I resign my g**a**ge.   R2 1.1.173

❧ ❧ ❧

UH SOUNDS (IN A STRESSED SYLLABLE)

LEWIS: Wh**a**t l**u**sty tr**u**mpet th**u**s d**o**th s**u**mmon **u**s?   JN 5.2.117

UH SOUNDS (IN AN UNSTRESSED SYLLABLE)

PANDARUS: **A**chilles? **A** drayman, **a** porter, **a** very camel.   TRO 1.2.249

REPEATED SYLLABLES
The repetition of the same syllable in neighboring words.

Sometimes Shakespeare will repeat entire *syllables* in a line, placing them close enough to one another so that they can resonate together—like identical wind chimes hanging from different branches of the same tree. It's important to note that these repetitions are not *rhymes*—they're words that have one or more *syllable* in common.

SHARED SYLLABLES

FRIAR: There is some strange mis**pri**sion in the **pri**nces.   ADO 4.1.185
    (misprison/princes)

GAUNT: Methinks I am a prophet new in**spir**ed,
And thus e**xpir**ing do foretell of him   R2 2.1.31
    (inspired/expiring)

BELARIUS: When we have supp'd,
We'll **man**nerly de**man**d thee of thy story   CYM 3.6.90
    (mannerly/demand)

OLIVIA: They say, poor gentleman, he's much dis**tract**.
A most ex**tract**ing frenzy of mine own
From my remembrance clearly banish'd his.   TN 5.1.280
    (distract/extracting)

JINGLES

Sometimes a short word sounds like part of a longer word used in the same sentence. The repetition of a syllable in this manner is called a *jingle*.

WARWICK: I'll **plant Plant**agenet, root him up who dares. — 3H6 1.1.48
 (plant/Plantagenet)

FALSTAFF: I **see** you are ob**se**quious in your love — WIV 4.2.2
 (see/obsequious)

LYSANDER: O, take the **sense**, sweet, of my inno**cence**! — MND 2.2.45
 (sense/innocence)

KING PHILIP: **Some** trumpet **summon** to the walls
These men of Angiers. — JN 2.1.198
 (Some/summon)

BUCKINGHAM: This is the day wherein I wish'd to **fall**
By the **fal**se faith of him whom most I trusted. — R3 5.1.16 (F)
 (fall/false)

YORK: For **Suffolk**'s duke, may he be **suffoc**ate
That dims the honor of this warlike isle. — 2H6 1.1.124
 (Suffolk/suffocate)

DESDEMONA: I cannot say "**whore**" —
It does ab**hor** me now I speak the word. — OTH 4.2.161
 (whore/abhor)

CONSTANCE: **Stay** for an answer to your embassy,
Lest unadvis'd you **stain** your swords with blood. — JN 2.1.44
 (stay/stain)

RICHARD: I, that am rudely stamp'd, and **want** love's majesty
To strut before a **want**on ambling nymph. — R3 1.1.16
 (want/wanton)

RICHARD: **Come**, lords, will you go
To c**om**fort Edward with our **com**pany?   R3 2.1.139
    (Come, comfort, company)

NORTHUMBERLAND: Three thousand men of war
Are making hither with all due expedience
And **short**ly mean to touch our northern **shore**.   R2 2.1.286
    (shortly/shore)

VIOLA: I'll bring you to a captain in this town,
Where lie my maiden weeds, by whose gentle help
I was pre**serve**d to **serve** this noble count.   TN 5.1.254
    (preserve/serve)

ANTONY: So it must be, for now
All length is **tort**ure; since the **torch** is out,
Lie down and stray no further.   ANT 4.1.4.46
    (torch/torture)

KING JOHN: We will heal up all,
For we'll create young Arthur Duke of Britain
And Earl of **Richmond**, and this **rich** fair town,
We make him lord of.   JN 2.1.550
    (Richmond/rich)

LADY MACBETH: [*Reading*] And I have learned from the perfect'st report
that they have **more** in them than **mor**tal knowledge.   MAC 1.5.2
    (more/mortal)

LEONATO: O, my lord, wisdom and blood combating in so **ten**der a body,
we have **ten** proofs to one that blood hath the victory.   ADO 2.3.164
    (tender/ten)

NEAR-RHYMES

Sometimes a syllable is repeated in a word in a final, but *unstressed* position, making the words very nearly rhyme, but not quite:

THESEUS: How shall we find the con**cord** of this dis**cord**?   MND 5.1.60
(*concord/discord*)

THESEUS: Such tricks hath strong imagination
That, if it would but ap**prehend** some joy,
It com**prehend**s some bringer of the joy.   MND 5.1.18
(*apprehend/comprehend*)

RHYME
A repetition of the final syllable or syllables in two or more words.

Shakespeare uses rhyme throughout his plays, although more often in his earlier works, and less so as he matured. Even so, Shakespeare's use of rhyme is nothing short of magical. It magnifies the power of speech, and binds us to the speaker with velvet cords of sound. It calls to the lost child within our hearts, and awakes the dormant imagination in our minds. It tickles us to laughter, enchants us through song, elevates our thinking above the mundane, breaks through the walls of cynicism, heightens our senses, magnifies emotions, weaves supernatural spells, harmonizes with the cosmos.

RHYMING COUPLETS
When Shakespeare rhymes the words at the end of a pair of verse lines, it's called a *rhyming couplet.*

HERMIA: Help me, Lysander, help me! Do thy **best**
To pluck this crawling serpent from my **breast**!   MND 2.2.145

KING RICHARD: What you will have, I'll give, and willing **too**;
For do we must what force will have us **do**.   R2 3.3.206

BOYET: Why all his behaviors did make their **retire**
To the court of his eye, peeping thorough **desire**.   LLL 2.1.234

FINAL COUPLETS (END OF A SCENE)

When Shakespeare uses a rhyme to finish a scene, it's a called a *final couplet*. A final couplet creates the sound of resolution just before the speaker exits—the metrical equivalent of a blackout on the stage.

> IAGO: 'Tis here, but yet **confus'd**.
> Knavery's plain face is never seen till **us'd**.   OTH 2.1.311

> DROMIO OF SYRACUSE: Thither I must, although against my **will**;
> For servants must their masters' minds **fulfill**.   ERR 4.1.112

> VIOLA: O Time, thou must untangle this, not **I**.
> It is too hard a knot for me t'**untie**.   TN 2.2.40

> ANGELO: Ever till **now**,
> When men were fond, I smil'd and wonder'd **how**.   MM 2.2.185

> RICHARD: Shine out, fair sun, till I have bought a **glass**,
> That I may see my shadow as I **pass**.   R3 1.2.262

FINAL COUPLETS (END OF A PLAY)

Shakespeare often uses final couplets to finish a play—the metrical equivalent of projecting the words "The End" on a movie screen:

> PRINCE: For never was a story of more **woe**,
> Than this of Juliet and her **Romeo**.   ROM 5.3.309

> PROSPERO: As you from crimes would pardon'd **be**,
> Let your indulgence set me **free**.   TMP ep.19

> DROMIO OF EPHESUS: We came into the world like brother and **brother**,
> And now let's go hand in hand, not one before **another**.   ERR 5.1.425

SHARED RHYMES

In Shakespeare's dialogue, rhyme is often *shared* between two characters speaking in verse:

DEMETRIUS: I say I love thee more than he can **do**.
LYSANDER: If thou say so, withdraw and prove it **too**.   MND 3.2.254

OBERON: How long within this wood intend you **stay**?
TITANIA: Perchance till after Theseus' wedding **day**.   MND 2.1.138

KING RICHARD: Why, uncle, thou hast many years to **live**.
GAUNT: But not a minute, King, that thou canst **give**.   R2 1.3.225

EXTON: From your own mouth, my lord, did I this **deed**.
KING HENRY: They love not poison that do poison **need**,
Nor do I thee.   R2 5.6.37

ROMEO: And we mean well in going to this **masque**,
But 'tis no wit to go.
MERCUTIO: Why, may one **ask**?
ROMEO: I dreamt a dream tonight.
MERCUTIO: And so did **I**.
ROMEO: Well, what was yours?
MERCUTIO: That dreamers often **lie**.
ROMEO: In bed asleep, while they do dream things **true**.
MERCUTIO: O, then I see Queen Mab hath been with **you**.   ROM 1.4.48

TALBOT: Shall all thy mother's hopes lie in one **tomb**?
JOHN: Ay, rather than I'll shame my mother's **womb**.
TALBOT: Upon my blessing, I command thee **go**.
JOHN: To fight I will, but not to fly the **foe**.
TALBOT: Part of thy father will be sav'd in **thee**.
JOHN: No part of him but will be sham'd in **me**.
TALBOT: Thou never hadst renown, nor canst not **lose it**.
JOHN: Yes, your renownèd name: shall flight **abuse it**?
TALBOT: Thy father's charge shall clear thee from that **stain**.
JOHN: You cannot witness for me, being **slain**.
If death be so apparent, then both **fly**.
TALBOT: And leave my foll'wers here to fight and **die**?
My age was never tainted with such **shame**.
JOHN: And shall my youth be guilty of such **blame**?

No more can I be sever'd from your **side**
Than can yourself yourself in twain **divide**.
Stay, go, do what you will, the like do **I**;
For live I will not, if my father **die**.

1H6 4.5.34

SHARED FINAL COUPLETS (END OF A SCENE)

Sometimes two characters conversing in verse will end their scene by rhyming each other, creating a *shared final couplet*:

JULIET: Sleep dwell upon thine eyes, peace in thy **breast**.
ROMEO: Would I were sleep and peace, so sweet to **rest**.

ROM 2.2.186

OBERON: And look thou meet me ere the first cock **crow**.
PUCK: Fear not, my lord. Your servant shall do **so**.

MND 2.1.267

SUFFOLK: Even as a splitted bark, so sunder **we**:
This way fall I to death.
QUEEN MARGARET: This way for **me**.

2H6 3.2.411

KING RICHARD: Set on toward London, cousin: is it **so**?
BOLINGBROKE: Yea, my good lord.
KING RICHARD: Then I must not say **no**.

R2 3.3.208

RHYMING TRIPLETS

Sometimes Shakespeare will rhyme *three* lines in a row, like this:

HELENA: Lo, she is one of this **confederacy**!
Now I perceive they have conjoin'd all **three**
To fashion this false sport in spite of **me**.

MND 3.2.192

SHARED TRIPLETS

Sometimes characters will *share* a triplet, like this:

ANTIPHOLUS OF EPHESUS: Are you there, wife? You might have come
before.
ADRIANA: [*Within*] Your wife, sir knave? Go, get you from the **door**.

DROMIO OF EPHESUS: If you went in pain, master, this knave would go **sore**.   ERR 3.1.63

COURTESAN: I hope you do not mean to cheat me **so**?
ANTIPHOLUS OF SYRACUSE: Avaunt, thou witch! Come, Dromio, let us **go**.
DROMIO OF SYRACUSE: "Fly pride," says the peacock. Mistress, that you **know**.   ERR 4.3.78

SHARED FINAL TRIPLETS

In these examples, two or three characters share a *final* triplet:

HELENA: Your hands than mine are quicker for a **fray**;
My legs are longer though, to run **away**.
HERMIA: I am amaz'd and know not what to **say**.   MND 3.2.342

DROMIO OF SYRACUSE: Master, shall I be porter at the **gate**?
ADRIANA: Ay, and let none enter, lest I break your **pate**.
LUCIANA: Come, come, Antipholus, we dine too **late**.   ERR 2.2.217

MIDLINE RHYMES

Occasionally, Shakespeare will embed a rhyme in the *middle* of a line. These mid-line rhymes are called, sometimes, *internal* rhymes:

In Verse

MERCUTIO: Speak but one rhyme and I am satisfied.
Cry but "Ay me!" Pronounce but "**love**" and "**dove**"   ROM 2.1.9

KING RICHARD: But, for the concord of my state and time,
Had not an **ear** to **hear** my true time broke.   R2 5.5.47

CAMILLO: I should leave **grazing,** were I of your flock,
And only live by **gazing**.   WT 4.4.109

KING PHILIP: Thy rage shall **burn** thee up, and thou shalt **turn**
To ashes, ere our blood shall quench that fire.   JN 3.1.344

CLEOPATRA: If you find him sad,
Say I am dancing; if in mirth, report
That I am sudden **sick**. **Quick**, and return.   ANT 1.3.3

ANNE: And be thy **wife** — if any be so mad —
More miserable by the **life** of thee
Than thou hast made me by my dear lord's death!   R3 4.1.74 (F)

BASTARD: Come lady, I will show thee to my kin;
And they shall **say**, when Richard me begot,
If thou hadst said him **nay**, it had been sin.   JN 1.1.273

KING RICHARD: But whate'er I be,
Nor I, nor any man that but man is,
With nothing shall be **pleas'd** till he be **eas'd**
With being nothing.   R2 5.5.38

BEROWNE: And then to sleep but three hours in the night,
And not be seen to **wink** of all the day,
When I was wont to **think** no harm all night,
And make a dark night too of half the day   LLL 1.1.42

In Prose

SHALLOW: If it be **confessed**, it is not **redressed**.   WIV 1.1.104

HOST: Shall I lose my doctor? No, he gives me the **potions** and the
motions.   WIV 3.1.102

LOST (OBSOLETE) RHYMES
There are many rhymes in Shakespeare that are lost to us because of pronunciation changes over the past four hundred years:

AUMERLE: No, good my lord. Let's fight with gentle **words**
Till time lends friends, and friends their helpful **swords**.   R2 3.3.131

KING RICHARD: Uncle, give me your hand. Nay, dry your **eyes**;
Tears show their love, but want their **remedies**.   R2 3.3.202

YORK: All is un**even**,
And everything is left at six and **seven**.   R2 2.2.121

KING HENRY: Sad-hearted man, much overgone with **care**,
Here sits a king more woeful than you **are**.   3H6 2.5.123

TYBALT: I will withdraw, but this intrusion **shall**,
Now seeming sweet, convert to bitter **gall**.   ROM 1.5.91 (F)

DUMAINE: To love, to wealth, to pomp, I pine and **die**,
With all these living in **philosophy**.   LLL 1.1.31

ULYSSES: Farewell, my lord; I as your lover **speak**:
The fool slides o'er the ice that you should **break**.   TRO 3.3.214

PUCK: Through the forest have I **gone**,
But Athenian found I **none**,
On whose eyes I might **approve**
This flower's force in stirring **love**.
Night and silence — Who is **here**?
Weeds of Athens he doth **wear**.
This is he, my master **said**,
Despisèd the Athenian **maid**;
And here the maiden, sleeping sound,
On the dank and dirty ground.
Pretty soul, she durst not **lie**
Near this lack-love, this kill-**courtesy**.   MND 2.2.66

ALTERNATING RHYMES

Sometimes Shakespeare will rhyme every other line in a four-line sequence in an alternating pattern, which can be described as ABAB. This alternating pattern is often called a *quatrain*:

TITANIA: Come, sit thee down upon this flow'ry **bed**,
While I thy amiable cheeks do **coy**,
And stick musk roses in thy sleek smooth **head**,
And kiss thy fair large ears, my gentle **joy**.   MND 4.1.1

❧ ❧ ❧

LUCIANA: If you did wed my sister for her **wealth**,
Then for her wealth's sake use her with more **kindness**;
Or if you like elsewhere, do it by **stealth**:
Muffle your false love with some show of **blindness**.

ERR 3.2.5

STAVE OF SIX

Here, the pattern ABAB is immediately followed by a couplet, CC. This is sometimes referred to as a *stave of six*:

HERMIA: Never so weary, never so in **woe**,
Bedabbled with the dew and torn with **briars**,
I can no further crawl, no further **go**.
My legs can keep no pace with my **desires**.
Here will I rest me till the break of **day**.
Heavens shield Lysander if they mean a **fray**!

MND 3.2.442

BEROWNE: Sweet lords, sweet lovers, O, let us **embrace**.
As true we are as flesh and blood can **be**.
The sea will ebb and flow, heaven show his **face**;
Young blood doth not obey an old **decree**.
We cannot cross the cause why we were **born**;
Therefore of all hands must we be **forsworn**.

LLL 4.3.210

SONNET FORM

Here, a speech is devised as a *sonnet*—a fourteen line pattern that, in Shakespeare's hands, begins with one quatrain of alternating rhymes (ABAB), followed by a second quatrain (CDCD), followed by third quatrain (EFEF), and finished with a couplet (GG):

BEROWNE: Study me how to please the eye **indeed**,
By fixing it upon a fairer **eye**,
Who dazzling so, that eye shall be his **heed**,
And give him light that it was blinded **by**.
Study is like the heaven's glorious **sun**,
That will not be deep search'd with saucy **looks**.
Small have continual plodders ever **won,**

Save base authority from other's **books**.
These earthly godfathers of heaven's **lights**,
That give a name to every fixèd **star**,
Have no more profit of their shining **nights**
Than those that walk and wot not what they **are**.
Too much to know is to know naught but **fame**,
And every godfather can give a **name**.

LLL 1.1.80

SHARED ALTERNATING RHYMES

Sometimes quatrains appear in dialogue, where alternating rhymed lines are *shared* between two or more speakers. Note the rhyme scheme (ABABCDCD)—shared by a quartet of men—in this bout of banter from *Love's Labor's Lost*:

BEROWNE: I'll prove her fair, or talk till doomsday **here**.
KING: No devil will fright thee then so much as **she**.
DUMAINE: I never knew man hold vile stuff so **dear**.
LONGAVILLE: Look, here's thy love, my foot and her face **see**.
BEROWNE: O, if the streets were pavèd with thine **eyes**,
Her feet were much too dainty for such **tread**.
DUMAINE: O vile! Then, as she goes, what upward **lies**,
The street should see as she walk'd **overhead**.

LLL 4.3.270

SHARED SONNET

Here's a rare treat—a *sonnet* shared by two speakers. In this dialogue, Romeo takes the first quatrain (ABAB), Juliet, the second quatrain (CDCD), and together they share a stave of six (EFEFGG):

ROMEO: If I profane with my unworthiest **hand**
This holy shrine, the gentler sin is **this**:
My lips, two blushing pilgrims, ready **stand**
To smooth that rough touch with a tender **kiss**.
JULIET: Good pilgrim, you do wrong your hand too **much**,
Which mannerly devotion shows in **this**,
For saints have hands that pilgrims hands do **touch**,
And palm to palm is holy palmer's **kiss**.

ROMEO: Have not saints lips, and holy palmers, **too**?
JULIET: Ay, pilgrim, lips that they must use in **prayer**.
ROMEO: O then, dear saint, let lips do what hands **do**:
They pray; grant thou, lest faith turn to **despair**.
JULIET: Saints do not move, though grant for prayers' **sake**.
ROMEO: Then move not while my prayer's effect I **take**.
Thus from my lips, by thine, my sin is **purg'd**.
JULIET: Then have my lips the sin that they have **took**.
ROMEO: Sin from my lips? O trespass sweetly **urg'd**!
Give me my sin again.
JULIET: You kiss by the **book**.

ROM 1.5.93

RHYMES IN SPELLS

Supernatural beings in Shakespeare use a potent mixture of rhythm and rhyme to create magic spells or incantations:

WITCHES: The wayward sisters, hand in **hand,**
Posters of the sea and **land,**
Thus do go **about**, **about**,
Thrice to **thine**, and thrice to **mine**,
And thrice again to make up **nine.**
Peace, the charm's wound up.
     (AABBCCC)

MAC 1.3.32

PUCK: On the **ground**
Sleep **sound**.
I'll **apply**
To your **eye**,
Gentle lover, **remedy**.
When thou **wak'st**,
Thou **tak'st**
True **delight**
In the **sight**
Of thy former lady's **eye**.
     (AABBBCCDDB)

MND 3.2.448

RHYMES IN SONGS

Add *melody* to lines that possess rhythm and rhyme, and you get a *song*. Here are excerpts from several Shakespearean songs, each demonstrating a different rhyme scheme:

BOTTOM: The finch, the sparrow, and the **lark**,
The plainsong cuckoo **gray**,
Whose note full many a man doth **mark**
And dare not answer "**nay**".   MND 3.1.130
    (ABAB)

GUIDERIUS: Fear no more the heat o' th' **sun**,
Nor the furious winter's **rages**;
Thou thy worldly task hast **done**,
Home art gone, and ta'en thy **wages**.
Golden lads and girls all **must**,
As chimney-sweepers, come to **dust.**   CYM 4.2.258
    (ABABCC)

SPRING: When daisies pied and violets **blue**,
And lady-smocks all silver **white**,
And cuckoo-buds of yellow **hue**,
Do paint the meadows with **delight**,
The cuckoo then on every **tree**
Mocks married men, for thus sings **he**:
"Cuckoo, cuckoo!" O word of **fear**,
Unpleasing to a married **ear**.   LLL 5.2.894
    (ABABCCDD)

AMIENS: Blow, blow, thou winter **wind**,
Thou art not so **unkind**,
As man's **ingratitude**.
Thy tooth is not so **keen**,
Because thou art not **seen**,
Although thy breath be **rude**.
Heigh-ho, sing heigh-ho, unto the green **holly**,
Most friendship is feigning, most loving mere **folly**.

Then heigh-ho, the **holly**,
This life is most **jolly**.   AYL 2.7.174
    (AABCCBDDDD)

REPEATED WORDS
The repetition of the same word in neighboring phrases or sentences.

For centuries, great orators have used the repetition of the same word in a speech to drive home a major point. One of the most famous twentieth-century examples of this device is Winston Churchill's address of May 13, 1940, preparing the British people for a hard fight against Hitler's war machine.

WINSTON CHURCHILL: You ask, what is our aim? I can answer in one word. It is **victory**. **Victory** at all costs, **victory** in spite of all terrors, **victory**, however long and hard the road may be. For without **victory**, there is no survival.   (Safire 1992, 132)

IN VERSE
As with Churchill, when one of Shakespeare's characters wants to illuminate a theme, or drive home a point, he will deliberately repeat himself:

PARIS: These **times** of woe afford no **times** to woo.   ROM 3.4.8

TROILUS: O virtuous fight,
When **right** with **right** wars who shall be most **right**.   TRO 3.2.171

MACBETH: If it were **done** when 'tis **done**, then 'twere well
It were **done** quickly.   MAC 1.7.1

POLONIUS: **Beware**
Of entrance to a quarrel, but being in,
Bear't that th' opposèd may **beware** of thee.   HAM 1.3.65

EMILIA: But **jealous** souls will not be answer'd so;
They are not ever **jealous** for the cause,
But **jealous** for they're **jealous**.   OTH 3.4.159

KING HENRY: For many a thousand widows
Shall this his **mock**, **mock** out of their dear husbands,
Mock mothers from their sons, **mock** castles down   H5 1.2.284

ANTONY: I will not do them **wrong**; I rather chose
To **wrong** the dead, to **wrong** myself and you,
Than I will **wrong** such honorable men.   JC 3.2.125

KING HENRY: I doubt **not** that; since we are well persuaded
We carry **not** a heart with us from hence
That grows **not** in a fair consent with ours,
Nor leave **not** one behind that doth **not** wish
Success and conquest to attend on us.   H5 2.2.20

NURSE: O woe! O woeful, woeful, woeful **day**!
Most lamentable **day**, most woeful **day**
That ever, ever I did yet behold!
O **day**, O **day**, O **day**, O hateful **day**!
Never was seen so black a **day** as this.
O woeful **day**, O woeful **day**!   ROM 4.5.49

CORIOLANUS: Here come more **voices**.
Your **voices**! For your **voices** I have fought,
Watch'd for your **voices**, for your **voices** bear
Of wounds two dozen odd; battles thrice six
I've seen and heard of; for your **voices** have
Done many things, some less, some more. Your **voices**!   COR 2.3.125

EDMUND: Well, then,
Legitimate Edgar, I must have your land.
Our father's love is to the bastard Edmund
As to th' **legitimate**. Fine word, "**legitimate**."
Well, my **legitimate**, if this letter speed
And my invention thrive, Edmund the base
Shall top th' **legitimate**.   LR 1.2.15

DUCHESS OF YORK: Nay, do not say "stand up."
Say "**pardon**" first, and afterwards, "stand up."

And if I were thy nurse, thy tongue to teach,
"**Pardon**" should be the first word of thy speech.
I never long'd to hear a word till now.
Say "**pardon**," King. Let pity teach thee how.
The word is short, but not so short as sweet;
No word like "**pardon**" for kings' mouths so meet.   R2 5.3.111

IN PROSE

Liberated from the meter, the repetition of a word in prose has less insistence, but carries great power nevertheless:

> FALSTAFF: Why, thou knowest I am as valiant as Hercules, but beware **instinct**. **Instinct** is a great matter. I was now a coward on **instinct**.   1H4 2.4.270

> PANDARUS: **Fair** be to you, my lord, and to all this **fair** company! **Fair** desires, in all **fair** measure, **fair**ly guide them! Especially to you, **fair** queen, **fair** thoughts be your **fair** pillow!   TRO 3.1.43

> FALSTAFF: 'Sblood, 'twas time to **counterfeit**, or that hot termagant Scot had paid me, scot and lot, too. **Counterfeit**? I lie, I am no **counterfeit**. To die is to be a **counterfeit**, for he is but the **counterfeit** of a man that hath not the life of a man; but to **counterfeit** dying, when a man thereby liveth, is to be no **counterfeit**, but the true and perfect image of life indeed.   1H4 5.4.113

IN DIALOGUE

The repetition of words in dialogue is a game of wits played by two clever opponents. The object of the game is to take up a particular word spoken by your adversary, and use it as the thrust of your response. The game is played the same way, regardless of whether it takes place in comedy, tragedy, history, or romance.

In Verse

> LEAR: I **gave** you all.
> REGAN: And in good time you **gave** it.   LR 2.4.250

> HIPPOLYTA: 'Tis **strange**, my Theseus, that these lovers speak of.
> THESEUS: More **strange** than true.   MND 5.1.1

PUCELLE: Christ's mother **helps** me, else I were too weak.
CHARLES: Whoe'er **helps** thee, 'tis thou that must help me.

1H6 1.2.106

GLOUCESTER: Be patient, gentle Nell; **forget** this grief.
ELEANOR: Ah, Gloucester, teach me to **forget** myself

2H6 2.4.26

SUFFOLK: **Jove** sometime went disguis'd, and why not I?
LIEUTENANT: But **Jove** was never slain, as thou shalt be.

2H6 4.1.48

PORTIA: Then **must** the Jew be merciful.
SHYLOCK: On what compulsion **must** I? Tell me that.

MV 4.1.182

ISABELLA: I am come to **know** your pleasure.
ANGELO: That you might **know** it would much better please me
Than to demand what 'tis.

MM 2.4.31

EXETER: The Dauphin crownèd king? All **fly** to him?
O, whither shall we **fly** from this reproach?
GLOUCESTER: We will not **fly**, but to our enemies' throats.

1H6 1.1.96

SUFFOLK: I go with message from the Queen to France;
I charge thee **waft** me safely cross the channel.
WHITMORE: Come, Suffolk, I must **waft** thee to thy death.

2H6 4.1.114

RICHARD: Think'st thou I am an **executioner**?
KING HENRY: If murd'ring innocents be executing,
Why, then thou art an **executioner**.

3H6 5.6.30

HERMIA: God speed, **fair** Helena. Whither away?
HELENA: Call you me "**fair**"? That "**fair**" again unsay.
Demetrius loves your **fair**. O happy **fair**!

MND 1.1.180

LEAR: Kent, on thy **life**, no more.
KENT: My **life** I never held but as a pawn
To wage against mine enemies, nor fear to lose it,
Thy safety being motive.

LR 1.1.154

DEMETRIUS: Let me go,
Or if thou follow me, do not believe

But I shall do thee **mischief** in the wood.
HELENA: Ay, in the temple, in the town, the field,
You do me **mischief**.

MND 2.1.235

LEONTES: My lord,
Is this the daughter of a king?
FLORIZEL: She is,
When **once** she is my wife.
LEONTES: That "**once**," I see, by your good father's speed,
Will come on very slowly.

WT 5.1.207

ORSINO: Come, away!
OLIVIA: Whither, my lord? Cesario, **husband**, stay.
ORSINO: **Husband**?
OLIVIA: Ay, **husband**. Can he that deny?
ORSINO: Her **husband**, sirrah?
VIOLA: No, my lord, not I.

TN 5.1.142

In Prose

Although prose offers a looser set of rules, the game of wits remains the same — to take a word used by your opponent, and toss it back to him like a radioactive spud:

MARIA: My purpose is indeed a **horse** of that color.
SIR ANDREW: And your **horse** now would make him an ass.

TN 2.3.167

OLIVER: Wilt thou lay hands on me, **villain**?
ORLANDO: I am no **villain**. I am the youngest son of Sir Rowland de Boys.
He was my father, and he is thrice a **villain** that says such a father begot
villains.

AYL 1.1.55

GADSHILL: There's money of the King's coming down the hill; 'tis going to
the **King's** Exchequer.
FALSTAFF: You lie, ye rogue, 'tis going to the **King's** Tavern.

1H4 2.2.54

LEAR: And you lie, sirrah, we'll have you **whipped**.
FOOL: I marvel what kin thou and thy daughters are: they'll have me
whipped for speaking true, thou'lt have me **whipped** for lying, and
sometimes I am **whipped** for holding my peace.

LR 1.4.181 (F)

SEBASTIAN: I prithee **vent** thy folly somewhere else. Thou know'st not me.

FESTE: **Vent** my folly? He has heard that word of some great man and now applies it to a fool. **Vent** my folly? I am afraid this great lubber the world will prove a cockney. I prithee now, ungird thy strangeness and tell me what I shall **vent** to my lady? Shall I **vent** to her that thou art coming?

TN 4.1.10

MARGARETON: Turn, slave, and fight.

THERSITES: What art thou?

MARGARETON: A **bastard** son of Priam's.

THERSITES: I am a **bastard**, too; I love **bastards**. I am **bastard** begot, **bastard** instructed, **bastard** in mind, **bastard** in valor, in everything illegitimate. One bear will not bite another, and wherefore should one **bastard**? Take heed, the quarrel's most ominous to us. If the son of a whore fight for a whore, he tempts judgment. Farewell, **bastard**!

TRO 5.7.13

A Series of Word Repetitions

A volley of a single word is sometimes not enough for someone to win a point. When this happens, another word is served and returned, followed by another, and then another—like a badminton match—until someone drops the shuttlecock:

ARTHUR: **Must** you with hot irons burn out both mine eyes?

HUBERT: Young boy, I **must**.

ARTHUR: And **will** you?

HUBERT: And I **will**.

JN 4.1.39

BENEDICK: Is there any **way** to show such friendship?

BEATRICE: A very even **way**, but no such friend.

BENEDICK: May a **man** do it?

BEATRICE: It is a **man**'s office, but not yours.

BENEDICK: I do love nothing in the world so well as you. Is not that **strange**?

BEATRICE: As **strange** as the thing I know not.

ADO 4.1.263

ANNE: Didst thou not kill this king?

RICHARD: I **grant** ye.

ANNE: Dost **grant** me, hedgehog? Then God **grant** too
Thou mayst be damnèd for that wicked deed.
O, he was gentle, mild and virtuous.

RICHARD: The better for the King of **Heav'n** that hath him.

ANNE: He is in **heav'n**, where thou shalt never come.
RICHARD: Let him thank me that help'd to send him thither;
For he was fitter for that **place** than earth.
ANNE: And thou unfit for any **place** but hell.
RICHARD: Yes, one **place** else if you will hear me name it.
ANNE: Some dungeon.
RICHARD: Your bedchamber.   R3 1.2.101

IAGO: My noble lord —
OTHELLO: What dost thou say, Iago?
IAGO: Did Michael Cassio, when you woo'd my lady,
Know of your love?
OTHELLO: He did, from first to last.
Why dost thou ask?
IAGO: But for a satisfaction of my **thought**,
No further harm.
OTHELLO: Why of thy **thought**, Iago?
IAGO: I did not think he had been acquainted with her.
OTHELLO: O yes, and went between us very oft.
IAGO: **Indeed**?
OTHELLO: **Indeed**? Ay, **indeed**. Discern'st thou aught in that?
Is he not **honest**?
IAGO: **Honest**, my lord?
OTHELLO: **Honest** — ay, **honest**.
IAGO: My lord, for aught I know.
OTHELLO: What dost thou **think**?
IAGO: **Think**, my lord?
OTHELLO: "**Think**, my lord?" By heaven, thou echo'st me
As if there were some monster in thy thought
Too hideous to be shown.   OTH 3.3.93

Two Words Repeated

Sometimes, in this game of wits, a superb player is able to hear two words and build a response around *both* of them:

RICHARD: But shall I **live** in **hope**?
ANNE: All men, I **hope**, **live** so.   R3 1.2.199
  (live, hope)

KING: **Fair** Princess, **welcome** to the court of Navarre.
PRINCESS: "**Fair**" I give you back again, and "**welcome**" I have not yet. LLL 2.1.90
    (fair, welcome)

MARGARET: I am **unworthy** to be Henry's **wife**.
SUFFOLK: No, gentle madam, I **unworthy** am
To woo so fair a dame to be his **wife** 1H6 5.3.122
    (unworthy, wife)

LADY GREY: Please you dismiss me with either "**ay**" or "**no**."
KING EDWARD: **Ay**, if thou wilt say "**ay**' to my request;
No, if thou dost say "**no**" to my demand. 3H6 3.2.78
    (ay, no)

REPEATED PHRASES
The repetition of a phrase in neighboring clauses or sentences.

As with repeated words, an orator may emphasize his thesis, or fortify his strongest argument, through the repetition of a *phrase*.

IN VERSE

KING JOHN: France, thou shalt rue **this hour** within **this hour**. JN 3.1.323

MACBETH: It **will have blood** they say; blood **will have blood**. MAC 3.4.121

MACBETH: Still it cried "**Sleep no more**!" to all the house;
"Glamis hath murder'd sleep, and therefore Cawdor
Shall **sleep no more**; Macbeth shall **sleep no more**." MAC 2.2.38

MARIANA: Sweet Isabel, take my part:
Lend me your knees, and **all my life** to come
I'll lend you **all my life** to do you service. MM 5.1.430

KING HENRY: The sum of all our answer is but this:
We would not seek a battle **as we are**,

Nor **as we are**, we say we will not shun it:
So tell your master.

H5 3.6.163

GLOUCESTER: And had I **twenty times** so many foes,
And each of them had **twenty times** their power,
All these could not procure me any scathe,
So long as I am loyal, true, and crimeless.

2H6 2.4.60

IN PROSE

In the looser structure of prose, a repeated phrase can not only drive home a point, but reveal a mind fixated on an idea to the point of obsession:

PANDARUS: I have had my labor for my travail; **ill thought on** of her and **ill thought on** of you

TRO 1.1.70

CLOWN: She being none of **your flesh and blood**, **your flesh and blood** has not offended the King, and so **your flesh and blood** is not to be punished by him.

WT 4.4.693

SHYLOCK: **Let him look to his bond**. He was wont to call me usurer. **Let him look to his bond**. He was wont to lend money for a Christian courtesy. **Let him look to his bond**.

MV 3.1.47

CLAUDIO: Hero thinks surely she will die; for she says **she will die** if he love her not, and **she will die** ere she will make her love known, and **she will die** if he woo her, rather than she will bate one breath of her accustomed crossness.

ADO 2.3.173

IAGO: **Put money in thy purse**. Follow thou the wars; defeat thy favor with an usurped beard. I say, **put money in thy purse**. It cannot be that Desdemona should long continue her love to the Moor — **put money in thy purse** — nor he his to her.

OTH 1.3.339

TOUCHSTONE: Truly, shepherd, **in respect** of itself, it is a good life; but **in respect** that it is a shepherd's life, it is naught. **In respect** that it is solitary, I like it very well; but **in respect** that it is private, it is a very vile life. Now **in respect** it is in the fields, it pleaseth me well; but **in respect** that it is not in the court, it is tedious.

AYL 3.2.13

IN DIALOGUE

In the same way that *words* can be taken up by an adversary to be used as a weapon in a game of wits, so can *phrases*:

BENVOLIO: Be rul'd by me. **Forget to think** of her.
ROMEO: O teach me how I should **forget to think**!

ROM 1.1.225

PRINCE: And I will die a **hundred thousand** deaths
Ere break the smallest parcel of this vow.
KING HENRY: A **hundred thousand** rebels die in this.

1H4 3.2.158

KING JOHN: Here **once again** we sit, **once again** crown'd,
And look'd upon, I hope, with cheerful eyes.
PEMBROKE: This "**once again**," but that your Highness pleas'd,
Was once superfluous.

JN 4.2.1

GLOUCESTER: Madam, the King is **old enough** himself
To give his censure. These are no women's matters.
QUEEN MARGARET: If he be **old enough**, what needs your Grace
To be Protector of his Excellence?

2H6 1.3.116

MESSENGER: **But yet**, madam —
CLEOPATRA: I do not like "**But yet**"; it does allay
The good precedence. Fie upon "**But yet**".
"**But yet**" is as a jailer to bring forth
Some monstrous malefactor.

ANT 2.5.49

AN ENTIRE LINE

Here, an *entire line* is swallowed whole and repeated as a retort:

BEROWNE: **Did not I dance with you in Brabant once?**
ROSALINE: **Did not I dance with you in Brabant once?**
BEROWNE: I know you did.
ROSALINE: How needless was it then
To ask the question!

LLL 2.1.114

CHAPTER 4

Reverberations

In music, themes are explored, expanded, and amplified through *repetition*. Think of the DOT-DOT-DOT—DASH of Beethoven's Fifth Symphony. The composer's repetition of that basic motif is carefully orchestrated throughout the opus. We sometimes hear it the *beginning* of a phrase, to launch a musical idea; sometimes in the *middle* of a phrase, to generate a build; sometimes at the *end* of a phrase, to create a climax; and sometimes we hear assorted combinations of all three, to produce texture and variety.

Shakespeare orchestrates the repetition of *words* and *phrases* in his lines in precisely the same manner that Beethoven does notes, using the music of the *spoken word* to create the harmonic relationships that provide information, meaning, and pleasure to the listener.

IMMEDIATE REPETITIONS
The immediate repetition of a word or phrase with no other words between.

Probably the most famous use of immediate repetition is found in Edgar Allan Poe's 1849 poem *The Bells*:

> Keeping **time, time, time**,
> As he **knells, knells, knells**,
> In a happy Runic rhyme,
> To the rolling of the bells —
> Of the **bells, bells, bells**:

To the tolling of the bells,
Of the **bells, bells, bells, bells,**
Bells, bells, bells —
To the moaning and the groaning of the bells.

(Harrison 1965, 7:119)

As in Poe, Shakespeare's characters immediately repeat the same word or phrase to express deep emotions, articulate big realizations, amplify strong actions, or all of the above.

REPEATED WORDS

Usually a word is repeated in this manner twice, or sometimes thrice, but sometimes many more:

Twice

MACBETH: **Out, out** brief candle!	MAC 5.5.23
DESDEMONA: O **falsely, falsely** murder'd.	OTH 5.2.117
MACDUFF: **Bleed, bleed** poor country!	MAC 4.3.31
HAMLET: **Rest, rest**, perturbèd spirit.	HAM 1.5.182
DON PEDRO: **Conclude, conclude**, he is in love.	ADO 3.2.62
IACHIMO: **Swift, swift** you dragons of the night	CYM 2.2.48
ANDROMACHE: **Unarm, unarm**, and do not fight today.	TRO 5.3.3
ANNE: **Blush, blush** thou lump of foul deformity	R3 1.2.57
CHORUS: **Work, work** your thoughts, and therein see a siege	H5 3.pr.25
CONSTANCE: **Arm, arm**, you heavens, against these perjur'd kings!	JN 3.1.107
LYSANDER: **Amen, amen**, to that fair prayer, say I.	MND 2.2.62
QUEEN MARGARET: **Fool, fool**, thou whet'st a knife to kill thyself.	R3 1.3.243

OTHELLO: **Cold, cold**, my girl?
Even like thy chastity.

OTH 5.2.275

LEONTES: **Stars, stars**,
And all eyes else, dead coals.

WT 5.1.67

PISANIO: **Flow, flow**,
You heavenly blessings, on her!

CYM 3.5.160

CORIOLANUS: O **mother, mother**!
What have you done?

COR 5.3.182

ISABELLA: **Seeming, seeming**!
I will proclaim thee, Angelo, look for't.

MM 2.4.150

HASTINGS: **Woe, woe**, for England; not a whit for me,
For I, too fond, might have prevented this.

R3 3.4.80

LEONATO: **Confirm'd, confirm'd**! O, that is stronger made
Which was before barr'd up with ribs of iron.

ADO 4.1.150

Triples

ENOBARBUS: But **why, why, why**?

ANT 3.7.2

OTHELLO: O **blood, blood, blood**!

OTH 3.3.451

BASTARD: **Sweet, sweet, sweet** poison for the age's tooth

JN 1.1.213

JULIET: **Sweet, sweet, sweet** nurse, tell me, what says my love?

ROM 2.5.54

PORTER: **Knock, knock, knock**! Who's there i' th' name of Beelzebub?

MAC 2.3.3

PANDARUS: O **world, world, world**! Thus is the poor agent despised.

TRO 5.10.36 (F)

CASSIO: **Reputation, reputation, reputation**! O, I have lost my reputation!

OTH 2.3.262

MACDUFF: O **horror, horror, horror**! Tongue nor heart
Cannot conceive nor name thee!

MAC 2.3.64

KING JOHN: Good **Hubert, Hubert, Hubert**, throw thine eye
On yon young boy.

JN 3.3.59

PROSPERO: Why that's my dainty Ariel. I shall miss thee.
But yet thou shalt have freedom. **So, so, so**.

TMP 5.1.95

LEAR: O **Lear, Lear, Lear**!
Beat at this gate that let thy folly in,
And thy dear judgment out.

LR 1.4.270 (F)

POLONIUS: What do you read, my lord?
HAMLET: **Words, words, words**.

HAM 2.2.192

Quadruples

LEAR: **Howl, howl, howl, howl**! O you are men of stones!

LR 5.3.258 (Q1)

CAPULET: **How, how, how, how**? Chopp'd logic! What is this?

ROM 3.5.149 (Q2)

PETRUCHIO: Sit down, Kate, and welcome. **Food, food, food, food**!

SHR 4.1.142

SHYLOCK: Why **there, there, there, there**! A diamond gone cost me two
thousand ducats in Frankfort.

MV 3.1.83

ISABELLA: O worthy prince, dishonor not your eye
By throwing it on any other object
Till you have heard my true complaint,
And given me **justice, justice, justice, justice**!

MM 5.1.25

Five Times

BOTTOM: Tongue, lose thy light!
Moon, take thy flight!
Now **die, die, die, die, die**.

MND 5.1.306

LEAR: Why should a dog, a horse, a rat have life,
And thou no breath at all? Thou'lt come no more,
Never, never, never, never, never.

LR 5.3.309 (F)

Six Times

LEAR: I'll put't in proof,
And when I have stol'n upon these son-in-laws,
Then **kill, kill, kill, kill, kill, kill**!   LR 4.6.187

REPEATED PHRASES
What works well for words, works well for phrases:

In Verse

LAERTES: **A touch, a touch,** I do confess.   HAM 5.2.286 (F)

ANNE: **Set down, set down** your honorable load   R3 1.2.1

EGEUS: I beg **the law, the law** upon his head!   MND 4.1.155

OTHELLO: **It is the cause, it is the cause** my soul.   OTH 5.2.1

KING RICHARD: **Too well, too well** thou tell'st a tale so ill.   R2 3.2.121

LEONTES: **Too hot, too hot!**
To mingle friendship far is mingling bloods.   WT 1.2.108

PHOEBE: O, **for shame, for shame,**
Lie not, to say mine eyes are murderers.   AYL 3.5.18

CONSTANCE: I am not mad. **Too well, too well**, I feel
The different plague of each calamity.   JN 3.4.48

PRINCESS: Come **challenge me, challenge me** by these deserts
And, by this virgin palm now kissing thine,
I will be thine.   LLL 5.2.805

HELENA: **Is't not enough, is't not enough**, young man,
That I did never, no, nor never can,
Deserve a sweet look from Demetrius' eye,
But you must flout my insufficiency?   MND 2.2.125

In Prose

HOLOFERNES: **What is the figure? What is the figure?**   LLL 5.1.64

FALSTAFF: **My womb, my womb, my womb** undoes me.   2H4 4.3.22

BOTTOM: I will roar, that I will make the Duke say, "**Let him roar again;
let him roar again!**"   MND 1.2.72

BOTTOM: **A calendar! A calendar!** Look in the almanac. **Find out moonshine, find out moonshine.**   MND 3.1.53

ROSALIND: Come, **woo me, woo me**; for now I am in a holiday humor and
like enough to consent.   AYL 4.1.68

HAMLET: You cannot take from me any thing that I will not more willingly
part withal — **except my life, except my life, except my life**.   HAM 2.2.215 (Q2)

DELAYED REPETITIONS
The repetition of a word or phrase with one or two words interposing.

Instead of repeating a word or phrase *immediately*, sometimes Shakespeare will fiddle with the
rhythm of a line by *delaying* the reverberation.

REPEATED WORDS

ANTONY: I am **dying**, Egypt, **dying**.   ANT 4.15.18

LEAR: **None** does offend, **none**, I say **none**.   LR 4.6.168 (F)

FALSTAFF: **Company**, villainous **company**, hath been the spoil of me.   1H4 3.3.9

HAMLET: O **villain, villain**, smiling, damnèd **villain**!   HAM 1.5.106

TROILUS: **Words, words**, mere **words**, no matter from the heart.   TRO 5.3.108

ENOBARBUS: **Naught, naught**, all **naught**! I can behold no longer.   ANT 3.10.1

BOURBON: **Shame**, and eternal **shame**, nothing but **shame**!   H5 4.5.10

TROILUS: O Cressid! O **false** Cressid! **False, false, false**!   TRO 5.2.178

THERSITES: **Lechery, lechery**, still wars and **lechery**; nothing else holds fashion.   TRO 5.2.194

SEBASTIAN: I can no other answer make but **thanks**,
And **thanks** and ever **thanks**   TN 3.3.14

EGEUS: **Thou, thou**, Lysander, **thou** hast given her rhymes
And interchang'd love tokens with my child.   MND 1.1.28

CELIA: O **wonderful**, **wonderful**! And most **wonderful wonderful**! And yet again **wonderful**! And after that out of all whooping.   AYL 3.2.191

ANTONY: Give me thy hand.
Thou hast been rightly honest. So hast **thou**,
And **thou**, and **thou**, and **thou**.   ANT 4.2.10

MACBETH: **Tomorrow**, and **tomorrow**, and **tomorrow**,
Creeps in this petty pace from day to day
To the last syllable of recorded time   MAC 5.5.19

REPEATED PHRASES

KING RICHARD: **A horse, a horse**! my kingdom for **a horse**!   R3 5.4.7

JAQUES: **A fool, a fool**! I met **a fool** i' th' forest,
A motley fool. AYL 2.7.12

PISTOL: Let us to France, like horse-leeches, my boys,
To suck, to suck, the very blood **to suck**! H5 2.3.55

SHYLOCK: **An oath, an oath**, I have **an oath** in heaven;
Shall I lay perjury upon my soul? MV 4.1.228

OTHELLO: **Damn her**, lewd minx! O, **damn her, damn her**! OTH 3.3.476

REPEATED ADJECTIVES

Another type of delayed word repetition is the *repeated adjective*—a device where the same adjective is used to describe two or more different objects or ideas in a series.

MACBETH: **False** face must hide what the **false** heart doth know. MAC 1.7.82

OLIVER: Good Monsieur Charles, what's the **new** news at the **new** court? AYL 1.1.96

DOCTOR: **Unnatural** deeds
Do breed **unnatural** troubles. MAC 5.1.71

EGEUS: Thou hast by moonlight at her window sung
With **feigning** voices verses of **feigning** love MND 1.1.30

PLANTAGENET: Thy **humble** servant vows obedience
And **humble** service to the point of death. 1H6 3.1.166

MISTRESS PAGE: Hang him, dishonest rascal! I would all of the **same** strain were in the **same** distress. WIV 3.3.185

CELIA: O, that's a **brave** man! He writes **brave** verses, speaks **brave** words, swears **brave** oaths, and breaks them bravely AYL 3.4.40

HAMLET: This counselor
Is now **most** still, **most** secret, and **most** grave,
Who was in life a foolish prating knave. HAM 3.4.213 (F)

TRANIO: 'Tis in my head to do my master good:
I see no reason but **supposed** Lucentio
Must get a father, called **supposed** Vincentio   SHR 2.1.406

AENEAS: This Ajax is **half** made of Hector's blood,
In love whereof, **half** Hector stays at home:
Half heart, **half** hand, **half** Hector comes to seek
This blended knight, **half** Trojan and **half** Greek.   TRO 4.5.83

HELENA: We Hermia, like two artificial gods,
Have with our needles created both **one** flower,
Both on one sampler, sitting on **one** cushion,
Both warbling of one song, both in **one** key,
As if our hands, our sides, voices, and minds,
Had been incorporate.   MND 3.2.203

KING HENRY: Tell me else
Could **such** inordinate and low desires,
Such poor, **such** barren, **such** lewd, **such** mean attempts,
Such barren pleasures, rude society,
As thou art match'd withal and grafted to,
Accompany the greatness of thy blood
And hold their level in thy princely heart?   1H4 3.2.11

INITIAL REPETITIONS

The repetition of the same word or phrase at the beginning of successive phrases or sentences.

This passage from Jesse Jackson's speech, delivered at the Democratic National Convention in Atlanta on July 17, 1988, is a superb example of the power of repeating the same words at the beginning of successive statements:

JESSE JACKSON: We must never surrender to inequality. **Women** cannot compromise ERA or comparable worth. **Women** are making sixty cents on the dollar to what a man makes. **Women** cannot buy meat cheaper. **Women** cannot buy bread cheaper. **Women** cannot buy milk cheaper. **Women** deserve to get paid for the work that you do. It's right and it's fair.

(Torricelli 1999, 375)

Robert F. Kennedy used the same device on April 4, 1968, speaking in Indianapolis three hours after the assassination of Martin Luther King, Jr.:

> ROBERT F. KENNEDY: **What we need in the United States is not** division. **What we need in the United States is not** hatred. **What we need in the United States is not** violence or lawlessness, but love and wisdom and compassion toward one another, and a feeling of justice toward those who still suffer within our country, whether they be white or they be black.
> (Torricelli 1999, 273)

Winston Churchill used the same device on June 4, 1940, to inspire the British to resist the German war machine:

> WINSTON CHURCHILL: **We shall** not flag nor fail. **We shall** go on to the end. **We shall** fight in France, **we shall** fight on the seas and oceans, **we shall** fight with growing confidence and growing strength in the air, **we shall** defend our island, whatever the cost may be; **we shall** fight on the beaches, **we shall** fight on the landing grounds, **we shall** fight in the fields and in the streets, **we shall** fight in the hills; w**e shall** never surrender
> (Cannadine 1989, 165)

Abraham Lincoln used it at Gettysburg, Pennsylvania, on November 19, 1863, to rededicate the union:

> ABRAHAM LINCOLN: But in a larger sense, **we cannot** dedicate, **we cannot** consecrate, **we cannot** hallow this ground. (Copeland 1942, 315)

And William Shakespeare used it countless times throughout the canon.

INITIAL REPETITION OF A WORD

In Verse

> BASTARD: **Mad** world, **mad** kings, **mad** composition! JN 2.1.561

> PROTEUS: **Sweet** love, **sweet** lines, **sweet** life! TGV 1.3.45

DUCHESS: **Bloody** thou art; **bloody** will be thy end.   R3 4.4.195

KING RICHARD: **Fool**, of thyself speak well. **Fool**, do not flatter.   R3 5.3.192

JULIET: Come weep with me: **pas**t hope, **past** cure, **past** help!   ROM 4.1.45

ORSINO: **One** face, **one** voice, **one** habit, and two persons!   TN 5.1.216

JAQUES: **Sans** teeth, **sans** eyes, **sans** taste, **sans** everything.   AYL 2.7.166

THESEUS: **Joy**, gentle friends! **Joy** and fresh days of love
Accompany your hearts!   MND 5.1.29

KING HENRY: **We** few, **we** happy few, **we** band of brothers;
For he today that sheds his blood with me
Shall be my brother   H5 4.3.60

TITUS: **Here** lurks no treason, **here** no envy swells,
Here grow no damnèd drugs, **here** are no storms,
No noise, but silence and eternal sleep.   TIT 1.1.153

HERO: I never yet saw man,
How wise, **how** noble, young, **how** rarely featur'd
But she would spell him backward.   ADO 3.1.59

THIRD CITIZEN: **When** clouds are seen, wise men put on their cloaks;
When great leaves fall, then winter is at hand;
When the sun sets, who doth not look for night?   R3 2.3.32 (F)

OTHELLO: O, now, forever,
Farewell the tranquil mind! **Farewell** content!
Farewell the plumèd troops and the big wars
That makes ambition virtue.   OTH 3.3.348

JULIA: But truer stars did govern Proteus' birth;
His words are bonds, **his** oaths are oracles,
His love sincere, **his** thoughts immaculate,

His tears pure messengers sent from his heart,
His heart as far from fraud as heav'n from earth.   TGV 2.7.74

WESTMERLAND: **Our** battle is more full of names than yours,
Our men more perfect in the use of arms,
Our armor all as strong, **our** cause the best;
Then reason will our hearts should be as good.
Say you not then our offer is compell'd.   2H4 4.1.148

KING RICHARD: For God's sake, let us sit upon the ground,
And tell sad stories of the death of kings —
How **some** have been depos'd, **some** slain in war,
Some haunted by the ghosts they have depos'd,
Some poison'd by their wives, **some** sleeping kill'd,
All murder'd.   R2 3.2.155

TITUS: I am not mad; I know thee well enough.
Witness this wretched stump, **witness** these crimson lines,
Witness these trenches made by grief and care,
Witness the tiring day and heavy night,
Witness all sorrow, that I know thee well
For our proud empress, mighty Tamora.   TIT 5.2.21

CASSIUS: But if you would consider the true cause
Why all these fires, why all these gliding ghosts,
Why birds and beasts from quality and kind,
Why old men, fools, and children calculate,
Why all these things change from their ordinance,
Their natures, and preformèd faculties
To monstrous quality, **why**, you shall find
That heaven hath infus'd them with these spirits
To make them instruments of fear and warning
Unto some monstrous state.   JC 1.3.62

❦ ❦ ❦

In Prose

PRINCE: **Wherein** is he good, but to taste sack and drink it? **Wherein** neat and cleanly, but to carve a capon and eat it? **Wherein** cunning, but in craft? **Wherein** crafty, but in villainy? **Wherein** villainous, but in all things? **Wherein** worthy, but in nothing?

1H4 2.4.455

GRUMIO: But hadst thou not crossed me, thou shouldst have heard how her horse fell, and she under her horse; thou shouldst have heard in how miry a place, **how** she was bemoiled, **how** he left her with her horse upon her, **how** he beat me because her horse stumbled, **how** she waded through the dirt to pluck him off me, **how** he swore, **how** she prayed that never prayed before, **how** I cried, **how** the horses ran away, **how** her bridle was burst, **how** I lost my crupper, with many things of worthy memory, which now shall die in oblivion, and thou return unexperienced to thy grave.

SHR 4.1.73

INITIAL REPETITION OF A PHRASE

In Verse

BOLINGBROKE: **The shadow of your** sorrow hath destroy'd **The shadow of your** face.

R2 4.1.292

SALISBURY: **They say**, by him the good Duke Humphrey died; **They say**, in him they fear your Highness' death.

2H6 3.2.248

ARAGON: **How much unlike** art thou to Portia! **How much unlike** my hopes and my deservings!

MV 2.9.56

TRANIO: **Though he be** blunt, I know him passing wise; **Though he be** merry, yet withal he's honest.

SHR 3.2.24

ROSALIND: **So was I when your Highness** took his Dukedom; **So was I when your Highness** banish'd him.

AYL 1.3.59

KING RICHARD: **Is the** chair empty? **Is the** sword unsway'd?
Is the King dead?   R3 4.4.469

CLAUDIO: **Is this** the Prince? **Is this** the Prince's brother?
Is this face Hero's? Are our eyes our own?   ADO 4.1.70

RICHARD: **Was ever woman in this humor** woo'd?
Was ever woman in this humor won?   R3 1.2.227

DEMETRIUS: **She is** a woman, therefore may be wooed;
She is a woman, therefore may be won;
She is Lavinia, therefore must be lov'd.   TIT 2.1.82

TITANIA: But she, being mortal, of that boy did die,
And for her sake do I rear up the boy,
And for her sake I will not part with him.   MND 2.1.135

MURELLUS: **And do you now** put on your best attire?
And do you now cull out a holiday?
And do you now strew flowers in his way
That comes in triumph over Pompey's blood?   JC 1.1.48

KING RICHARD: **With mine own** tears I wash away my balm,
With mine own hands I give away my crown,
With mine own tongue deny my sacred state,
With mine own breath release all duteous oaths   R2 4.1.207

RICHARD: **Your beauty** was the cause of that effect —
Your beauty, that did haunt me in my sleep
To undertake the death of all the world,
So I might live one hour in your sweet bosom.   R3 1.2.121 (F)

ORLANDO: **If ever** you have look'd on better days;
If ever been where bells have knoll'd to church;
If ever sat at any good man's feast;
If ever from your eyelids wip'd a tear,
And know what 'tis to pity and be pitied,
Let gentleness my strong enforcement be   AYL 2.7.113

MARIANA: **This is** that face, thou cruel Angelo,
Which once thou swor'st was worth the looking on;
This is the hand, which with a vow'd contract
Was fast belock'd in thine; **this is** the body
That took away the match from Isabel,
And did supply thee at thy garden-house
In her imagin'd person.   MM 5.1.207

ANTONIO: I pray you think you question with the Jew.
You may as well go stand upon the beach
And bid the main flood bate his usual height;
You may as well use question with the wolf,
Why he hath made the ewe bleat for the lamb;
You may as well forbid the mountain pines
To wag their high tops, and to make no noise
When they are fretten with the gusts of heaven   MV 4.1.70

MARTIUS: **If any** such be here —
As it were sin to doubt — that love this painting
Wherein you see me smear'd; **if any** fear
Lesser his person than an ill report;
If any think brave death outweighs bad life,
And that his country's dearer than himself,
Let him alone, or so many so minded,
Wave thus to express his disposition,
And follow Martius.   COR 1.6.67

KING HENRY: When this is known, then to divide the times:
So many hours must I tend my flock,
So many hours must I take my rest,
So many hours must I contemplate,
So many hours must I sport myself,
So many days my ewes have been with young,
So many weeks ere the poor fools will ean,
So many years ere I shall shear the fleece.   3H6 2.5.30

❦ ❦ ❦

In Prose

HOST: **To see thee** fight, **to see thee** foin, **to see thee** traverse, **to see thee** here, **to see thee** there, **to see thee** pass thy punto, thy stock, thy reverse, thy distance, thy montant.

WIV 2.3.24

HAMLET: Why, look you, how unworthy a thing you make of me! **You would** play upon me, **you would** seem to know my stops, **you would** pluck out the heart of my mystery, **you would** sound me from my lowest note to the top of my compass

HAM 3.2.363

INITIAL REPETITIONS IN DIALOGUE

When used in dialogue, initial repetitions smack of overt wordplay. Whether it be witty banter between lovers, verbal jousting between friends, or a pithy exchange between deadly enemies, the method is the same — the listener parries the words of the speaker by using them as the beginning of a riposte.

Words

KING RICHARD: **Harp** not on that string, madam. That is past.
QUEEN ELIZABETH: **Harp** on it still shall I till heartstrings break.

R3 4.4.364 (Q1)

DEMETRIUS: **Well** roared, lion.
THESEUS: **Well** run, Thisby.
HIPPOLYTA: **Well** shone, moon.

MND 5.1.265

RICHARD: **Clifford**, ask mercy and obtain no grace.
EDWARD: **Clifford**, repent in bootless penitence.
WARWICK: **Clifford**, devise excuses for thy faults.

3H6 2.6.69

LEAR: What can you say to draw
A third more opulent than your sisters? Speak.
CORDELIA: **Nothing**, my Lord.
LEAR: **Nothing**.
CORDELIA: **Nothing**.
LEAR: **Nothing** will come of nothing, speak again.

LR 1.1.85 (F)

Phrases

ORSINO: **Still so** cruel?
OLIVIA: **Still so** constant, lord.   TN 5.1.110

LANCASTER: **This is the strangest** tale that ever I heard.
PRINCE: **This is the strangest** fellow, brother John.   1H4 5.4.154

PROTEUS: **So, by your circumstance**, you'll call me fool.
VALENTINE: **So, by your circumstance**, I fear you'll prove.   TGV 1.1.37

PLANTAGENET: **Hath not thy rose a** canker, Somerset?
SOMERSET: **Hath not thy rose a** thorn, Plantagenet?   1H6 2.4.68

DROMIO OF SYRACUSE: **I, sir, am Dromio**. Command him away.
DROMIO OF EPHESUS: **I, sir, am Dromio**. Pray let me stay.   ERR 5.1.336

ELEANOR: **There's a good** mother, boy, that blots thy father.
CONSTANCE: **There's a good** grandam, boy, that would blot thee.   JN 2.1.132

DUKE SENIOR: **If there be truth in sight, you are my** daughter.
ORLANDO: **If there be truth in sight, you are my** Rosalind.   AYL 5.4.118

JAQUES: **I pray you, mar no more** trees with writing love songs in their barks.
ORLANDO: **I pray you, mar no more** of my verses with reading them ill-favoredly.   AYL 3.2.259

ANTONIO: **If you will not** murder me for your love, let me be your servant.
SEBASTIAN: **If you will not** undo what you have done, that is, kill him whom you have recovered, desire it not.   TN 2.1.35

AENEAS: **If not Achilles**, sir,
What is your name?
ACHILLES: **If not Achilles**, nothing.   TRO 4.5.75

❦ ❦ ❦

SON: **Was ever** son so rued his father's death?
FATHER: **Was ever** father so bemoan'd his son?
KING HENRY: **Was ever** King so griev'd for subject's woe?   3H6 2.5.109

AUMERLE: I do beseech your grace to pardon me.
It is a matter of small consequence,
Which for some reasons I would not have seen.
YORK: **Which for some reasons**, sir, I mean to see.   R2 5.2.60

LADY BONA: **Tell him**, in hope he'll prove a widower shortly,
I'll wear the willow garland for his sake.
QUEEN MARGARET: **Tell him**, my mourning weeds are laid aside,
And I am ready to put armor on.
WARWICK: **Tell him** from me that he hath done me wrong,
And therefore I'll uncrown him ere't be long.   3H6 4.1.99

DUKE: **I'm sorry** one so learnèd and so wise
As you, Lord Angelo, have still appear'd,
Should slip so grossly, both in the heat of blood,
And lack of temper'd judgment afterward.
ANGELO: **I'm sorry** that such sorrow I procure,
And so deep sticks it in my penitent heart
That I crave death more willingly than mercy;
'Tis my deserving, and I do entreat it.   MM 5.1.470

LORENZO: The moon shines bright. **In such a night** as this,
When the sweet wind did gently kiss the trees,
And they did make no noise, in such a night
Troilus methinks mounted the Troyan walls,
And sigh'd his soul toward the Grecian tents,
Where Cressid lay that night.
JESSICA: **In such a night**
Did Thisby fearfully o'ertrip the dew,
And saw the lion's shadow ere himself,
And ran dismay'd away.
LORENZO: **In such a night**
Stood Dido with a willow in her hand
Upon the wild sea-banks, and waft her love
To come again to Carthage.

JESSICA: **In such a night**
Medea gather'd the enchanted herbs
That did renew old Aeson.
LORENZO: **In such a night**
Did Jessica steal from the wealthy Jew,
And with an unthrift love did run from Venice
As far as Belmont.
JESSICA: **In such a night**
Did young Lorenzo swear he lov'd her well,
Stealing her soul with many vows of faith,
And ne'er a true one.
LORENZO: **In such a night**
Did pretty Jessica, like a little shrew,
Slander her love, and he forgave it her.
JESSICA: I would out-night you, did nobody come;
But hark, I hear the footing of a man.

MV 5.1.1

FINAL REPETITIONS
The repetition of the same word or phrase at the end of several successive phrases or sentences.

Judge Clarence Thomas, appearing before the Senate Judiciary Committee on October 11, 1991, blasted accusations of sexual harassment brought against him by former employee Anita Hill by repeating the same words at the end of a series of phrases:

CLARENCE THOMAS: Mr. Chairman, I am a victim of this process and my
name has **been harmed**, my integrity has **been harmed**, my character
has **been harmed**, my family has **been harmed**, my friends have **been
harmed**. There is nothing this committee, this body, or this country can do
to give me my good name back—nothing.   (Torricelli 1999, 394)

In the same manner, in a lecture delivered in Rochester, New York, in 1850, the African-American abolitionist Frederick Douglass used final repetition to denounce the cruelties of the slave system:

FREDERICK DOUGLASS: To ensure good behavior, the slaveholder **relies
on the whip**; to induce proper humility, he **relies on the whip**; to rebuke
what he is pleased to term insolence, he **relies on the whip**; to supply the

place of wages, as an incentive to toil, he **relies on the whip**; to bind down the spirit of the slave, to imbrute and to destroy his manhood, he **relies on the whip**

(Foner and Taylor 1999, 167)

Note how these final repetitions work like a linguistic whip, where each successive phrase ends with the same resounding crack.

Shakespeare uses this device, too, throughout his plays, to achieve the same powerful effect.

FINAL REPETITIONS IN VERSE

Words

PRINCE: Do not think **so**. You shall not find it **so**.

1H4 3.2.129

OTHELLO: A fine **woman**, a fair **woman**, a sweet **woman**!

OTH 4.1.179

ANNE: Thy deeds inhuman and **unnatural**
Provokes this deluge most **unnatural**.

R3 1.2.60 (F)

RICHARD: He that bereft thee, lady, of thy **husband**
Did it to help thee to a better **husband**.

R3 1.2.138

SALISBURY: What other harm have I, good lady, **done**,
But spoke the harm that is by others **done**?

JN 3.1.38

BLANCHE: O, well did he become that lion's **robe**
That did disrobe the lion of that **robe**!

JN 2.1.141

RICHARD: This hand, which for thy **love**, did kill thy **love**,
Shall for thy **love**, kill a far truer **love**.

R3 1.2.189 (F)

NURSE: Tybalt is gone, and Romeo **banishèd**.
Romeo that kill'd him, he is **banishèd**.

ROM 3.2.69

PORTIA: We do pray for **mercy**,
And that same prayer doth teach us all to render
The deeds of **mercy**.

MV 4.1.200

QUEEN MARGARET: Have naught to do with **him**; beware of **him**;
Sin, death, and hell have set their marks on **him**,
And all their ministers attend on **him**.   R3 1.3.291

PROTEUS: To leave my Julia, shall I be **forsworn**;
To love fair Sylvia, shall I be **forsworn**;
To wrong my friend, I shall be much **forsworn**.   TGV 2.6.1

PRINCE: If all the year were playing holidays
To sport would be as tedious as to work;
But when they seldom **come**, they wish'd-for **come**   1H4 1.2.204

CONSTANCE: Thou shalt be punish'd for thus frighting me,
For I am sick and capable of **fears**,
Oppress'd with wrongs, and therefore full of **fears**,
A widow, husbandless, subject to **fears**,
A woman, naturally born to **fears**   JN 3.1.11

LEONTES: Is this **nothing**?
Why then the world and all that's in't is **nothing**,
The cov'ring sky is nothing, Bohemia **nothing**,
My wife is **nothing**, nor nothing have these nothings,
If this be **nothing**.   WT 1.2.292

HOTSPUR: He said he would not ransom **Mortimer**,
Forbade my tongue to speak of **Mortimer**,
But I will find him when he lies asleep,
And in his ear I'll holler "**Mortimer**!"
Nay, I'll have a starling shall be taught to speak
Nothing but "**Mortimer**," and give it him
To keep his anger still in motion.   1H4 1.3.219

Phrases

LADY MACBETH: To beguile **the time**,
Look like **the time**.   MAC 1.5.63

ADRIANA: In bed he slept not **for my urging it**;
At board he fed not **for my urging it**   ERR 5.1.63

SUFFOLK: The King will labor still **to save his life**,
The commons haply rise **to save his life**   2H6 3.1.239

DESDEMONA: Why I should fear **I know not**,
Since guiltiness **I know not**; but yet I feel I fear.   OTH 5.2.38

CHIRON: I care not, I, knew she and **all the world**:
I love Lavinia more than **all the world**.   TIT 2.1.71

SHYLOCK: I'll have **my bond**! Speak not against **my bond**!
I have sworn an oath that I shall have **my bond**!   MV 3.3.4

PROTEUS: Longer than I prove loyal to **your grace**
Let me not live to look upon **your grace**.   TGV 3.2.20

PETRUCHIO: I come to wive it wealthily **in Padua**;
If wealthily, then happily **in Padua**.   SHR 1.2.75

QUEEN ISABEL: God, the best maker of all marriages,
Combine your hearts **in one**, your realms **in one**!   H5 5.2.359

ROSS: The commons hath he pill'd with grievous taxes,
And quite lost their hearts. The nobles he hath fin'd
For ancient quarrels, **and quite lost their hearts**.   R2 2.1.246

HAMLET: This was **your husband**. Look you now what follows.
Here is **your husband**, like a mildew'd ear
Blasting his wholesome brother.   HAM 3.4.63 (Q2)

ANGELO: Answer to this:
I, now the voice of the recorded law,
Pronounce a sentence on your **brother's life**;
Might there not be a charity in sin
To save this **brother's life**?   MM 2.4.60

FRIAR LAURENCE: What, rouse thee, man! Thy Juliet is alive,
For whose dear sake thou wast but lately dead:
There art thou happy. Tybalt would kill thee,

But thou slew'st Tybalt: **there art thou happy**.
The law that threaten'd death becomes thy friend,
And turns it to exile: **there art thou happy**.

ROM 3.3.135

SILVIUS: If thou remember'st not the slightest folly
That ever love did make thee run into,
Thou hast not lov'd.
Or if thou hast not sat as I do now,
Wearying thy hearer in thy mistress' praise,
Thou hast not lov'd.
Or if thou hast not broke from company
Abruptly as my passion now makes me,
Thou hast not lov'd.

AYL 2.4.34

FINAL REPETITIONS IN PROSE

Words

SHALLOW: Nay, she must be **old**; she cannot choose but be **old**; certain she's **old**.

2H4 3.2.207

BENEDICK: I can find no rhyme to "lady" but "baby," an innocent **rhyme**; for "scorn," "horn," a hard **rhyme**; for "school," "fool," a babbling **rhyme**; very ominous endings.

ADO 5.2.37

PRINCE: See now, whether pure fear and entire cowardice doth not make thee wrong this virtuous gentlewoman. Is she of the **wicked**? is thine hostess here of the **wicked**? or is this boy of the **wicked**? or honest Bardolph, whose zeal burns in his nose, of the **wicked**?

2H4 2.4.325

KING HENRY: Put off your maiden blushes, take me by the hand, and say, "Harry of England, I am **thine**," which word thou shalt no sooner bless mine ear withal, but I will tell thee aloud, "England is **thine**, Ireland is **thine**, France is **thine**, and Henry Plantagenet is **thine**."

H5 5.2.235

Phrases

THERSITES: Agamemnon **is a fool**, Achilles **is a fool**, Thersites **is a fool**, and, as aforesaid, Patroclus **is a fool**.

TRO 2.3.58 (F)

SHYLOCK: I will buy **with you**, sell **with you**, talk **with you**, walk **with you**, and so following; but I will not eat **with you**, drink **with you**, nor pray **with you**.

MV 1.3.35

BENEDICK: One woman is fair, **yet I am well**; another is wise, **yet I am well**; another virtuous, **yet I am well**

ADO 2.3.27

BENEDICK: You are a villain; I jest not; I will make it good how **you dare**, with what **you dare**, and when **you dare**. Do me right, or I will protest your cowardice.

ADO 5.1.145

ROSALIND: A lean cheek, **which you have not**; a blue eye and sunken, **which you have not**; an unquestionable spirit, **which you have not**; a beard neglected, **which you have not**

AYL 3.2.373

FINAL REPETITIONS IN DIALOGUE

In dialogue, final repetitions behave like brazen pirates. Mark how the listener pilfers the last words of the speaker, then shamelessly employs that same ending to tell a completely different tale.

Words

PARIS: Happily met, my lady and my **wife**.
JULIET: That may be, sir, when I may be a **wife**.

ROM 4.1.18

PARIS: Younger than she are happy mothers **made**.
CAPULET: And too soon marr'd are those so early **made**.

ROM 1.2.12

CLARENCE: Bid Gloucester think on this, and he will **weep**.
FIRST MURDERER: Ay, millstones, as he lesson'd us to **weep**.

R3 1.4.239 (F)

Phrases

JULIA: They do not love that do not show **their love**.
LUCETTA: O, they love least that let men know **their love**.

TGV 1.2.31

ALL: Welcome high prince, the mighty **Duke of York**!
SOMERSET: [*Aside*] Perish, base prince, ignoble **Duke of York**.

1H6 3.1.176

QUEEN MARGARET: O Henry, let me plead for **gentle Suffolk**!
KING HENRY: Ungentle queen, to call him **gentle Suffolk**!

2H6 3.2.289

PETRUCHIO: I say it is the moon **that shines so bright**.
KATHERINA: I know it is the sun **that shines so bright**.

SHR 4.5.4

QUEEN: Hamlet, thou hast thy **father much offended**.
HAMLET: Mother, you have my **father much offended**.

HAM 3.4.9

KATHERINA: Asses **are made to bear, and so are you**.
PETRUCHIO: Women **are made to bear, and so are you**.

SHR 2.1.199

KING PHILIP: The yearly course that brings this day about
Shall never see it but **a holy day**.
CONSTANCE: A wicked day, and not **a holy day**!

JN 3.1.81

PETRUCHIO: I say **it is the moon**.
KATHERINA: I know **it is the moon**.
PETRUCHIO: Nay, then you lie; **it is the blessèd sun**.
KATHERINA: Then God be blest, **it is the blessèd sun**!

SHR 4.5.16

BASSANIO: Sweet Portia,
If you did know to whom I gave **the ring**,
If you did know for whom I gave **the ring**,
And would conceive for what I gave **the ring**,
And how unwillingly I left **the ring**,
When naught would be accepted but **the ring**,

You would abate the strength of your displeasure.
PORTIA: If you had known the virtue of **the ring**,
Or half her worthiness that gave **the ring**,
Or your own honor to contain **the ring**,
You would not then have parted with **the ring**.

MV 5.1.192

DIVIDED COUPLES

The repetition of one word or phrase at the beginning, and of another at the end, of successive phrases or sentences.

By combining the two previous devices—*initial* repetition and *final* repetition—and using them *simultaneously*, we get a new device: a *divided couple*. Divided couples are *couples*, because they always appear at the party together; they are *divided*, because they are kept apart by the crowd of text that comes between them.

DIVIDED COUPLES IN VERSE

RICHARD: I have **no brother**; I am like **no brother**

3H6 5.6.80

JULIET: **Come**, gentle **night**; **come**, loving, black-brow'd **night**,
Give me my Romeo

ROM 3.2.20

KING RICHARD: **It** cannot **be avoided but by this**:
It will not **be avoided but by this**.

R3 4.4.410

ISABELLA: **That Angelo's** forsworn, **is it not strange**?
That Angelo's a murd'rer, **is't not strange**?

MM 5.1.38

EDWARD: **Had he been** ta'en **we should have heard the news**;
Had he been slain **we should have heard the news**.

3H6 2.1.4

QUEEN MARGARET: **I had** an Edward, **till a Richard kill'd him**;
I had a Harry, **till a Richard kill'd him**.

R3 4.4.40

CLEOPATRA: **I laugh'd** him out of **patience**, and that night
I laugh'd him into **patience**, and next morn,
Ere the ninth hour, I drunk him to his bed

ANT 2.5.19

DUCHESS: **Go thou to** Richmond, and good fortune guide **thee.**
Go thou to Richard, and good angels tend **thee.**
Go thou to sanctuary, and good thoughts possess **thee.**   R3 4.1.91 (F)

CITIZEN: **If** lusty love should go in quest of beauty,
Where should he find it fairer **than in Blanche**?
If zealous love should go in search of virtue,
Where should he find it purer **than in Blanche**?   JN 2.1.426

DIANA: If you shall marry,
You give away this hand, and that is **mine;**
You give away heaven's vows, and those are **mine;**
You give away myself, which is known **mine**   AWW 5.3.169

HORATIO: Stay illusion!
If thou hast any sound, or use of voice,
Speak to me.
If there be any good thing to be done,
That may to thee do ease, and grace to me,
Speak to me.   HAM 1.1.127

DIVIDED COUPLES IN PROSE

ROSALIND: I'll tell you **who Time** ambles **withal, who Time** trots **withal,
who Time** gallops **withal,** and who he stands still withal.   AYL 3.2.310

BENEDICK: Why, i' faith, methinks she's **too** low for a high **praise, too**
brown for a fair **praise,** and **too** little for a great **praise**.   ADO 1.1.171

ROSALIND: [*To Phoebe*] **I will** marry you, if ever I marry woman, and I'll be
married tomorrow. [*To Orlando*] **I will** satisfy you, if ever I satisfy man,
and you shall be **married tomorrow**. [*To Silvius*] **I will** content you, if what
pleases you contents you, and you shall be **married tomorrow**.   AYL 5.2.113

BRUTUS: **Who is here so** base that he would be a bondman? **If any,
speak, for him have I offended. Who is here so** rude that would not be
a Roman? **If any, speak, for him have I offended. Who is here so** vile
that will not love his country? **If any, speak, for him have I offended.**   JC 3.2.29

DIVIDED COUPLES IN DIALOGUE

When do divided couples appear in dialogue?
When the listener wants to make a snappy comeback in dialogue!

ADRIANA: **Go back again**, thou slave, and fetch him **home**!
DROMIO OF EPHESUS: **Go back again** and be new beaten **home**?   ERR 2.1.75

BENEDICK: **They swore that you were** almost sick **for me**.
BEATRICE: **They swore that you were** well-nigh dead **for me**.   ADO 5.4.80

KING: **This maid** will not serve your **turn, sir**.
COSTARD: **This maid** will serve my **turn, sir**.   LLL 1.1.298

FORD: **Want no** money, Sir John, **you shall want none**.
FALSTAFF: **Want no** Mistress Ford, Master Brook, **you shall want none**.   WIV 2.2.258

ELEANOR: **Thou monstrous** slanderer **of heaven and earth**!
CONSTANCE: **Thou monstrous** injurer **of heaven and earth**!
Call not me slanderer.   JN 2.1.173

SON: **How will** my mother for a father's death
Take on with me, and ne'er **be satisfied**!
FATHER: **How will** my wife for slaughter of my son
Shed seas of tears, and ne'er **be satisfied**!
KING HENRY: **How will** the country for these woeful chances
Misthink the King, and not **be satisfied**!   3H6 2.5.103

BOOKENDS

The repetition at the end of a phrase or sentence of the word or words with which it began.

It's easy to see why this device is called a *bookend*—on the page, the repeated word looks just like a pair of identical bookends placed at each end of a row of books.

❧ ❧ ❧

BOOKENDS OVER ONE LINE OF VERSE

Bookends are easiest to spot when they occur in a complete sentence over a single line of verse:

KING HENRY: **Much** is your sorrow; mine ten times so **much**.	3H6 2.5.112
HAMLET: "**Seems**," madam? Nay, it is. I know not "**seems**."	HAM 1.2.76
PROVOST: **Drunk** many times a day, if not many days entirely **drunk**.	MM 4.2.149
CASSIUS: **Cassius** from bondage will deliver **Cassius**.	JC 1.3.90
RICHMOND: **Kings** it makes gods, and meaner creatures **kings**.	R3 5.2.24
EMILIA: **Moor**, she was chaste. She lov'd thee, cruel **Moor**.	OTH 5.2.249
POLONIUS: **Thus** it remains, and the remainder **thus**.	HAM 2.2.104
HELENA: **Weigh** oath with oath, and you will nothing **weigh**.	MND 3.2.131
MERCUTIO: **I** will not budge for no man's pleasure, **I**.	ROM 3.1.55
LEAR: **Blow**, winds, and crack your cheeks! Rage, **blow**!	LR 3.2.1
GAUNT: **Old** Gaunt indeed, and gaunt in being **old**.	R2 2.1.74
SUFFOLK: **Dead** in his bed, my lord; Gloucester is **dead**.	2H6 3.2.29
SUFFOLK: **Comfort**, my sov'reign; gracious Henry, **comfort**.	2H6 3.2.38
OLIVIA: **Hold**, Toby! On thy life, I charge thee, **hold**!	TN 4.1.45

BOOKENDS WITH SPILL-OVER

Sometimes there's not enough room between the bookends to hold all of the books, forcing a few volumes to spill out on one side or the other. In these examples, although the bookends neatly hold one line of verse in place, the *thought* being communicated is too big to be contained by them, and "spills over" into the neighboring line or lines.

BOLINGBROKE: **You** are my father, for methinks in **you**
I see old Gaunt alive.   R2 2.3.117

DUKE: So our decrees,
Dead to infliction, to themselves are **dead**   MM 1.3.27

SUFFOLK: **Consent**, and for thy honor give **consent**,
Thy daughter shall be wedded to my king.   1H6 5.3.136

KATHERINE: **Come** when the King doth to my lady **come**;
Then if I have much love, I'll give you some.   LLL 5.2.829

OCTAVIA: O my good lord,
Believe not all, or if you must **believe**,
Stomach not all.   ANT 3.4.10

PARIS: Then, I say,
Well may we fight for her whom we know **well**
The world's large spaces cannot parallel.   TRO 2.2.160

VIOLA: **Love** make his heart of flint that you shall **love**,
And let your fervor, like my master's, be
Plac'd in contempt.   TN 1.5.286

BOOKENDS OVER TWO LINES

In these examples, the books held by the bookends take up *two* shelves — that is, the repeated word happens in the line *below* rather than in the *same* line of verse.

AGRIPPA: **Truths** would be tales,
Where now half-tales be **truths**.   ANT 2.2.133

※ ※ ※

ULYSSES: **Pride** hath no other glass
To show itself but **pride**.

TRO 3.3.47

CORIOLANUS: **Purpose** so barr'd, it follows
Nothing is done to **purpose**.

COR 3.1.148

CAPULET: **Earth** hath swallow'd all my hopes but she:
She's the hopeful lady of my **earth**.

ROM 1.2.14

POLONIUS: **Mad** call I it, for to define true madness,
What is't but to be nothing else but **mad**?

HAM 2.2.93

KING PHILIP: **Peace** be to England, if that war return
From France to England, there to live in **peace**.

JN 2.1.89

CONSTANCE: **Law** cannot give my child his kingdom here,
For he that holds his kingdom holds the **law**

JN 3.1.187

KING HENRY: **Wither** one rose, and let the other flourish;
If you contend, a thousand lives must **wither**.

3H6 2.5.101

HECTOR: **Life** every man holds dear, but the dear man
Holds honor far more precious, dear, than **life**.

TRO 5.3.27

BOOKEND OVER THREE LINES
This is a rare example of a three-line bookend:

FIRST SENATOR: **Immediate** are my needs, and my relief
Must not be toss'd and turn'd to me in words,
But find supply **immediate**.

TIM 2.1.25

MULTIPLE BOOKENDS
These examples contain more than one bookend in a line. As in a Calder *mobile*, each element seems suspended from a branch, exquisitely counterpoised by a copy of itself.

KING HENRY: **Woe** above **woe**! **grief** more than common **grief**!

3H6 2.5.94

BUCKINGHAM: Come, lead me, officers, to the block of shame;
Wrong hath but **wrong**, and **blame** the due of **blame**.

R3 5.1.28 (F)

CITIZEN: **Blood** hath bought **blood**, and **blows** have answer'd **blows**;
Strength match'd with **strength**, and **power** confronted **power**.

JN 2.1.329

DUCHESS: The conquerors
Make war upon themselves, **brother** to **brother**,
Blood to **blood**, **self** against **self**.

R3 2.4.61 (F)

DUKE: An Angelo for Claudio, **death** for **death**;
Haste still pays **haste**, and **leisure** answers **leisure**;
Like doth quit **like**, and **measure** still for **measure**.

MM 5.1.409

REPEATED PHRASES AS BOOKENDS

These bookends are repeated *phrases* rather than repeated words.

IAGO: **I am** not what **I am**.

OTH 1.1.65

DESDEMONA: **My lord** is not **my lord**

OTH 3.4.124

OTHELLO: **Put out the light**, and then **put out the light**.

OTH 5.2.7

RICHARD: **We are not safe**, Clarence, **we are not safe**.

R3 1.1.70

KING HENRY: **Once more** unto the breach, dear friends, **once more**

H5 3.1.1

HOTSPUR: **The King** is kind, and well we know **the King**
Knows at what time to promise, when to pay.

1H4 4.3.52

BEROWNE: Come on then, I will swear to study so,
To know the thing I am forbid **to know**

LLL 1.1.59

MACBETH: The spring, the head, the fountain of your blood
Is stopp'd; the very source of it **is stopp'd**.

MAC 2.3.98

LUCETTA: I have no other than a woman's reason:
I think him so because **I think him so**.

TGV 1.2.23

VIOLA: **Prove true**, imagination, O, **prove true**,
That I, dear brother, be now ta'en for you.

TN 3.4.375

EDGAR: **The worst** is not,
So long as we can say, "This is **the worst**."

LR 4.1.27

BOOKENDS IN PROSE

Although far less common, a bookend will sometimes appear in prose.

TOUCHSTONE: "**So-so**" is good, very good, very excellent good; and yet
it is not, it is but "**so-so**."

AYL 5.1.27

A MIRRORED PHRASE

In this example, the words in the repeated phrase are reversed, creating a mirrored effect:

BRUTUS: **Remember March**, the ides of **March remember**

JC 4.3.18

BOOKENDS IN DIALOGUE

Sometimes bookends appear in dialogue, where the speaker's first word or phrase is repeated as the last word or words of the listener's response.

CYMBELINE: **Past grace**? obedience?
IMOGEN: Past hope, and in despair; that way, **past grace**.

CYM 1.1.136

HERMIA: **Methinks** I see these things with parted eye,
When everything seems double.
HELENA: So **methinks**.

MND 4.1.189

❧ ❧ ❧

LANDINGS
The last word or words of a phrase repeated as the beginning of the next phrase.

You'll understand why this device is called a *landing* if you imagine that the repeated word or phrase is the *top* of one flight of stairs, as well as the *bottom* of the next flight of stairs. A landing requires the climber to place both feet down securely before proceeding upward on the next set of steps. Landings are easiest to spot when they occur in the middle of a line of verse.

REPEATED WORDS AS LANDINGS

SHALLOW: Death, as the Psalmist saith, is certain to **all**, **all** shall die.

2H4 3.2.37

ORSINO: But for thee, **fellow**: **fellow**, thy words are madness.

TN 5.1.98

DON PEDRO: The former **Hero**! **Hero** that is dead!

ADO 5.4.65

DUCHESS OF YORK: Dost thou teach **pardon**, **pardon** to destroy?

R2 5.3.120

GAUNT: Watching breeds **leanness**, **leanness** is all gaunt.

R2 2.1.78

KING: O speak of **that**! **That** do I long to hear.

HAM 2.2.50

CLEOPATRA: Give me some **music**; **music**, moody food
Of us that trade in love.

ANT 2.5.1

JOHN: No more can I be sever'd from your side,
Than can **yourself yourself** in twain divide.

1H6 4.5.48

OTHELLO: That I have ta'en away this old man's daughter,
It is most **true**; **true** I have married her.

OTH 1.3.78

LYSANDER: She sees not **Hermia**. **Hermia**, sleep thou there,
And never mayst thou come Lysander near.

MND 2.2.135

PHILOSTRATE: I have heard it over,
And it is **nothing**, **nothing** in the world.

MND 5.1.77

HUMFREY: For, as we think,
You are the **king King** Edward hath depos'd

3H6 3.1.68 (F)

DON PEDRO: My love is thine to **teach**. **Teach** it but how,
And thou shalt see how apt it is to learn
Any hard lesson that may do thee good.

ADO 1.1.291

OCTAVIA: Husband **win**, **win** brother,
Prays and destroys the prayer; no midway
'Twixt these extremes at all.

ANT 3.4.18

OTHELLO: I know, Iago,
Thy honesty and love doth mince this matter,
Making it light to **Cassio**. **Cassio**, I love thee,
But never more be officer of mine.

OTH 2.3.246

REPEATED PHRASES AS LANDINGS

VIOLA: I see you what **you are, you are** too proud

TN 1.5.250

OTHELLO: Sweet soul, **take heed**, **take heed** of perjury.

OTH 5.2.50

SHYLOCK: You knew, **none so well**, **none so well** as you, of my daughter's flight.

MV 3.1.24

BENEDICK: But till all graces be in **one woman**, **one woman** shall not come in my grace.

ADO 2.3.30

ANTONIO: Muse not that I thus suddenly proceed,
For what **I will**, **I will**, and there an end.

TGV 1.3.64

BOLINGBROKE: As **I was banish'd**, **I was banish'd** Herford;
But as **I come**, **I come** for Lancaster.

R2 2.3.113

❦ ❦ ❦

LANDINGS IN DIALOGUE

Landings also appear in dialogue—more often than not, when the listener immediately restates the last word or words of the speaker as a *question*, an *exclamation*, or a *curt reply*.

MESSENGER: Madam,
She was a **widow** —
CLEOPATRA: **Widow**? Charmian, hark.   ANT 3.3.27

CITIZEN: Who is it that hath warn'd us to the walls?
KING PHILIP: 'Tis France for **England**.
KING JOHN: **England** for itself.   JN 2.1.201

PERICLES: Well, speak on. Where were you born?
And wherefore **call'd Marina**?
MARINA: **Call'd Marina**
For I was born **at sea**.
PERICLES: **At sea**! What mother?
MARINA: My mother was the daughter of a king;
Who died the minute I was born   PER 5.1.154

LANDINGS AND BOOKENDS USED TOGETHER

When landings and bookends appear together—as in these lines—the second half of the line seems to reflect back on the first.

LEAR: **Adultery**? Thou shalt not **die**: die for **adultery**?   LR 4.6.110 (F)

CONSTANCE: **War**, war, no **peace**! **Peace** is to me a **war**.   JN 3.1.113

LUCIUS: **Thy name** well fits **thy faith**; **thy faith thy name**.   CYM 4.2.381

BOLINGBROKE: **This** and **much more**, **much more** than twice all **this**,
Condemns you to the death.   R2 3.1.28

ENDLINE LANDINGS

Rather than occurring in the *middle* of a line of verse, as in the examples above, these landings are split over *two* lines—using the word or phrase at the very end of one line as the beginning of the next line.

Words Used as Endline Landings

LYSANDER: Why should you think that I should woo in **scorn**?
Scorn and derision never come in tears.   MND 3.2.122

KING RICHARD: Come, I have learn'd that fearful commenting
Is leaden servitor to dull **delay**;
Delay leads impotent and snail-pac'd beggary.   R3 4.3.51

SUFFOLK: She is content to be at your **command**;
Command, I mean, of virtuous chaste intents,
To love and honor Henry as her lord.   1H6 5.5.19

Phrases Used as Endline Landings

QUEEN ELIZABETH: O no, my reasons are **too deep and dead**:
Too deep and dead, poor infants, in their graves.   R3 4.4.362

KING HENRY: O thou that judgest all things, stay **my thoughts**,
My thoughts that labor to persuade my soul
Some violent hands were laid on Humphrey's life.   2H6 3.2.136

Endline Landings in Dialogue

In dialogue? Yes, endline landings also appear in dialogue, usually—just as with midline landings—as a *question*, an *exclamation*, or a *curt reply*.

Words

JULIA: And is that paper **nothing**?
LUCETTA: **Nothing** concerning me.   TGV 1.2.72

ANGELO: He must die **tomorrow**.
ISABELLA: **Tomorrow**? O, that's sudden — spare him, spare him!   MM 2.2.82

HELENA: Yet Hermia still loves you. Then be **content**.
LYSANDER: **Content** with Hermia? No, I do repent
The tedious minutes I with her have spent.   MND 2.2.110

⚜ ⚜ ⚜

LUCIO: If you will hang me for it, you may, but I had rather it would please you I might be **whipped**.

DUKE: **Whipped** first, and hanged after.

MM 5.1.505

CLEOPATRA: He's friends with Caesar,
In state of health, thou sayst; and thou sayst, **free**.

MESSENGER: **Free**, madam? No, I made no such report.
He's bound unto Octavia.

ANT 2.5.55

NORTHUMBERLAND: My lord, in the base court he doth attend
To speak with you. May it please you to come **down**?

KING RICHARD: **Down, down** I come, like glist'ring Phaeton,
Wanting the manage of unruly jades.

R2 3.3.176

Phrases

CORNWALL: Fetch forth the stocks!
As I have life and honor, there shall he sit **till noon**.

REGAN: **Till noon**? Till night, my lord, and all night too.

LR 2.2.125

PRINCE: **What's the matter**?

FALSTAFF: **What's the matter**? There be four of us here have ta'en a thousand pound this day morning.

PRINCE: Where is it, Jack? **Where is it**?

FALSTAFF: **Where is it**? Taken from us it is. A hundred upon poor four of us.

1H4 2.4.157

KING HENRY: No, on the barren mountains let him starve;
For I shall never hold that man my friend
Whose tongue shall ask me for one penny cost
To ransom home **revolted Mortimer**.

HOTSPUR: **Revolted Mortimer**!
He never did fall off, my sov'reign liege,
But by the chance of war.

1H4 1.3.89

LADDERS

A progression where the word or words at the end of each phrase in a sequence is repeated at the beginning of the next.

You'll understand why this device is called a *ladder*, if you imagine that the repeated word is a *rung* that requires the climber to place one foot securely down upon it, and then the other, before proceeding upward.

Here's a wonderful example of a ladder attributed to Benjamin Franklin:

BENJAMIN FRANKLIN: A little neglect may breed great mischief … for want of a nail, the **shoe** was lost; for want of a **shoe,** the **horse** was lost, and for want of a **horse**, the rider was lost.   (Bartlett 2002, 320)

Here's how Shakespeare's characters climb ladders of their own:

LADDERS IN VERSE

QUEEN: She's a lady
So tender of rebukes, that words are **strokes**,
And **strokes** death to her.   CYM 3.5.40

QUEEN MARGARET: O Buckingham, take heed of yonder dog.
Look when he fawns, **he bites**; and when **he bites**,
His venom tooth will rankle to the death.   R3 1.3.288 (F)

KING RICHARD: My brain I'll prove the female to **my soul,**
My soul the father, and these two beget
A generation of still breeding thoughts   R2 5.5.6

TITUS: Why 'tis no matter man: if they did hear,
They would not **mark** me; or if they did **mark**,
They would not pity me   TIT 3.1.33

KING RICHARD: My conscience hath a thousand several **tongues,**
And every **tongue** brings in a several **tale,**
And every **tale** condemns me for a villain.   R3 5.3.193

QUEEN: Be thou assur'd: if words be made of **breath**,
And **breath** of **life**, I have no **life** to breathe
What thou hast said to me.   HAM 3.4.197

KING RICHARD: The love of wicked men converts to **fear**;
That **fear** to **hate**, and **hate** turns one or both
To worthy danger and deservèd death.   R2 5.1.66

OTHELLO: No, Iago,
I'll see before I **doubt**; when I **doubt**, **prove**;
And on the **proof**, there is no more but this;
Away at once with love or jealousy.   OTH 3.3.189

KING: And let the kettle to the **trumpet** speak,
The **trumpet** to the **cannoneer** without,
The **cannons** to the **heavens**, the **heavens** to earth,
"Now the King drinks to Hamlet."   HAM 5.2.275

DROMIO OF EPHESUS: She is so hot because **the meat is cold**.
The meat is cold because **you come not home**.
You come not home because **you have no stomach**.
You have no stomach, having broke your fast   ERR 1.2.47

TROILUS: This she? No, this is Diomed's Cressida.
If beauty have a **soul**, this is not she;
If **souls** guide **vows**, if **vows** are **sanctimony**,
If **sanctimony** be the gods' delight,
If there be unity in rule itself,
This is not she.   TRO 5.2.137

HOTSPUR: I better brook the loss of brittle life
Than those proud titles thou hast won of me;
They wound my **thoughts** worse than thy sword my flesh.
But **thoughts**, the slaves of **life**, and **life**, **time's** fool,
And **time**, that takes survey of all the world,
Must have a stop.   1H4 5.4.78

☙ ☙ ☙

KING HENRY: O God! methinks it were a happy life
To be no better than a homely swain;
To sit upon a hill, as I do now,
To carve out dials quaintly, point by point,
Thereby to see the minutes how they run:
How many makes the **hour** full complete,
How many **hours** brings about the **day**,
How many **days** will finish up the **year**,
How many **years** a mortal man may live.   3H6 2.5.21

LADDERS IN PROSE

KING HENRY: If thou would have such a one, **take me**. And **take me**, **take a soldier**. **Take a soldier**, take a king.   H5 5.2.165

PARIS: He eats nothing but doves, love, and that breeds **hot blood**, and **hot blood** begets **hot thoughts**, and **hot thoughts** beget **hot deeds**, and **hot deeds** is love.   TRO 3.1.128

BEATRICE: Foul words is but **foul wind**, and **foul wind** is but **foul breath**, and **foul breath** is noisome; therefore I will depart unkissed.   ADO 5.2.52

HAMLET: Alexander died, Alexander was buried, Alexander returneth to **dust**; the **dust** is **earth**; of **earth** we make **loam**; and why of that **loam** whereto he was converted might they not stop a beer-barrel?   HAM 5.1.208 (Q2)

TOUCHSTONE: Why, if thou never wast at court, thou **never saw'st good manners**; if thou **never saw'st good manners**, then thy manners must be **wicked**, and **wickedness** is **sin**, and **sin** is damnation.   AYL 3.2.40

HAMLET: Farewell, dear mother.
KING: Thy loving father, Hamlet.
HAMLET: My mother. Father and mother is **man and wife**, **man and wife** is one flesh, and so, my mother.   HAM 4.3.49 (F)

PANTHINO: Tut, man, I mean thou'lt **lose the flood**, and in **losing the flood**, **lose the voyage**, and in **losing thy voyage**, **lose thy master**, and in **losing thy master**, **lose thy service**, and in **losing thy service** — [*Launce puts his hand over Panthino's mouth.*] Why dost thou stop my mouth?   TGV 2.3.41

ROSALIND: For your brother and my sister no sooner met but they **looked**; no sooner **looked** but they **loved**; no sooner **loved** but they **sighed**; no sooner **sighed** but they asked one another **the reason**; no sooner knew **the reason** but they sought the remedy; and in these degrees have they made a pair of stairs to marriage   AYL 5.2.32

A LADDER IN DIALOGUE

PANDARUS: He that will have a cake out of the wheat must needs **tarry the grinding**.
TROILUS: Have I not tarried?
PANDARUS: Ay, **the grinding**; but you must tarry **the bolting**.
TROILUS: Have I not tarried?
PANDARUS: Ay, **the bolting**; but you must tarry **the leavening**.
TROILUS: Still have I tarried.
PANDARUS: Ay, to **the leavening**; but here's yet in the word "hereafter" the kneading, the making of the cake, the heating the oven, and the baking. Nay, you must stay the cooling, too, or ye may chance burn your lips.   TRO 1.1.15

CHAPTER 5

Transformations

At the risk of sounding repetitive, Shakespeare has still more devices that use repetition in his lines. Rather than the *exact* repetition of a word or phrase, however, these methods involve a *transformation* of one kind or another—a verbal metamorphosis, if you will, to a different form, a different meaning, or a different order. In other words, a word may be introduced as a fat caterpillar, but the next time we hear it, it's a fluttering butterfly. Or a phrase may be introduced as an appetizing apple, but the next time we hear it, it's compost.

SENSE SHIFTING
The repetition of the same spelling of a word using different senses.

Perhaps the most famous modern example of sense shifting is from Franklin D. Roosevelt's inaugural address, given on March 4, 1933:

> FRANKLIN D. ROOSEVELT: So, first of all, let me assert my firm belief that the only thing we have to **fear** is **fear** itself — nameless, unreasoning, unjustified terror which paralyzes needed efforts to convert retreat into advance.   (Safire 1992, 779)

The first time FDR uses the word "fear," he uses it as a *verb*, meaning "to be afraid of." The second time he uses the word "fear," he uses it as a *noun*, meaning "terror" or "panic." The spelling of the word is the exactly the same in both instances, but the meaning of the word changes. That's a sense shift.

Note how Shakespeare uses this same device in his plays to strike a note of sophistication in the speaker.

SENSE SHIFTING IN SPEECHES

KING HENRY: You have good **leave** to **leave** us. 1H4 1.3.20

ULYSSES: Therefore 'tis **meet** Achilles **meet** not Hector. TRO 1.3.333

CAESAR: The cause is in my **will**; I **will** not come JC 2.2.71

GAUNT: Old **Gaunt** indeed, and **gaunt** in being old. R2 2.1.74

PISTOL: To England will I **steal**, and there I'll **steal** H5 5.1.87

DUKE: Look that you love your wife, her **worth worth** yours. MM 5.1.497

KING: Thy own **wish wish** I thee in ev'ry place. LLL 2.1.178

BENVOLIO: We'll **measure** them a **measure**, and be gone. ROM 1.4.10

FALSTAFF: O, give me the **spare** men, and **spare** me the great ones. 2H4 3.2.269

CONSTABLE: A very **little little** let us do,
And all is done. H5 4.2.33

LEONTES: Go **play**, boy, play: thy mother **plays**, and I
Play too WT 1.2.187

PERCY: My gracious lord, I **tender** you my service,
Such as it is, being **tender**, raw, and young R2 2.3.41

ISABELLA: I am a woeful suitor to your **honor**,
Please but your **honor** hear me. MM 2.2.27

DON PEDRO: Look what will serve is **fit**. 'Tis once, thou lovest,
And I will **fit** thee with the remedy. ADO 1.1.318

VALENTINE: He is complete in feature and in mind
With all good **grace** to **grace** a gentlemen.   TGV 2.4.73

HASTINGS: I'll have this **crown** of mine cut from my shoulders
Before I'll see the **crown** so foul misplac'd.   R3 3.2.43 (F)

KING RICHARD: Swell'st thou, proud heart? I'll give thee scope to **beat**,
Since foes have scope to **beat** both thee and me.   R2 3.3.140

PORTIA: Let me give **light**, but let me not be **light**;
For a light wife doth make a heavy husband.   MV 5.1.129

JULIA: Be calm good wind, blow not a word away,
Till I have found each **letter** in the **letter**   TGV 1.2.115

FALSTAFF: Mistress **Ford**? I have had **ford** enough. I was thrown into the
ford. I have my belly full of **ford**.   WIV 3.5.35

DUKE FREDERICK: Bring him dead or **living**
Within this twelvemonth, or turn thou no more
To seek a **living** in our territory.   AYL 3.1.6

FIRST GUARD: This is an aspic's trail, and these fig **leaves**
Have slime upon them, such as th' aspic **leaves**
Upon the caves of Nile.   ANT 5.2.351

SENSE SHIFTING IN DIALOGUE

Sometimes it makes sense, for a canny speaker hoping to score points, to echo a word already used in the dialogue, but with a different sense.

GREY: To who in all this presence speaks your **Grace**?
RICHARD: To thee, that hast nor honesty nor **grace**.   R3 1.3.54 (F)

NESTOR: Our **gen'ral** doth salute you with a kiss.
ULYSSES: Yet is the kindness but particular;
'Twere better she were kiss'd in **general**.   TRO 4.5.19

KING HENRY: Do you **like** me, Kate?
KATHERINE: *Pardonnez-moi*, I cannot tell vat is "**like** me."
KING HENRY: An angel is **like** you, Kate, and you are **like** an angel.   H5 5.2.107

POLONIUS: What is the **matter**, my lord?
HAMLET: Between who?
POLONIUS: I mean the **matter** that you read, my lord.
HAMLET: Slanders, sir   HAM 2.2.193

HAMLET: Give us the **foils**. Come on.
LAERTES: Come, one for me.
HAMLET: I'll be your **foil**, Laertes; in mine ignorance
Your skill shall, like a star i' th' darkest night,
Stick fiery off indeed.   HAM 5.2.254 (F)

ELEANOR: I can produce
A **will** that bars the title of thy son.
CONSTANCE: Ay, who doubts that? A **will**, a wicked **will**,
A woman's **will**, a canker'd grandam's **will**!   JN 2.1.191

ANTIPHOLUS OF SYRACUSE: Where is the thousand **marks** thou hadst
of me?
DROMIO OF EPHESUS: I have some **marks** of yours upon my pate,
Some of my mistress' **marks** upon my shoulders,
But not a thousand **marks** between you both.   ERR 1.2.81

Sense Shifting of a Phrase in Dialogue
Here's a rare example of a *phrase* repeated in dialogue, but with a different sense:

KING RICHARD: Ha, am I king? 'Tis so. But Edward lives.
BUCKINGHAM: **True, noble prince.**
KING RICHARD: O bitter consequence,
That Edward still should live, "**true noble prince**."   R3 4.2.14

REVERSE ORDER
The repetition of words in reverse order.

Probably the best-known example of *reverse order* is from John F. Kennedy's inaugural speech, delivered on January 20, 1961:

> JOHN F. KENNEDY: And so, my fellow Americans, ask not what your **country** can do for **you** — ask what **you** can do for your **country**.
> (Torricelli and Carroll 1999, 224)

Note how the words "country" and "you" are introduced in the first half of the sentence, and then elegantly restated — in *reverse order* — in the second half.

Realizing the power of the figure, Kennedy uses it again in the same speech:

> JOHN F. KENNEDY: Let us never **negotiate** out of **fear**, but let us never **fear** to **negotiate**.
> (Torricelli and Carroll 1999, 223)

And again in September 25 of same year, 1961, in a speech to the United Nations General Assembly:

> JOHN F. KENNEDY: **Mankind** must put an end to **war**, or **war** will put an end to **mankind**.
> (Ratcliffe 2000, 403)

Reversals tend to make memorable maxims:

> CONSTANTIN STANISLAVSKI: Love the **art** in **yourself**, not **yourself** in the **art**.
> (Grothe 1999, 43)

And great bumper stickers:

> CHIEF SEATTLE: This we know — the **earth** does not belong to **man**, **man** belongs to the **earth**.
> (Grothe 1999, 15)

❧ ❧ ❧

And pithy political platforms:

> HILARY RODHAM CLINTON: It is not enough to preach about **family values**. We must **value families**.   (Grothe 1999, 47)

In Shakespeare — as on bumpers and platforms — this device gets its punch by making a terse assertion, an assertion that is immediately turned on its head by reversing the position of its two major elements.

REVERSE ORDER IN SPEECHES

WITCHES: **Fair** is **foul**, and **foul** is **fair**	MAC 1.1.11
CONSTANCE: **War**, war, no **peace**! **Peace** to me is a **war**.	JN 3.1.113
HAMLET: Suit the **action** to the **word**, the **word** to the **action**	HAM 3.2.17
DUKE: **Love** talks with better **knowledge**, and **knowledge** with dearer **love**.	MM 3.2.150
LEONATO: How much better is it to **weep** at **joy**, than to **joy** at **weeping**.	ADO 1.1.28
PLAYER KING: For 'tis a question left us yet to prove, Whether **love** lead **fortune**, or else **fortune love**.	HAM 3.2.202
QUEEN MARGARET: Thy **friends** suspect for **traitors** while thou liv'st, And take deep **traitors** for thy dearest **friends**.	R3 1.3.222 (F)
FALSTAFF: O powerful love, that in some respects makes a **beast** a **man**, in some other a **man** a **beast**!	WIV 5.5.4
FESTE: **Virtue** that transgresses is but patched with **sin**, and **sin** that amends is but patched with **virtue**.	TN 1.5.48
ESCALUS: Rather **rejoicing** to see another **merry**, than **merry** at any thing which professed to make him **rejoice**.	MM 3.2.235
TOUCHSTONE: I do now remember a saying: "The **fool** doth think he is **wise**, but the **wise** man knows himself to be a **fool**."	AYL 5.1.30

FALSTAFF: A **pox** of this **gout**! Or, a **gout** of this **pox**! For the one or the
other plays the rogue with my big toe.   2H4 1.2.243

DUKE SENIOR: What would you have? Your **gentleness** shall **force**,
More than your **force** move us to **gentleness**.   AYL 2.7.102

HAMLET: For this same lord,
I do repent; but heav'n hath pleas'd it so
To punish **me** with **this,** and **this** with **me**
That I must be their scourge and minister.   HAM 3.4.172

DUKE: Dear Isabel,
I have a motion much imports your good,
Whereto if you'll a willing ear incline,
What's **mine** is **yours**, and what is **yours** is **mine**.   MM 5.1.534

REVERSE ORDER IN DIALOGUE

In dialogue, reverse order shows the speaker the flip side of his own argument — like turning a
man's well-worn coat inside out to show him a brand new lining.

CHIEF JUSTICE: You have **misled** the **youthful prince**.
FALSTAFF: The **youthful prince** hath **misled** me.   2H4 1.2.144

CHIEF JUSTICE: Well, God send the **prince** a better **companion**.
FALSTAFF: God send the **companion** a better **prince**. I cannot rid my
hands of him.   2H4 1.2.199

MARIA: That last is Berowne, the merry madcap lord.
No **word** with him but a **jest**.
BOYET: And every **jest** but a **word**.   LLL 2.1.215

REVERSE ORDER WITH RELATED WORDS

Although these examples are not "pure" — for they fail to repeat the *exact* same words — they
still fit the bill, for the *related words* involved are repeated in reverse order.

STANLEY: **Richmond** is on the **seas**.
KING RICHARD: There let him sink, and be the **seas** on **him**.   R3 4.4.462

TIMON: What dost thou **think** 'tis **worth**?
APEMANTUS: Not **worth** my **thinking**.   TIM 1.1.213

FORM SHIFTING
The repetition of the root of a word or words with different grammatical functions or forms.

A classic example of form shifting is this aphorism by William Penn (1644–1718):

WILLIAM PENN: Let the people think they **govern**, and they will be **governed**.
(Andrews 1993, 230)

Note how Penn uses the verb "govern" in the first part of the sentence, and "governed" in the second part. The root of the word is the same in each instance, but the grammatical form of the word changes. This is *form shifting*.

Another good example of this device is a quotation attributed to Robert Frost:

ROBERT FROST: Love is an **irresistible desire** to be **irresistibly desired**.
(Quinn 1982, 75)

This quote contains not just one, but *two* form shifts. First, Frost uses the word "irresistible" as an adjective, and then repeats it as an adverb, "irresistibly." He also uses the noun "desire," which he then repeats as a verb, "desired."

This device is one of Shakespeare's favorites, most often appearing in the text as closely related word pairs such as these—like fraternal twins being pushed in the same stroller by their devoted mother.

TWO FORMS OF A WORD

LYSANDER: I followed **fast**; but **faster** did he fly   MND 3.2.416

PROTEUS: **Unheedful** vows may **heedfully** be broken   TGV 2.6.11

ANNE: Thou **bloodless** remnant of that royal **blood**   R3 1.2.7

DUCHESS: Then **patiently** hear my **impatience**.   R3 4.4.157

DUMAINE: **Proceeded** well, to stop all good **proceeding**.   LLL 1.1.95

BASTARD: Straight let us **seek**, or straight we shall be **sought**   JN 5.7.79

GUILDENSTERN: **Happy** in that we are not **overhappy**.   HAM 2.2.228 (F)

THESEUS: Our sport shall be to **take** what they **mistake**.   MND 5.1.90

GLOUCESTER: Is it but **thought** so? What are they that **think** it? 2H6 3.1.107

KING RICHARD: I **wasted** time, and now doth time **waste** me   R2 5.5.49

HAMLET: **Conception** is a blessing; but as your daughter may **conceive**,
friend, look to't.   HAM 2.2.184

BENEDICK: So much for **praising** myself, who, I myself will bear witness,
is **praiseworthy**.   ADO 5.2.87

JULIET: He was not born to shame:
Upon his brow **shame** is **asham'd** to sit   ROM 3.2.91

KING JOHN: How oft the sight of means to do **do** ill deeds
Make deeds ill **done**.   JN 4.2.219

LEAR: I am a man
More **sinn'd** against than **sinning**.   LR 3.2.60 (F)

IMOGEN: **Society** is no comfort
To one not **sociable**.   CYM 4.2.12

NESTOR: In the **reproof** of chance
Lies the true **proof** of men.   TRO 1.3.33

BRACKENBURY: I will not reason what is **meant** hereby,
Because I will be guiltless of the **meaning**.   R3 1.4.93 (Q1)

FRENCH KING: Think we King Harry **strong**;
And princes, look you **strongly** arm to meet him.   H5 2.4.48

DECIUS: But when I tell him he hates **flatterers**
He says he does, being then most **flatterèd**.   JC 2.1.207

MELUN: What in the world should make me now **deceive**,
Since I must lose the use of all **deceit**?   JN 5.4.26

TITUS: Speak, Lavinia, what accursèd **hand**
Hath made thee **handless** in thy father's sight?   TIT 3.1.66

ANTONY: If it were so, it was a **grievous** fault,
And **grievously** hath Caesar answer'd it.   JC 3.2.79

ENOBARBUS: The loyalty well held to **fools** does make
Our faith mere **folly**.   ANT 3.13.42

KING HENRY: O, be sick, **great greatness**,
And bid thy ceremony give thee cure!   H5 4.1.251

BEROWNE: Therefore this article is made in **vain**,
Or **vainly** comes th' admired Princess hither.   LLL 1.1.139

PRINCE: I'll so **offend** to make **offense** a skill,
Redeeming time when men think least I will.   1H4 1.2.216

JULIA: Now trust me, 'tis an **office** of great worth,
And you an **officer** fit for the place.   TGV 1.2.44

CORDELIA: For thee, oppressèd King, I am cast down,
Myself could else **outfrown** false fortune's **frown**.   LR 5.3.5

CHATILLION: The proud control of fierce and bloody war,
To **enforce** these rights so **forcibly** withheld.   JN 1.1.17

KING JOHN: Go, Faulconbridge: now hast thou thy desire;
A **landless** knight makes thee a **landed** squire.

JN 1.1.176

KING RICHARD: Fair cousin, you **debase** your princely knee
To make the **base** earth proud with kissing it.

R2 3.3.190

TITUS: O, **handle** not the theme, to talk of **hands**,
Lest we remember still that we have none.

TIT 3.2.29

NESTOR: I would my arms could match thee in **contention**
As they **contend** with thee in courtesy.

TRO 4.5.205

KING: Come, Gertrude, we'll call up our wisest friends
And let them know both what we mean to **do**
And what's untimely **done**.

HAM 4.1.38

BEROWNE: Go to, it is a plague
That Cupid will impose for my neglect
Of his **almighty** dreadful little **might**.

LLL 3.1.201

HAMLET: Rightly to be great
Is not to stir without **great** argument,
But **greatly** to find quarrel in a straw
When honor's at the stake.

HAM 4.4.53 (Q2)

LADY PERCY: Him did you leave,
Second to none, **unseconded** by you,
To look upon the hideous god of war
With disadvantage

2H4 2.3.33

THREE FORMS OF A WORD

Add — *gasp!* — another child to the stroller, and the doting mom will push fraternal triplets.

DUCHESS OF YORK: A **beggar begs** that never **begg'd** before.

R2 5.3.78

LEONATO: Canst thou so daff me? Thou hast **kill'd** my child.
If thou **kill'st** me, boy, thou shalt **kill** a man.

ADO 5.1.78

ANGELO: The **tempter** or the **tempted**, who sins most, ha?
Not she, nor doth she **tempt**

MM 2.2.163

KING RICHARD: Is this the **face** that **fac'd** so many follies
That was at last **out-fac'd** by Bolingbroke?

R2 4.1.285

QUEEN MARGARET: Ah, little **joy enjoys** the queen thereof,
For I am she, and altogether **joyless**.

R3 1.3.154

BALTHASAR: **Note** this before my **notes**:
There's not a **note** of mine that's worth the **noting**.

ADO 2.3.54

ARMADO: I do affect the very ground, which is **base**, where her shoe,
which is **baser**, guided by her foot, which is **basest**, doth tread.

LLL 1.2.167

KATHERINA: **Moved**? In good time! Let him that **moved** you hither
Remove you hence. I knew you at the first
You were a **movable**.

SHR 2.1.195

KING RICHARD: Then crushing penury
Persuades me I was better when a **king**;
Then am I **king'd** again, and by and by
Think that I am **unking'd** by Bolingbroke,
And straight am nothing.

R2 5.5.34

RICHARD: Look how I am **bewitch'd**! Behold, mine arm
Is like a blasted sapling wither'd up.
And this is Edward's wife, that monstrous **witch**,
Consorted with that harlot strumpet Shore,
That by their **witchcraft** thus have markèd me.

R3 3.4.68 (F)

ELEANOR: Give with our niece a dowry large enough,
For by this match thou shalt so **surely** tie
Thy now **unsur'd assurance** to the crown,

That yon green boy shall have no sun to ripe
The bloom that promiseth a mighty fruit.   JN 2.1.469

PORTIA: **Happy** in this, she is not yet so old
But she may learn; **happier** than this,
She is not bred so dull but she can learn;
Happiest of all, is that her gentle spirit
Commits itself to yours to be directed,
As from her lord, her governor, her king.   MV 3.2.160

TWO FORMS OF TWO WORDS

To push the "child" metaphor just a little further, here we see two sets of fraternal twins — that
is, two forms of two words — all happily playing together in the same sandbox.

JULIET: I'll **look** to **like**, if **looking liking** move   ROM 1.3.97

FESTE: Better a **witty fool** than a **foolish wit**.   TN 1.5.36

PORTIA: You **taught** me first to **beg**, and now methinks
You **teach** me how a **beggar** should be answer'd.   MV 4.1.439

DUCHESS: **Rest** thy **unrest** on England's **lawful** earth,
Unlawfully made drunk with innocent blood.   R3 4.4.29

PANDULPH: All **form** is **formless, order orderless**,
Save what is opposite to England's love   JN 3.1.253

KING RICHARD: Plead what I will **be**, not what I have **been**,
Not my **deserts**, but what I will **deserve**.   R3 4.4.414

MESSENGER: He hath indeed **better bettered expectation** than you
must **expect** of me to tell you how.   ADO 1.1.15

YORK: O, my liege,
Pardon me if you **please**; if not, I, **pleas'd**
Not to be **pardon'd**, am content withal.   R2 2.1.186

QUEEN MARGARET: Urge neither **charity** nor **shame** to me:
Uncharitably with me have you dealt,
And **shamefully** my hopes by you are butcher'd.

R3 1.3.273 (F)

TWO FORMS OF THREE WORDS

Add yet *another* pair of fraternal twins to the sandbox, however, and things can get a bit chaotic.

TROILUS: The Greeks are **strong**, and **skillful** to their **strength**,
Fierce to their **skill**, and to their **fierceness** valiant.

TRO 1.1.7

TWO FORMS OF A WORD IN DIALOGUE

In dialogue, the listener borrows a word from the speaker, deliberately alters it to fit his or her own ends, and gives it back again, refashioned.

SYLVIA: Is she not passing **fair**?
JULIA: She hath been **fairer**, madam, than she is.

TGV 4.4.148

FRIAR: Lady, what man is he you are **accus'd** of?
HERO: They know that do **accuse** me. I know none.

ADO 4.1.176

HERMIA: I would my father **look'd** but with my eyes.
THESEUS: Rather your eyes must with his judgment **look**.

MND 1.1.56

HIPPOLYTA: He says they can do nothing in this **kind**.
THESEUS: The **kinder** we, to give them thanks for nothing.

MND 5.1.88

TALBOT: Thou never hadst **renown**, nor canst not lose it.
JOHN: Yes, your **renownèd** name: shall flight abuse it?

1H6 4.5.40

PARIS: Come you to make **confession** to this father?
JULIET: To answer that, I should **confess** to you.

ROM 4.1.22

❧ ❧ ❧

LEAR: Out of my **sight**!
KENT: **See** better Lear, and let me still remain
The true blank of thine eye.   LR 1.1.157

DEMETRIUS: I'll run from thee and hide me in the brakes,
And leave thee to the mercy of **wild** beasts.
HELENA: The **wildest** hath not such a heart as you.   MND 2.1.227

THREE FORMS OF A WORD IN DIALOGUE

KATHERINA: Where did you study all this goodly speech?
PETRUCHIO: It is extempore, from my mother **wit**.
KATHERINA: A **witty** mother! **Witless** else her son.   SHR 2.1.262

KING JOHN: Alack, thou dost **usurp** authority.
KING PHILIP: Excuse it is to beat **usurping** down.
ELEANOR: Who is it thou dost call **usurper**, France?   JN 2.1.118

PRINCESS: Haste, signify so much, while we attend,
Like humble-visag'd suitors, his high **will**.
BOYET: Proud of employment, **willingly** I go.
PRINCESS: All pride is **willing** pride, and yours is so.   LLL 2.1.33

KING RICHARD: Wrong not her birth; she is a royal princess.
QUEEN ELIZABETH: To **save** her life, I'll say she is not so.
KING RICHARD: Her life is **safest** only in her birth.
QUEEN ELIZABETH: And only in that **safety** died her brothers.   R3 4.4.212 (F)

REPEATED STRUCTURES
The repetition of the same grammatical pattern using different words.

One of the best examples of this device is Julius Caesar's famous boast:

JULIUS CAESAR: I came, I saw, I conquered.   (Ratcliffe 2000, 368)

Here, a simple grammatical pattern is clearly repeated three times: I **Verb**, I **Verb**, I **Verb**. This is sometimes called *parallel structure.*

Another fine example is ascribed to Charles V of Spain (1500–1558), who reportedly said:

> CHARLES V: I speak Spanish to God, Italian to women, French to men, and German to my horse.
> (Bartlett 2002, 149)

Again, note the repeated structure: I speak **Noun** to **Noun**, **Noun** to **Noun**, **Noun** to **Noun**, and **Noun** to my **Noun**. Note also how each phrase is of approximately equal length, which is another feature of the device.

Here's a modern example from Edward Kennedy's memorial tribute to his brother Robert F. Kennedy, given on June 8, 1968:

> EDWARD KENNEDY: My brother need not be idealized, or enlarged in death beyond what he was in life, to be remembered simply as a good and decent man, who saw wrong and tried to right it, saw suffering and tried to heal it, saw war and tried to stop it.
> (Torricelli 1999, 276)

Again, note how the basic structure is repeated: "who saw **Noun** and tried to **Verb** it, saw **Noun** and tried to **Verb** it, saw **Noun** and tried to **Verb** it."

Shakespeare, too, used these repeated structures in his language:

REPEATED STRUCTURES IN VERSE

> MERCUTIO: He heareth not, he stirreth not, he moveth not;
> The ape is dead, and I must conjure him.
> ROM 2.1.15

> BUCKINGHAM: Thou art sworn as deeply to effect what we intend
> As closely to conceal what we impart.
> R3 3.1.158

> BELARIUS: O, this life
> Is nobler than attending for a check,
> Richer than doing nothing for a bribe,
> Prouder than rustling in unpaid-for silk
> CYM 3.3.21

HOTSPUR: For he made me mad
To see him shine so brisk, and smell so sweet,
And talk so like a waiting gentlewoman
Of guns and drums and wounds   1H4 1.3.53

BLANCHE: Husband, I cannot pray that thou mayst win;
Uncle, I needs must pray that thou mayst lose;
Father, I may not wish the fortunes thine;
Grandam, I will not wish thy wishes thrive.   JN 3.1.331

RICHARD: And therefore, since I cannot prove a lover
To entertain these fair well-spoken days,
I am determinèd to prove a villain,
And hate the idle pleasures of these days.   R3 1.1.28

LEAR: 'Tis not in thee
To grudge my pleasures, to cut off my train,
To bandy hasty words, to scant my sizes,
And in conclusion, to oppose the bolt
Against my coming in.   LR 2.4.173

KING JOHN: Behold, the French amaz'd vouchsafe a parle,
And now instead of bullets wrapp'd in fire
To make a shaking fever in your walls,
They shoot but calm words folded up in smoke,
To make a faithless error in your ears   JN 2.1.226

PRIAM: Come, Hector, come. Go back.
Thy wife hath dreamt, thy mother hath had visions,
Cassandra doth foresee, and I myself
Am like a prophet suddenly enrapt
To tell thee that this day is ominous.   TRO 5.3.62

POLONIUS: Which done, she took the fruits of my advice,
And he, repell'd (a short tale to make),
Fell into a sadness, then into a fast,
Thence to a watch, thence into a weakness,
Thence into a lightness, and, by this declension,

Into the madness wherein now he raves
And all we mourn for.

HAM 2.2.145 (Q2)

REPEATED STRUCTURES IN PROSE

In prose, freed from the rhythmical strictures of verse, these repeated structures take on a looser musical quality— more Satchmo than Strauss, more Gershwin than Gluck, more Brubeck than Bach.

SHYLOCK: If you prick us, do we not bleed? If you tickle us, do we not laugh? If you poison us, do we not die? And if you wrong us, shall we not revenge?

MV 3.1.64

SHYLOCK: No ill luck stirring but what lights o' my shoulders, no sighs but o' my breathing, no tears but o' my shedding.

MV 3.1.95

BEROWNE: Well, she hath one o' my sonnets already: the clown bore it, the fool sent it, and the lady hath it.

LLL 4.3.15

BRUTUS: As Caesar loved me, I weep for him; as he was fortunate, I rejoice at it; as he was valiant, I honor him; but, as he was ambitious, I slew him.

JC 3.2.25

BRUTUS: There is tears for his love; joy for his fortune; honor for his valor; and death for his ambition.

JC 3.2.27

NATHANIEL: Your reasons at dinner have been sharp and sententious: pleasant without scurrility, witty without affection, audacious without impudency, learned without opinion, and strange without heresy.

LLL 5.1.2

KENT: I do profess to be no less than I seem, to serve him truly that will put me in trust, to love him that is honest, to converse with him that is wise and says little, to fear judgment, to fight when I cannot choose, and to eat no fish.

LR 1.4.13

SECOND MURDERER: I'll not meddle with it. It makes a man a coward: a man cannot steal but it accuseth him; a man cannot swear but it checks him; a man cannot lie with his neighbor's wife but it detects him.

R3 1.4.134

SHYLOCK: He hath disgraced me, and hindered me half a million, laughed at my losses, mocked at my gains, scorned my nation, thwarted my bargains, cooled my friends, heated mine enemies — and what's his reason?

MV 3.1.54

DON JOHN: I cannot hide what I am: I must be sad when I have cause and smile at no man's jests, eat when I have stomach and wait for no man's leisure, sleep when I am drowsy and tend on no man's business, laugh when I am merry, and claw no man in his humor.

ADO 1.3.13

REPEATED STRUCTURES IN DIALOGUE

In dialogue, the listener not only receives the *words* of the speaker, but also saves the *package* they came in. That same customized package is then carefully reloaded with different words, and sent off as a return message to the speaker.

GREMIO: O, this learning, what a thing it is!
GRUMIO: O, this woodcock, what an ass it is!

SHR 1.2.159

RICHARD: Never came poison from so sweet a place.
ANNE: Never hung poison on a fouler toad.

R3 1.2.146

KING: Sir, I will pronounce your sentence: you shall fast a week with bran and water.
COSTARD: I had rather pray a month with mutton and porridge.

LLL 1.1.300

DON PEDRO: O day untowardly turned!
CLAUDIO: O mischief strangely thwarting!
DON JOHN: O plague right well prevented!

ADO 3.2.131

ROSALINE: Shall I come upon thee with an old saying, that was a man when King Pepin of France was a little boy, as touching the hit it?
BOYET: So I may answer thee with one as old, that was a woman when Queen Guinevere of Britain was a little wench, as touching the hit it.

LLL 4.1.119

RICHARD: Fairer than tongue can name thee, let me have
Some patient leisure to excuse myself.
ANNE: Fouler than heart can think thee, thou canst make
No excuse current but to hang thyself.

R3 1.2.81

RICHARD: Vouchsafe, divine perfection of a woman,
Of these supposèd crimes to give me leave
By circumstance but to acquit myself.
ANNE: Vouchsafe, defus'd infection of a man,
Of these known evils but to give me leave
By circumstance t' accuse thy cursèd self.

R3 1.2.75

SOUND-ALIKES

The use of two or more words in neighboring phrases that sound alike, but differ in spelling and meaning.

The English language is loaded with homophones, words that sound alike but are spelled differently and have different meanings—words like "aisle" and "isle"; "blue" and "blew"; "cent" and "scent"; "days" and "daze"; "earn" and "urn"; "flour" and "flower," and so on.

Although puns have for centuries been much maligned as the lowest form of humor, they were much enjoyed and admired in Shakespeare's time.

The examples below fall into the category of repetition, because Shakespeare deliberately uses *both* forms of the sound-alike close enough to each other so that we very clearly hear the repetition of *one* pronunciation, but with two meanings. Note how Shakespeare uses these sound-alikes not just in comedy, but in *dramatic* scenes as well.

SOUND-ALIKES IN SPEECHES

COBBLER: Truly, sir, **all** that I live by is with the **awl**.

JC 1.1.21

BEROWNE: O, what a **scene** of fool'ry have a **seen**

LLL 4.3.161

LEAR: Look, look, a mouse! **Peace, peace;** this **piece** of toasted cheese
will do it.

LR 4.6.89 (F)

GRATIANO: Not on thy **sole**, but on thy **soul**, harsh Jew,
Thou mak'st thy knife keen.   MV 4.1.123

ANNE: Lo, in these windows that let forth thy life,
I **pour** the helpless balm of my **poor** eyes.   R3 1.2.12 (F)

TALBOT: Sell every man his life as **dear** as mine,
And they shall find **dear deer** of us, my friends.   1H6 4.2.53

MARIA: I heard my lady talk of it yesterday; and of a foolish **knight** that
you brought in one **night** here to be her wooer.   TN 1.3.15

FALSTAFF: Indeed I am in the **waist** two yards about, but I am now about
no **waste**; I am about thrift.   WIV 1.3.42

KING RICHARD: Bid him bring his power
Before **sun**-rising, lest his **son** George fall
Into the blind cave of eternal night.   R3 5.3.60

VIOLA: O Time, thou must untangle this, **not** I;
It is too hard a **knot** for me t'untie.   TN 2.2.40

ROMEO: You have dancing shoes
With nimble **soles**. I have a **soul** of lead
So stakes me to the ground I cannot move.   ROM 1.4.14

GUIDERIUS: With his own sword,
Which he did wave against my **throat**, I've ta'en
His head from him. I'll **throw't** into the creek
Behind our rock, and let it to the sea   CYM 4.2.149

SOUND-ALIKES IN DIALOGUE

In dialogue, the listener takes advantage of these dual pronunciations to win a duel of wits.

In Verse

WINCHESTER: **Rome** shall remedy this.
GLOUCESTER: **Roam** thither then.   1H6 3.1.51

NURSE: O, tell me, did you see Aaron the **Moor**?
AARON: Well, **more** or less, or ne'er a whit at all   TIT 4.2.52

PETRUCHIO: What's this? Mutton?
FIRST SERVANT: **Ay**.
PETRUCHIO: Who brought it?
PETER: **I**.   SHR 4.1.160

KING: But now, my cousin Hamlet and my **son** —
HAMLET: [*Aside*] A little more than kin and less than kind.
KING: How is it that the clouds still hang on you?
HAMLET: Not so, my lord, I am too much in the **sun**.   HAM 1.2.64 (F)

MERCUTIO: You are a lover; borrow Cupid's wings,
And **soar** with them above a common bound.
ROMEO: I am too **sore** enpiercèd with his shaft
To **soar** with his light feathers   ROM 1.4.17

MARCUS: O, thus I found her straying in the park,
Seeking to hide herself, as doth the **deer**
That hath receiv'd some unrecuring wound.
TITUS: It was my **dear**, and he that wounded her
Hath hurt me more than had he kill'd me dead   TIT 3.1.88

In Prose

SPEED: "Item: She can **sew**."
LAUNCE: That's as much as to say, "Can she **so**?"   TGV 3.1.306

POLONIUS: I did enact Julius Caesar. I was kill'd i' th' **Capitol**. Brutus
kill'd me.
HAMLET: It was brute part of him to kill so **capital** a calf there.   HAM 3.2.103

CHIEF JUSTICE: Your means are very slender, and your **waste** is great.
FALSTAFF: I would it were otherwise; I would my means were greater, and my **waist** slender.   2H4 1.2.140

PANTHINO: Away, ass! You'll lose the **tide** if you tarry any longer.
LAUNCE: It is no matter if the **tied** were lost, for it is the unkindest **tied** that ever any man **tied**.
PANTHINO: What's the unkindest **tide**?
LAUNCE: Why he that's **tied** here, Crab, my dog.   TGV 2.3.36

OBSOLETE SOUND-ALIKES

Sometimes, due to changes in pronunciation over the past four hundred years, sound-alikes no longer sound alike.

DEMETRIUS: Thou told'st me they were stol'n unto this **wood**,
And here am I, and **woo'd** within this wood
Because I cannot meet my Hermia.   MND 2.1.191

GONZALO: When every grief is entertained that's offered, comes to the entertainer —
SEBASTIAN: **A dollar**.
GONZALO: **Dolour** comes to him indeed. You have spoken truer than you purposed.   TMP 2.1.16

CHAPTER 6

Substitutions

Children are wizards at making imaginative substitutions—like using a blanket as a set of wings, or a towel as a super-hero's cape; turning a thick stick into a baseball bat, or a long skirt into a mermaid's tail; making a rocket ship out of a cardboard box, or a clubhouse out of a pile of sofa cushions.

Shakespeare practices a similar kind of wizardry in his plays, making substitutions in his language to spark the listener's childlike imagination—like using a familiar noun as a verb, or an invented title as a nickname; presenting a small part of something as the thing itself, or a wild exaggeration as the truth; replacing proper words with fabulously mangled ones, or lucid sentences with ridiculously florid ones.

PARTS OF SPEECH
The substitution of one part of speech for another.

In modern life, it's not uncommon to hear one part of speech substituted for another. For example, we take for granted that certain brand names can be used as verbs, such as Google, meaning "to perform an internet search"; Xerox, meaning "to photocopy"; FedEx, meaning "to ship overnight"; and Spam, meaning "to send unsolicited e-mail." We do not fall apart when we hear a verb phrase used as a noun, like "teardown"—an older house fated to be demolished and replaced by a new house. Nor do we fret when we discover a noun dressed up as an adjective, like the word "angsty."

It shouldn't surprise us, then, when Shakespeare substitutes one part of speech for another in precisely the same way, such as using the noun "dog" as a verb, meaning "to track like a hound"; the noun "candy" as an adjective, meaning "sugary and flattering"; and the verb "annoy" as a noun, meaning "pain and suffering."

NOUNS USED AS VERBS

THESEUS: Well **moused**, lion.	MND 5.1.269
EDGAR: He **childed** as I father'd.	LR 3.6.110 (Q1)
CLEOPATRA: He **words** me girls, he **words** me	ANT 5.2.191
LEWIS: I am too high-born to be **propertied**	JN 5.2.79
MONTANO: But, good lieutenant, is your gen'ral **wiv'd**?	OTH 2.1.60
KING HENRY: Destruction straight shall **dog** them at the heels.	R2 5.3.139
MACBETH: Come, seeling night, **Scarf** up the tender eye of pitiful day	MAC 3.2.46
POMPEY: Julius Caesar, Who at Philippi the good Brutus **ghosted**	ANT 2.6.12
FIRST QUEEN: Give us the bones Of our dead kings, that we may **chapel** them	TNK 1.1.49
MACBETH: Accursèd be that tongue that tells me so, For it hath **cow'd** my better part of man!	MAC 5.8.17

MACBETH: Here had we now our country's honor **roof'd,**
Were the grac'd person of our Banquo present

MAC 3.4.39

LEAR: When the thunder would not **peace** at my bidding, there I found
'em, there I smelt 'em out.

LR 4.6.102 (F)

MENENIUS: You shall perceive that a Jack guardant cannot **office** me
from my son Coriolanus.

COR 5.2.62

EDGAR: My face I'll grime with filth,
Blanket my loins, **elf** all my hair in knots

LR 2.3.9 (F)

EDGAR: The crows and choughs that **wing** the midway air
Show scarce so gross as beetles.

LR 4.6.13

KING HENRY: Why, what read you there
That have so **cowarded** and chas'd your blood
Out of appearance?

H5 2.2.74

FRANCE: Sure, her offence
Must be of such unnatural degree
That **monsters** it

LR 1.1.218

ANTONY: Wouldst thou be **window'd** in great Rome, and see
Thy master thus with pleach'd arms, bending down
His corrigible neck

ANT 4.14.72

ANTONY: Henceforth,
The white hand of a lady **fever** thee;
Shake thou to look on't.

ANT 3.13.137

ALONSO: I wish
Myself were **mudded** in that oozy bed
Where my son lies.

TMP 5.1.150

CLEOPATRA: And I shall see
Some squeaking Cleopatra **boy** my greatness
In the posture of a whore.

ANT 5.2.219

CALIBAN: And here you **sty** me
In this hard rock, whiles you do keep from me
The rest o' th' island.

TMP 1.2.342

CORDELIA: And wast thou fain, poor father,
To **hovel** thee with swine and rogues forlorn
In short and musty straw?

LR 4.7.37

ARIEL: Be't to fly,
To swim, to dive into the fire, to ride
On the curl'd clouds, to thy strong bidding **task**
Ariel and all his quality.

TMP 1.2.190

HAMLET: Nay, but to live
In the rank sweat of an enseamèd bed,
Stew'd in corruption, **honeying**, and making love
Over the nasty sty!

HAM 3.4.92

LEAR: Will you, with those infirmities she owes,
Unfriended, new-adopted to our hate,
Dower'd with our curse and **stranger'd** with our oath,
Take her or leave her?

LR 1.1.202 (F)

AUFIDIUS: Though in this city he
Hath **widow'd** and unchilded many a one,
Which to this hour bewail the injury,
Yet he shall have a noble memory.

COR 5.6.151

ADJECTIVES USED AS VERBS

SIMONIDES: Your presence **glads** our days.

PER 2.3.21

CAPULET: Thank me no thankings, nor **proud** me no prouds

ROM 3.5.152

MACBETH: Good things of day begin to droop and **drowse**,
Whiles night's black agents to their preys do rouse. MAC 3.2.52

ANTONY: My more particular
And that which most with you should **safe** my going,
Is Fulvia's death. ANT 1.3.55

ALEXAS: So he nodded,
And soberly did mount an arm-gaunt steed,
Who neigh'd so high that what I would have spoke
Was beastly **dumbed** by him. ANT 1.5.47

LEONTES: I chose
Camillo for the minister to poison
My friend Polixenes; which had been done,
But that the mind of good Camillo **tardied**
My swift command WT 3.2.159

VERBS USED AS NOUNS

CRESSIDA: I true? How now? What wicked **deem** is this? TRO 4.4.59

KING EDWARD: Sound drums and trumpets! Farewell sour **annoy**!
For here, I hope, begins our lasting joy. 3H6 5.7.45

GLOUCESTER: And doggèd York, that reaches at the moon,
Whose overweening arm I have pluck'd back,
By false **accuse** doth level at my life. 2H6 3.1.158

DUKE: Again, if any Syracusan born
Come to the bay of Ephesus — he dies,
His goods confiscate to the Duke's **dispose** ERR 1.1.18

NOUNS USED AS ADJECTIVES

POMPEY: But all the charms of love,
Salt Cleopatra, soften thy wan'd lip!

ANT 2.1.20

HOTSPUR: Why, what a **candy** deal of courtesy
This fawning greyhound then did proffer me!

1H4 1.3.251

A TITLE USED AS A VERB

LUCIO: Lord Angelo **dukes** it well in his absence

MM 3.2.94

BODY PARTS USED AS VERBS

DOUGLAS: No man so potent breathes upon the ground
But I will **beard** him.

1H4 4.1.11

POSTHUMUS: 'Tis still a dream, or else such stuff as madmen
Tongue and **brain** not

CYM 5.4.145

CLEOPATRA: A hand that kings
Have **lipp'd**, and trembled kissing.

ANT 2.5.29

HAMLET: But if indeed you find him not within this month, you shall **nose**
him as you go up the stairs into the lobby.

HAM 4.3.35 (Q2)

MENENIUS: Go you that banish'd him;
A mile before his tent fall down, and **knee**
Your way into his mercy.

COR 5.1.4

A PRONOUN USED AS A VERB

SIR TOBY: If thou **thou'st** him some thrice, it shall not be amiss

TN 3.2.45

⸗ ⸗ ⸗

A PRONOUN USED AS A NOUN

ORLANDO: Run, run, Orlando, carve on every tree
The fair, the chaste, and unexpressive **she**.　　　　　　　　AYL 3.2.9

IMOGEN: Or I could make him swear
The **shes** of Italy should not betray
Mine interest and his honor　　　　　　　　CYM 1.3.28

ANTONY: Whip him. Were't twenty of the greatest tributaries
That do acknowledge Caesar, should I find them
So saucy with the hand of **she** here — what's her name,
Since she was Cleopatra?　　　　　　　　ANT 3.13.96

A PRONOUN USED AS ANOTHER PRONOUN

KING RICHARD: **Me** rather had my heart might feel your love,
Than my unpleas'd eye see your courtesy.　　　　　　　　R2 3.3.192

ELEANOR: Come to thy grandam, child.
CONSTANCE: Do, child, go to **it** grandma, child.
Give grandam kingdom, and **it** grandam will
Give **it** a plum, a cherry, and a fig.
There's a good grandam.　　　　　　　　JN 2.1.159

RELATED WORDS
The substitution of a word or phrase for a related word or phrase.

When we hear the saying "the pen is mightier than the sword," we readily comprehend the meaning — that writing can have greater force than armies — despite the substitutions used in the line. We understand that "the pen" is standing in for the power of the written word, and that the "the sword" is a proxy for the power of military force.

So, too, in our everyday lives, we understand, when we hear someone speak of a part of a thing, or an item related to a thing, that a substitution has occurred. We readily understand that "a line" is a letter, "wheels" are an automobile, "threads" are clothes, "heads" are persons, "hands" are workers, "smokes" are cigarettes, "sweat" is hard labor, "a bottle" is an alcoholic drink, "Wall Street" is the financial world, "Hollywood" is the film industry, and "the White House" is the President.

Shakespeare does the same thing in his plays. We know, for example, when we hear "the crown," that it often means more than an imperial headpiece—it means the King or the Queen. When we hear "the scepter," we know that it often means more than the regal staff—it means the power of the monarchy. And when we hear "the throne," we know that it often means more than than the royal seat—it means the kingship of England.

SUBSTITUTING AN ELEMENT OR PART OF A THING FOR THE THING ITSELF

MACBETH: Take thy **face** hence. MAC 5.3.19
(Face for self)

LEONTES: No **foot** shall stir. WT 5.3.98
(Foot for person)

ROSS: Your **eye** in Scotland
Would create soldiers MAC 4.3.186
(Eye for leadership, oversight, presence)

HAMLET: I'll lug the **guts** into the neighbor room. HAM 3.4.212
(Guts for Polonius's body)

MARINA: Never was **waves** nor **wind** more violent PER 4.1.59
(Waves and wind for the sea)

CORNWALL: Lest it see more, prevent it. Out, vile **jelly**! LR 3.7.83
(Jelly for Gloucester's eye)

FOOL: For there was never yet fair woman but she made **mouths** in a glass. LR 3.2.36
(Mouths for faces)

BENEDICK: Is it not strange that **sheep's guts** should hale souls out of men's bodies? ADO 3.2.59
(Sheep's guts for lute strings)

BEATRICE: Would it not grieve a woman to be overmastered with a piece of valiant **dust**? ADO 2.1.61
> *(Dust for a man)*

VOLUMNIA: These are the ushers of Martius. Before him he carries **noise**, and behind him he leaves **tears**. COR 2.1.158
> *(Noise for the sound of the army; tears for the sound of women mourning)*

SCROOP: **White-beards** have arm'd their thin and hairless scalps Against thy majesty R2 3.2.112
> *(White beards for old men)*

HAMLET: Two thousand souls and twenty thousand ducats Will not debate the question of **this straw**. HAM 4.4.25 (Q 2)
> *(This straw for the disputed land)*

PRINCE EDWARD: Speak like a subject, proud ambitious York! Suppose that I am now **my father's mouth**; Resign thy chair, and where I stand, kneel thou 3H6 5.5.17
> *(My father's mouth for the King's voice)*

ANTONIO: She that from Naples Can have no note, unless the sun were post — The man i' th' moon's too slow — till **new-born chins** Be rough and razorable TMP 2.1.247
> *(New-born chins for babies' faces)*

SUBSTITUTING RELATED ITEMS FOR THE THING ITSELF

ANTONY: Friends, Romans, countrymen, lend me your **ears**! JC 3.2.73
> *(Ears for attention)*

HAMLET: And do still, by these **pickers and stealers**. HAM 3.2.336 (Q2)
> *(Pickers and stealers for hands)*

❧ ❧ ❧

PROSPERO: At first sight
They have chang'd **eyes.**   TMP 1.2.441
   (Eyes for loving looks)

ISABELLA: There spake my brother! There my **father's grave**
Did utter forth a voice.   MM 3.1.85
   (Father's grave for dead father)

ROSALIND: But I must comfort the weaker vessel, as **doublet and hose**
ought to show itself courageous to **petticoat**   AYL 2.4.6
   (Men's clothes for men; women's clothes for women)

BASTARD: **Bell, book, and candle** shall not drive me back
When **gold and silver** becks me to come on.   JN 3.3.12
   (Bell book and candle for excommunication; gold and silver for profit)

ELEANOR: Could I come near your beauty with my nails,
I'd set my **ten commandments** in your face.   2H6 1.3.141
   (Commandments for fingers)

SUBSTITUTING A QUALITY FOR A PROPER NAME

VIOLA: Farewell, fair **cruelty.**   TN 1.5.288
   (A quality for Olivia's name)

PROSPERO: Shrug'st thou, **malice**?   TMP 1.2.367
   (A quality for Caliban's name)

PROSPERO: Bravely, my **diligence.**   TMP 5.1.241
   (A quality for Ariel's name)

AUTOLYCUS: **Age**, thou hast lost thy labor.   WT 4.4.760
   (A quality to address the Shepherd)

⁂ ⁂ ⁂

SUBSTITUTING A QUALITY OF THE THING FOR THE THING ITSELF

VIOLA: How easy is it for the **proper-false**
In women's waxen hearts to set their forms.   TN 2.2.29
  (Proper-false for handsome and deceitful men)

LEAR: Know that we have divided
In three our kingdom; and 'tis our fast intent
To shake all cares and business from our age,
Conferring them on younger **strengths**   LR 1.1.37 (F)
  (Strengths for men and women)

UNRELATED WORDS

The substitution of a word or phrase for an unrelated word or phrase in order to suggest a likeness or analogy between them.

In the examples above, the substitution occurs *inside* the family—like a grandfather or a brother walking the bride down the aisle instead of her father. In the examples below, the substitution occurs *outside* the family—that is, a completely *unrelated* object or idea is used in place of another. This type of substitution is used to force a comparison between two dissimilar things—to suggest hidden qualities, to reveal new facets, or to offer a fresh perspective on the original.

In this parallel universe, a spoon can walk the bride down the aisle so she can marry a potato, and a bicycle pump can be the preacher. This is made possible by a type of verbal alchemy known as *metaphor*. And in this mystical art, Shakespeare is a sorcerer of the highest order.

HAMLET: I will speak **daggers** to her, but use none.   HAM 3.2.396
  (Words are daggers)

MACBETH: I have supp'd full with **horrors**   MAC 5.5.13
  (Horrors are food, fuel, sustenance)

LEAR: Peace, Kent!
Come not between the **dragon** and his wrath.   LR 1.1.121
  (Lear is a dragon)

IMOGEN: Prithee, dispatch:
The **lamb** entreats the **butcher**: where's thy knife?   CYM 3.4.95
    (Imogen is a lamb; Pisanio is a butcher)

CLAUDIO: There, Leonato, take her back again.
Give not this **rotten orange** to your friend   ADO 4.1.31
    (Hero is a rotten orange)

JULIA: Injurious **wasps**, to feed on such sweet **honey**
And kill the bees that yield it with your stings!   TGV 1.2.103
    (Julia's fingers are wasps; Proteus's words are honey)

GLOUCESTER: Thus is the **shepherd** beaten from thy side,
And **wolves** are gnarling who shall gnaw thee first.   2H6 3.1.191
    (Gloucester is a shepherd; the courtiers are wolves)

MARIA: Will you hoist sail, sir? Here lies your way.
VIOLA: No, good **swabber**, I am to hull here a little longer.   TN 1.5.202
    (Maria is a sailor)

HAMLET: Besides, to be demanded of a **sponge**, what replication should
be made by the son of a King?   HAM 4.2.12
    (Rosencrantz is a sponge)

BUCKINGHAM: Had you not come upon your **cue**, my lord,
William Lord Hastings had **pronounc'd your part**   R3 3.4.26 (F)
    (Richard is an actor)

PETRUCHIO: My **falcon** now is sharp and passing empty,
And till she stoop she must not be full gorg'd,
For then she never looks upon her lure.   SHR 4.1.190
    (Katherine is a falcon)

❧ ❧ ❧

MACDUFF: Most sacrilegious murder hath broke ope
The Lord's anointed **temple** and stole thence
The life o' th' building.   MAC 2.3.67
    (King Duncan is a temple)

QUEEN: Ah, thou the **model** where old Troy did stand,
Thou **map** of honor, thou King Richard's **tomb**,
And not King Richard.   R2 5.1.11
    (Richard is a model, a map, a tomb)

IAGO: This **broken joint** between you and her husband entreat her to
splinter, and, my fortunes against any lay worth naming, this crack of your
love shall grow stronger than it was before.   OTH 2.3.322
    (A marital quarrel is a broken bone)

ROMEO: If I profane with my unworthiest hand
This **holy shrine**, the gentler sin is this:
My lips, **two blushing pilgrims**, ready stand
To smooth that rough touch with a holy kiss.   ROM 1.5.93
    (Juliet's hand is a holy shrine; Romeo's lips are blushing pilgrims)

NICKNAMES

The substitution of a term of affection, familiarity, or contempt for a proper name.

People like to use nicknames to express their feelings for other human beings. We give common nicknames to important people, like "Jack" for John F. Kennedy, "Jackie" for Jacqueline Kennedy, and "Di" for Princess Diana. We truncate and compress names, such as "Dubya" for George W. Bush, "Ike" for Dwight D. Eisenhower, and "Jacko" for Michael Jackson. We create contemptuous nicknames, such as "Tricky Dick" for Richard M. Nixon and "Slick Willie" for Bill Clinton. We bestow honorary titles, such as "Lady Day" for Billie Holiday, "Duke" for John Wayne, and "The Chairman of the Board" for Frank Sinatra. And we invent affectionate names, like "Magic" for Earvin Johnson and "Lady Bird" for LBJ's wife Claudia Taylor Johnson.

The Bard's characters use nicknames in just the same fashion.

AFFECTIONATE NICKNAMES
The substitution of a familiar name for a proper name.

KING HENRY: I thank thee, **Meg**; these words content me much.　　2H6 3.2.26
   (Queen Margaret as Meg)

KING EDWARD: Come, hither, **Bess**, and let me kiss my boy.　　3H6 5.7.15
   (Queen Elizabeth as Bess)

GLOUCESTER: Come, **Nell**, thou wilt ride with us?　　2H6 1.2.59
   (Dame Eleanor as Nell)

QUEEN MARGARET: O, **Ned**, sweet, **Ned**, speak to thy mother, boy.　　3H6 5.5.51
   (Edward, Prince of Wales as Ned)

FALSTAFF: God save thy Grace, King **Hal**, my royal **Hal**.　　2H4 5.5.41
   (Henry the Fifth as Hal)

PETRUCHIO: You lie, in faith, for you are called plain **Kate**,
And bonny **Kate**, and sometimes **Kate** the curst　　SHR 2.1.185
   (Katherina as Kate)

NICKNAMES MADE FROM FORMAL TITLES
The substitution of a mock title for a proper name.

BEATRICE: I pray you, is **Signior Mountanto** returned from the wars or
no?　　ADO 1.1.30
   (Of Benedick)

BENEDICK: What, my dear **Lady Disdain**! Are you yet living?　　ADO 1.1.118
   (Of Beatrice)

BENEDICK: I cannot endure my **Lady Tongue**.　　ADO 2.1.275
   (Of Beatrice)

BENEDICK: Ha! The Prince and **Monsieur Love**! ADO 2.3.36
    (Of Claudio)

BEATRICE: Surely, a princely testimony, a goodly count, **Count Comfect**, a sweet gallant, surely. ADO 4.1.316
    (Of Claudio; comfect means candy, or confection)

BENEDICK: For my **Lord Lackbeard** there, he and I shall meet, and till then peace be with him. ADO 5.1.192
    (Of Claudio)

STEPHANO: We'll not run, **Monsieur Monster**. TMP 3.2.18
    (Of Caliban)

LUCIO: Behold, behold, where **Madam Mitigation** comes! MM 1.2.44
    (Of Mistress Overdone, who "mitigates" by relieving lust and desire)

ANTONIO: This ancient morsel, this **Sir Prudence** TMP 2.1.286
    (Of Gonzalo)

POINS: What says **Monsieur Remorse**? 1H4 1.2.113
    (Of Falstaff)

LUCIO: Come hither, **Goodman Baldpate**, do you know me? MM 5.1.326
    (Of the Duke)

BEROWNE: This is the ape of form, **Monsieur the Nice**,
That when he plays at tables chides the dice
In honorable terms. LLL 5.2.325
    (Of Boyet)

Nicknames in Dialogue

JAQUES: I'll tarry no longer with you. Farewell, good **Signior Love**.
ORLANDO: I am glad of your departure. Adieu, good **Monsieur Melancholy**. AYL 3.2.292

❧ ❧ ❧

TERMS OF ENDEARMENT
The substitution of an affectionate term or "pet name" for a proper name.

SIR TOBY: Good night, **Penthesilea**.   TN 2.3.177
    (To Maria, referring to the Queen of the Amazons)

STEPHANO: Open your mouth. Here is that which will give language to
you, **cat**.   TMP 2.2.83
    (To Caliban)

STEPHANO: **Moon-calf**, speak once in thy life, if thou beest a good
moon-calf.   TMP 3.2.21
    (To Caliban)

PANDARUS: Ah, poor **capocchia**, has't not slept tonight?   TRO 4.2.31
    (To Cressida, using the Italian for "dolt" or "simpleton")

MACBETH: Be innocent of the knowledge, dearest **chuck**,
Till thou applaud the deed.   MAC 3.2.45
    (To Lady Macbeth)

PISTOL: Trust none,
For oaths are straws, men's faiths are wafer-cakes,
And hold-fast is the only dog, **my duck**.   H5 2.3.52
    (To Hostess Quickly)

TERMS OF CONTEMPT
The substitution of an abusive or diminutive term for a proper name.

PRINCE: Here comes **lean Jack**, here comes **bare-bone**.   1H4 2.4.326
    (Meaning, Falstaff)

FALSTAFF: Peace, good **pint-pot**; peace, good **tickle-brain**.   1H4 2.4.397
    (Meaning, Mistress Quickly)

MACBETH: What soldiers, **patch**?
Death of thy soul, those linen cheeks of thine
Are counselors to fear. What soldiers, **whey-face**? MAC 5.3.15
    (Meaning, the Servant)

QUEEN MARGARET: And where's that valiant crookback prodigy
Dicky your boy, that with his grumbling voice
Was wont to cheer his dad in mutinies? 3H6 1.4.76
    (Meaning, Richard, Duke of Gloucester)

MOCK TITLES USING "OF"
The substitution of a mock title using "of" for a proper name.

PRINCE: I am not yet of Percy's mind, the **Hotspur of the north** 1H4 2.4.102
    (Meaning, Harry Percy)

CAMILLO: Good sooth, she is
The **queen of curds and cream**. WT 4.4.161
    (Meaning, Perdita)

LUCIO: By my troth, Isabel, I loved thy brother; if the old fantastical **Duke
of dark corners** had been at home, he had lived. MM 4.3.156
    (Meaning, Duke Vincentio)

YORK: **She-wolf of France**, but worse than wolves of France,
Whose tongue more poisons than the adder's tooth! 3H6 1.4.111
    (Meaning, Queen Margaret)

BENVOLIO: Why, what is Tybalt?
MERCUTIO: More than **prince of cats**. O, he's the courageous **captain
of compliments**. ROM 2.4.19
    (Meaning, Tybalt)

❧ ❧ ❧

EXAGGERATIONS

The substitution of a deliberate and obvious exaggeration for an accurate, precise, or literal statement.

Sometimes the truth is not enough to get the point across. Sometimes it's necessary to use a deliberate and obvious exaggeration, to overstate the truth for effect:

"I've told you a thousand times to clean up your room."

"I could eat a million of these."

"I could sleep for a week."

"This book weighs a ton."

"He's the most beautiful man alive."

"It's the greatest love story ever filmed."

"This is the most important piece of legislation of our lifetime."

These deliberate distortions of the truth are sometimes referred to as *hyperbole*, and Shakespeare uses the device a thousand times better than anyone who ever wrote anything since the Sumerians invented cuneiform.

CLEOPATRA: His legs bestrid the ocean; his rear'd arm
Crested the world.

ANT 5.2.82

HAMLET: I lov'd Ophelia. Forty thousand brothers
Could not with all their quantity of love
Make up my sum.

HAM 5.1.269

DOLL: Ah, rogue, i' faith, I love thee. Thou art as valorous as Hector of Troy,
worth five of Agamemnon, and ten times better than the Nine Worthies.
Ah, villain!

2H4 2.4.218

LAERTES: Now pile your dust upon the quick and dead,
Till of this flat a mountain you have made

T' o'ertop old Pelion or the skyish head
Of blue Olympus.   HAM 5.1.251

ROSALIND: Break an hour's promise in love? He that will divide a minute
into a thousand parts and break but a part of the thousandth part of a
minute in the affairs of love, it may be said of him that Cupid hath clapped
him o' the shoulder, but I'll warrant him heart-whole.   AYL 4.1.44

PAULINA: A thousand knees
Ten thousand years together, naked, fasting,
Upon a barren mountain, and still winter
In storm perpetual, could not move the gods
To look that way thou wert.   WT 3.2.210

SUFFOLK: Now, by the ground that I am banish'd from,
Well could I curse away a winter's night,
Though standing naked on a mountain top,
Where biting cold would never let grass grow,
And think it but a minute spent in sport.   2H6 3.2.334

PORTIA: Yet for you
I would be trebled twenty times myself,
A thousand times more fair, ten thousand times more rich
That only to stand high in your account
I might in virtues, beauties, livings, friends
Exceed account.   MV 3.2.152

MOCK RHETORIC

The deliberate substitution of florid, affected, imprecise, or courtly words for straightforward ones.

Shakespeare's characters will sometimes use *mock rhetoric*—courtly language that is meant to sound sophisticated, intellectual, and mannered, but is nothing but a sham. Mock rhetoric is used to obscure the truth, as with Hamlet's enigmatic confession to Rosencrantz and Guildenstern; or to intimidate, as with Touchstone's attempts to repel a rival for Audrey's affections; or to con the listeners, as when Autolycus lords over the shepherd and his son; or to ridicule the use of courtly language itself, as when Kent confronts Cornwall.

HAMLET: I am but mad north-north-west. When the wind is southerly, I know a hawk from a handsaw.

HAM 2.2.378

FESTE: I did impeticos thy gratility, for Malvolio's nose is no whipstock, my lady has a white hand, and the Myrmidons are no bottle-ale houses.

TN 2.3.26

TOUCHSTONE: Then learn this of me: to have, is to have; for it is a figure in rhetoric that drink, being pour'd out of a cup into a glass, by filling the one doth empty the other. For all your writers do consent that *ipse* is he. Now, you are not *ipse*, for I am he.

AYL 5.1.40

FESTE: Bonos dies, Sir Toby; for, as the old hermit of Prague, that never saw pen and ink, very wittily said to a niece of King Gorboduc, "That that is, is"; so I, being Master Parson, am Master Parson; for what is "that" but "that," and "is" but "is"?

TN 4.2.12

AUTOLYCUS: Whether it like me or no, I am a courtier. Seest thou not the air of the court in these enfoldings? Hath not my gait in it the measure of the court? Receives not thy nose court-odor from me? Reflect I not on thy baseness court-contempt? Think'st thou, for that I insinuate to toze from thee thy business, I am therefore no courtier? I am courtier *cap-a-pe*; and one that will either push on or pluck back thy business there; whereupon I command thee to open thy affair.

WT 4.4.730

KENT: Sir, in good faith, in sincere verity,
Under th' allowance of your great aspect,
Whose influence, like the wreath of radiant fire
On flick'ring Phoebus front —
CORNWALL: What mean'st by this?
KENT: To go out of my dialect, which you discommend so much.

LR 2.2.105 (F)

HAMLET: Sir, his definement suffers no perdition in you, though I know to divide him inventorially would dozy th' arithmetic of memory, and yet but yaw neither in respect of his quick sail. But in the verity of extolment, I take him to be a soul of great article, and his infusion of such dearth and rareness

as, to make true diction of him, his semblable is his mirror, and who else
would trace him, his umbrage, nothing more. HAM 5.2.112 (Q2)

EUPHEMISM
The substitution of an inoffensive term for an offensive one.

In civilized company, euphemisms are part of everyday conversation, where politeness dictates using mild, indirect, or vague terms rather than risk offending someone with harsh, blunt, or coarse language. Two subjects that regularly inspire euphemistic speech are death and bodily functions. Instead of death, we talk about passing away, being called home, and meeting one's maker. To avoid discussing specific bodily functions, we excuse ourselves to freshen up, powder our noses, and visit the rest room.

Shakespeare's characters make similar substitutions to avoid uttering something unpleasant.

OLIVIA: **'Tis not that time of moon with me** to make one in so skipping
a dialogue. TN 1.5.200
    (Meaning, she's having her period)

AUTOLYCUS: Walk before toward the sea-side, go on the right hand. **I
will but look upon the hedge,** and follow you. WT 4.4.825
    (Meaning, he needs to urinate)

CLEOPATRA: And it is great
To do **that thing that ends all other deeds** ANT 5.2.4
    (Meaning, suicide)

KING: Where is Polonius?
HAMLET: In heaven. Send thither to see. If your messenger find him not
there, **seek him i' th' other place yourself**. HAM 4.3.32
    (Meaning, go to hell)

❧ ❧ ❧

CHIEF JUSTICE: How doth the King?

WARWICK: Exceeding well. **His cares are now all ended**.

CHIEF JUSTICE: I hope, not dead.

WARWICK: **He's walked the way of nature**,

And to our purposes he lives no more.   2H4 5.2.2

    (Meaning, the King is dead)

MALAPROPS
The use of good words ill-applied, or wrongly placed.

The word "malaprop" originally comes from the French *mal à propos*, meaning "inappropriate." The use of the word to describe perfectly good words used imperfectly can be traced back to the appearance of Mrs. Malaprop in 1775 in the play *The Rivals* by Richard Brinsley Sheridan:

MRS. MALAPROP: He is the very **pine-apple** of politeness!

                    (Sheridan, 3.3.25)

    (She means pinnacle)

MRS. MALAPROP: She's as headstrong as an **allegory** on the banks of the Nile.   (Sheridan, 3.3.217)

    (She means an alligator)

Malaprops can still be heard in modern life as well. Our forty-third president, for example, has created a cottage industry with his prolific use of malaprops—often dubbed *Bushisms*—that continually begets books, calendars, magnets, posters, T-shirts, mugs, and tote bags.

GEORGE W. BUSH: Reading is the **basics** for all learning.

                    (Weisberg 2004, 26)

    (He means basis)

GEORGE W. BUSH: We cannot let terrorists and rogue nations hold this nation **hostile** or hold our allies **hostile**.   (Weisberg 2004, 48)

    (He means hostage)

GEORGE W. BUSH: I am mindful not only of preserving executive powers for myself, but for **predecessors** as well.   (Weisberg 2004, 95)
> *(He means successors)*

Of course, Shakespeare, never having seen *The Rivals*, and never having heard George W. Bush, would not have called these slips of the tongue "malaprops" — but he used them just the same. Most often we hear them in the comedies, voiced by characters like Dogberry, who is, without question, the very pine-apple of Shakespeare's malaprop-makers. But malaprops occur in the histories, romances, and tragedies as well.

MUCH ADO ABOUT NOTHING

DOGBERRY: You are thought here to be the most **senseless** and fit man for the constable of the watch; therefore bear you the lantern.   ADO 3.3.23
> *(He means sensible)*

DOGBERRY: You shall also make no noise in the streets; for, for the watch to babble and to talk is most **tolerable** and not to be endured.   ADO 3.3.35
> *(He means intolerable)*

DOGBERRY: Marry, sir, I would have some **confidence** with you that **discerns** you nearly.   ADO 3.5.2
> *(He means conference and concerns)*

DOGBERRY: Comparisons are **odorous**.   ADO 3.5.16
> *(He means odious)*

DOGBERRY: Only get the learned writer to set down our **excommunication**, and meet me at the jail.   ADO 3.5.63
> *(He means examination, or communication)*

※ ※ ※

DOGBERRY: O villain! Thou wilt be condemned into everlasting **redemption** for this.

(He means damnation)

ADO 4.2.57

DOGBERRY: Dost thou not **suspect** my place? Dost thou not **suspect** my years?

(He means respect)

ADO 4.2.74

DOGBERRY: No, thou villain, thou art full of **piety**, as shall be proved upon thee by good witness.

(He means impiety)

ADO 4.2.79

DOGBERRY: By this time our sexton hath **reformed** Signor Leonato of the matter.

(He means informed)

ADO 5.1.254

VERGES: Yea, or else it were pity but they should suffer **salvation**, body and soul.

(He means damnation)

ADO 3.3.2

FIRST WATCH: We here have **recovered** the most dangerous piece of **lechery** that was ever known in the commonwealth.

(He means discovered and treachery)

ADO 3.3.167

A MIDSUMMER NIGHT'S DREAM

BOTTOM: But I will **aggravate** my voice so that I will roar you as gently as any sucking dove. I will roar you an 'twere any nightingale.

(He means moderate, or mitigate)

MND 1.2.81

BOTTOM: We will meet, and there we may rehearse most **obscenely** and courageously.

(Perhaps Bottom means unseen, without being seen?)

MND 1.2.108

BOTTOM: O, wherefore, Nature, didst thou lions frame,
Since lion vile hath here **deflower'd** my dear

(He means devoured)

MND 5.1.292

BOTTOM: But I pray you, let none of your people stir me. I have an **exposition** of sleep come upon me.

MND 4.1.39

(He means disposition)

QUINCE: Ay, or else one must come in with a bush of thorns and a lantern, and say he comes to **disfigure**, or to **present**, the person of Moonshine.

MND 3.1.60

(He means figure and represent)

THE MERRY WIVES OF WINDSOR

BARDOLPH: Why, sir, for my part, I say the gentleman had drunk himself out of his **five sentences**.

WIV 1.1.175

(He means five senses)

HOST: For the which, I will be thy **adversary** toward Anne Page.

WIV 2.3.94

(He means emissary, or advocate)

SLENDER: But if you say, "Marry her," I will marry her; that I am freely **dissolved**, and **dissolutely**.

WIV 1.1.251

(He means resolved and resolutely)

QUICKLY: She does so take on with her men; they mistook their **erection**.

WIV 3.5.40

(She means direction)

QUICKLY: Good faith, it is such another Nan; but, I **detest**, an honest maid as ever broke bread.

WIV 1.4.150

(She means protest)

THE MERCHANT OF VENICE

GOBBO: He hath a great **infection**, sir, as one would say, to serve.

MV 2.2.125

(He means affection)

LAUNCELOT: In very brief, the suit is **impertinent** to myself, as your worship shall know by this honest old man

MV 2.2.137

(He means pertinent)

GOBBO: That is the very **defect** of the matter, sir.   MV 2.2.143
  (He means effect)

LAUNCELOT: I do beseech you, sir, go. My young master doth expect
your **reproach**.   MV 2.5.20
  (He means approach)

MEASURE FOR MEASURE

ELBOW: My wife, sir, whom I **detest** before heaven and your honor   MM 2.1.69
  (He means protest)

ELBOW: I do lean upon justice, sir, and do bring in here before your good
honor two notorious **benefactors**.   MM 2.1.50
  (He means malefactors)

ELBOW: First, and it like you, the house is a **respected** house; next, this
is a **respected** fellow; and his mistress is a **respected** woman.   MM 2.1.162
  (He means suspected)

LOVE'S LABOR'S LOST

COSTARD: Sir, the **contempts** thereof are as touching me.   LLL 1.1.190
  (He means contents)

COSTARD: And therefore welcome the sour cup of **prosperity**.   LLL 1.1.313
  (He means adversity)

DULL: I myself **reprehend** his own person, for I am his Grace's farborough.   LLL 1.1.183
  (He means represent)

HENRY THE FOURTH, PART TWO

HOSTESS QUICKLY: And he is **indited** to dinner to the Lubber's Head in
Lumbert Street, to Master Smooth's, the silkman.   2H4 2.1.28
  (She means invited)

HOSTESS QUICKLY: Murder! Murder! Ah, thou **honeysuckle** villain, wilt thou kill God's officers and the King's?
> (*Perhaps she means homicidal?*)

2H4 2.1.50

TWO GENTLEMEN OF VERONA

LAUNCE: Sir, there is a proclamation that you are **vanished**.
> (*He means banished*)

TGV 3.1.218

KING HENRY THE FIFTH

HOSTESS: O well-a-day, Lady, if he be not hewn now, we shall see willful **adultery** and murder committed.
> (*Perhaps she means assault, or battery?*)

H5 2.1.37

THE WINTER'S TALE

CLOWN: Ay; or else 'twere hard luck, being in so **preposterous estate** as we are.
> (*He means prosperous a state*)

WT 5.2.148

ANTONY AND CLEOPATRA

CLOWN: Truly I have him, but I would not be the party that should desire you to touch him, for his biting is **immortal**. Those that do die of it do seldom or never recover.
> (*He means mortal, or deadly*)

ANT 5.2.247

MALAFORMS
The unintended creation of a new word by a speaker who has mangled the pronunciation of a perfectly good existing word.

George W. Bush is also famously prone to another linguistic gaffe—creating a word that sounds like the word he intended to say, but isn't. The distinction here is important: while malaprops are good words that have been misused, a *malaform* is the mangling of a good word into something you won't find in the dictionary.

> GEORGE W. BUSH: They **misunderestimated** the compassion of our country. I think they **misunderestimated** the will and determination of the commander-in-chief, too. (Weisberg 2004, 100)
> *(He means underestimated)*

> GEORGE W. BUSH: The United States and Russia are in the midst of a **transformationed** relationship that will yield peace and progress.
> (Weisberg 2004, 52)
> *(He means transformational, or transforming?)*

> GEORGE W. BUSH: Governor Bush will not stand for the **subsidation** of failure. (Weisberg 2004, 35)
> *(He means subsidization)*

> GEORGE W. BUSH: Whether it **resignates** or not doesn't matter to me, because I stand for doing what's the right thing, and what the right thing is hearing the voices of people who work. (Weisberg 2004, 12)
> *(He means resonates)*

In Shakespeare, it is Dogberry—already the canon's maestro-of-malaprops—who holds the high office of malaform-maker-in-chief. As evidence, witness each of the examples below, in which the officer abuses a completely innocent word. Witness, too, how other characters, such as Mistress Quickly in *Merry Wives*, are quick to corrupt perfectly virtuous words into malaforms as well.

MUCH ADO ABOUT NOTHING

> DOGBERRY: Adieu. Be **vigitant**, I beseech you. ADO 3.3.94
> *(He means vigilant)*

> DOGBERRY: Yea, marry, that's the **eftest** way. Let the watch come forth. ADO 4.2.36
> *(He means deftest)*

※ ※ ※

DOGBERRY: Our watch, sir, have indeed comprehended two **aspicious** persons   ADO 3.5.46
    (He means suspicious)

DOGBERRY: This is your charge: you shall comprehend all **vagrom** men   ADO 3.3.25
    (He means vagrant)

DOGBERRY: It shall be **suffigance**.   ADO 3.5.52
    (He means sufficient)

DOGBERRY: Is our whole **dissembly** appeared?   ADO 4.2.1
    (He means assembly)

THE MERRY WIVES OF WINDSOR

QUICKLY: But indeed she is given too much to **allicholy** and musing.   WIV 1.4.154
    (She means melancholy)

QUICKLY: She's as **fartuous** a civil modest wife, and one, I tell you, that will not miss you morning nor evening prayer, as any is in Windsor   WIV 2.2.97
    (She means virtuous)

EVANS: You must speak **possitable**, if you can carry her your desires towards her.   WIV 1.1.236
    (He means positively)

HENRY THE FOURTH, PART TWO

HOSTESS QUICKLY: Your **pulsidge** beats as extraordinarily as heart would desire   2H4 2.4.23
    (She means pulse)

THE TAMING OF THE SHREW

GRUMIO: Is there any man has **rebused** your worship?   SHR 1.2.7
    (He means abused)

TWELFTH NIGHT

SIR ANDREW: We took him for a coward, but he's the very devil **incardinate**.   TN 5.1.182
   (He means incarnate)

ANTONY AND CLEOPATRA

LEPIDUS: Nay, certainly I have heard the Ptolemies' **pyramises** are very goodly things; without contradiction I have heard that.   ANT 2.7.35
   (He means pyramids)

CHAPTER 7

Omissions

Shakespeare sometimes omits words in his lines, asking readers or listeners to supply the omitted language in their own minds. In many ways these devices are among the most difficult to grasp, for they demand that one recognize what's been left out, and fill in the blanks appropriately. Like jazz, these omissions give meaning to the spaces *in between* the words. They make silence eloquent, as in a Miles Davis solo, coaxing the listener to feel them as part of a larger pattern, to understand them as an unsounded part of a larger idea.

OMITTED CONNECTING WORDS
The omission of connecting words, which must be supplied by the listener.

The omission of connecting words in a line—words like "and," "or," and "but"—creates a kind of verbal bluntness, as Winston Churchill clearly understood when he said this about the notorious Munich Agreement in 1938:

WINSTON CHURCHILL: Silent, mournful, abandoned, broken, Czechoslovakia recedes into darkness.   (Cannadine 1989, 134)

Rewritten, with the connecting word "and" inserted, Churchill's words seem more poetic than harsh:

Silent, mournful, abandoned, **and** broken, Czechoslovakia recedes into darkness.

Stark, direct, impassioned, bold, this same method of omitting connecting words is used by Shakespeare's characters, too, most often in passages conveying strong emotions.

OMITTED "AND"

KING RICHARD: So weeping, smiling, greet I thee, my earth   R2 3.2.10
    (*Rewritten: So weeping* **and** *smiling*)

BASTARD: Hew them to pieces, hack their bones asunder,
Whose life was England's glory, Gallia's wonder.   1H6 4.7.47
    (*Rewritten: Whose life was England's glory,* **and** *Gallia's wonder*)

FERDINAND: I,
Beyond all limit of what else i' th' world,
Do love, prize, honor you.   TMP 3.1.71
    (*Rewritten: Do love, prize,* **and** *honor you*)

LEAR: Thou better know'st
The offices of nature, bond of childhood,
Effects of courtesy, dues of gratitude.   LR 2.4.177
    (*Rewritten: Effects of courtesy,* **and** *dues of gratitude*)

ANTONY: O mighty Caesar! Dost thou lie so low?
Are all thy conquests, glories, triumphs, spoils,
Shrunk to this little measure?   JC 3.1.148
    (*Rewritten: Are all thy conquests, glories, triumphs,* **and** *spoils*)

IAGO: Witness that here Iago doth give up
The execution of his wit, hands, heart,
To wrong'd Othello's service!   OTH 3.3.465
    (*Rewritten: his wit, hands,* **and** *heart*)

VALENTINE: She is my essence, and I leave to be
If I be not by her fair influence
Foster'd, illumin'd, cherish'd, kept alive.   TGV 3.1.182
    (*Rewritten: Foster'd, illumin'd, cherish'd,* **and** *kept alive*)

OMITTED "BUT"

POLIXENES: I pray thee, good Camillo, be no more importunate: 'Tis a
sickness denying thee anything, a death to grant this.   WT 4.2.1
    *(Rewritten: **but** a death to grant this)*

COUNTESS: [*Reading a letter*] "I have wedded her, not bedded her, and
sworn to make the 'not' eternal."   AWW 3.2.21
    *(Rewritten: I have wedded her, **but** not bedded her)*

ROSS: Alas, poor country,
Almost afraid to know itself. It cannot
Be call'd our mother, but our grave, where nothing
But who knows nothing is once seen to smile;
Where sighs and groans and shrieks that rent the air
Are made, not mark'd   MAC 4.3.164
    *(Rewritten: Are made, **but** not mark'd)*

OMITTED "OR"

KING RICHARD: Cry woe, destruction, ruin, loss, decay:
The worst is death, and death will have his day.   R2 3.2.102 (F)
    *(Rewritten: Cry woe, destruction, ruin, loss, **or** decay)*

ARIEL: All hail, great master, grave sir, hail! I come
To answer thy best pleasure; be't to fly,
To swim, to dive into the fire, to ride
On the curl'd clouds, to thy strong bidding task
Ariel and all his quality.   TMP 1.2.189
    *(Rewritten: be't to fly, **or** to swim, **or** to dive into the fire, **or** to ride on
the curl'd clouds)*

OMITTED "NEITHER"

ANTONY: The miserable change now at my end
Lament nor sorrow at
    (Rewritten: **Neither** *lament nor sorrow at)*

ANT 4.15.51

OMITTED "RATHER"

LEPIDUS: His faults in him seem as the spots of heaven,
More fiery by night's blackness; hereditary
Rather than purchas'd; what he cannot change
Than what he chooses.
    (Rewritten: **Rather** *than what he chooses)*

ANT 1.4.12

OMITTED "LIKE"

CAESAR: The wife of Antony
Should have an army for an usher. Nay the dust
Should have ascended to the roof of heaven,
Rais'd by your populous troops. But you are come
A market maid to Rome.
    (Rewritten: But you are come **like** *a market maid to Rome)*

ANT 3.6.44

OMITTED "AGAINST"

ARCHBISHOP: I have in equal balance justly weigh'd
What wrongs our arms may do, what wrongs we suffer,
And find our griefs heavier than our offences.
    (Rewritten: What wrongs our arms may do **against** *what wrongs we suffer)*

2H4 4.1.67

❧ ❧ ❧

OMITTED "AND THEREFORE"

KATHERINA: A woman mov'd is like a fountain troubled,
Muddy, ill-seeming, thick, bereft of beauty   SHR 5.2.142
    *(Rewritten: Muddy, ill-seeming, thick, **and therefore**, bereft of beauty)*

OMITTED NOUNS
The omission of nouns so that one noun is used as the subject in several phrases.

When children first hear the old saying "a stitch in time saves nine," they usually ask: saves nine *what*? Grown-ups, who have learned to spot the omission, understand the meaning: that a single stitch, made in time, can save nine stitches. So, too, a single noun, used in the right place in the line, saves Shakespeare from having to use that noun more than once.

ONE NOUN

One Noun in Verse

ENOBARBUS: No, I will go seek
Some **ditch** wherein to die. The foul'st best fits
My latter part of life.   ANT 4.6.36
    (Carried over: ditch)
    *(Rewritten: The foul'st **ditch** best fits my latter part of life)*

ANTONY: Not Caesar's **valor**
Hath o'erthrown Antony, but Antony's
Hath triumph'd on itself.   ANT 4.15.14
    (Carried over: valor)
    *(Rewritten: But Antony's **valor** hath triumph'd on itself)*

One Noun in Prose

JAQUES: I have neither the scholar's **melancholy**, which is emulation; nor the musician's, which is fantastical; nor the courtier's, which is proud; nor

the soldier's, which is ambitious; nor the lawyer's, which is politic; nor the
lady's, which is nice; nor the lover's, which is all these   AYL 4.1.10

> *(Carried over: melancholy)*
> *(Rewritten: nor the musician's* **melancholy**, *which is fantastical; nor
> the courtier's* **melancholy**, *which is proud; nor the soldier's* **melan-
> choly**, *which is ambitious; nor the lawyer's* **melancholy**, *which is
> politic; nor the lady's* **melancholy**, *which is nice; nor the lover's*
> **melancholy**, *which is all these)*

One Noun in Dialogue

In dialogue, the noun stated by the speaker is omitted — but strongly implied — in the response
of the listener.

> ROSALIND: Not true in **love**?
> CELIA: Yes, when he is in, but I think he is not in.   AYL 3.4.26
>
> > *(Carried over: love)*
> > *(Rewritten: when he is in* **love**, *but I think he is not in* **love**)*

> MIRANDA: And now **farewell**
> Till half an hour hence.
> FERDINAND: A thousand thousand.   TMP 3.1.90
>
> > *(Carried over: farewell)*
> > *(Rewritten: A thousand thousand* **farewells**)

NO NOUNS

And, once in a great while, nouns are omitted altogether.

> CAESAR: Go,
> And with your speediest bring us what she says
> And how you find of her.   ANT 5.1.66
>
> > *(Omitted: haste? return?)*
> > *Rewritten: And with your speediest haste)*

⌘ ⌘ ⌘

OMITTED VERBS

The omission of verbs so that one verb governs a number of clauses.

Sometimes one verb is asked to do all the heavy lifting in a sentence, such as the word "took" in this sentence from Charles Dickens's 1837 novel *The Pickwick Papers*:

> At length Mr. Stiggins, with several most indubitable symptoms of having quite as much pine-apple rum and water about him as he could comfortably accommodate, took his hat, and his leave; and Sam was, immediately afterwards, shown to bed by his father. (Dickens 1998, 372)

Rewritten, the phrase might read:

> At length Mr. Stiggins **…took** his hat, and **took** his leave

Shakespeare often places the same demands on his verbs, asking *one* verb to do the work of *many* in a sentence.

ONE VERB

One Verb in Speeches

> KING RICHARD: Good uncle, let this end where it begun;
> We'll **calm** the Duke of Norfolk, you your son. R2 1.1.158
>   *(Carried over: calm)*
>   *(Rewritten: you **calm** your son)*

> AUMERLE: No, good my lord, let's fight with gentle words,
> Till time **lend** friends, and friends their helpful swords. R2 3.3.131
>   *(Carried over: lend)*
>   *(Rewritten: and friends **lend** their helpful swords)*

> BRABANTIO: Look to her, Moor, if thou hast eyes to see;
> She has **deceiv'd** her father, and may thee. OTH 1.3.292
>   *(Carried over: deceiv'd)*
>   *(Rewritten: and may **deceive** thee)*

BENEDICK: Let's have a dance ere we are married, that we may lighten
our own hearts and our wives' heels.   ADO 5.4.118
>   (*Carried over: lighten*)
>   (*Rewritten: and* **lighten** *our wives' heels*)

VALENTINE: To be in love, where scorn is **bought** with groans,
Coy looks with heartsore sighs, one fading moment's mirth
With twenty watchful, weary, tedious nights.   TGV 1.1.29
>   (*Carried over: bought*)
>   (*Rewritten: Coy looks* **bought** *with heartsore sighs, and one fad-
>   ing moment's mirth* **bought** *with twenty watchful, weary, tedious
>   nights*)

VIOLA: And all those sayings will I overswear,
And all those swearings **keep** as true in soul
As doth the orbèd continent the fire
That severs day from night.   TN 5.1.269
>   (*Carried over: keep*)
>   (*Rewritten: As the orbèd continent doth* **keep** *the fire*)

GONZALO: In one voyage
Did Claribel her husband find at Tunis,
And Ferdinand her brother **found** a wife
Where he himself was lost; Prospero his duchy
In a poor isle, and all of us ourselves,
When no man was his own.   TMP 5.1.208
>   (*Carried over: found*)
>   (*Rewritten: Prospero* **found** *his duchy in a poor isle, and all of us
>   **found** ourselves, when no man was his own*)

WESTMERLAND: Wherefore do you so ill translate yourself
Out of the speech of peace that bears such grace,
Into the harsh and boist'rous tongue of war —
Turning your books to graves, your ink to blood,
Your pens to lances, and your tongue divine
To a loud trumpet and a point of war?   2H4 4.1.47
>   (*Carried over: turning*)
>   (*Rewritten:* **turning** *your ink to blood,* **turning** *your pens to lances,*

*and **turning** your tongue divine to a loud trumpet and a point of war?)*

One Verb in Dialogue

In dialogue, the verb used by the speaker may become the unspoken foundation of the listener's reply.

> DUNCAN: **Dismay'd** not this our captains, Macbeth and Banquo?
> CAPTAIN: Yes, as sparrows eagles, or the hare the lion.   MAC 1.2.33
> *(Carried over: Dismayed)*
> *(Rewritten: as sparrows **dismay** eagles, or the hare **dismays** the lion)*

NO VERBS

Sometimes Shakespeare omits verbs altogether, leaving us to fill in the blank with a best guess based on the context.

> PARIS: For what, alas, can these my single arms?   TRO 2.2.135
> *(Omitted: do?)*
> *(Rewritten: For what, alas, can these my single arms **do**?)*

> FRIAR LAURENCE: Wisely and slow; they stumble that run fast.   ROM 2.3.94
> *(Omitted: proceed?)*
> *(Rewritten: **Proceed** wisely and slowly)*

> KING: I your commision will forthwith dispatch,
> And he to England shall along with you.   HAM 3.3.3
> *(Omitted: go?)*
> *(Rewritten: And he to England shall **go** along with you)*

> MACDUFF: What, all my pretty chickens, and their dam,
> At one fell swoop?   MAC 4.3.218
> *(Omitted: Killed?)*
> *(Rewritten: **killed** at one fell swoop?)*

❧ ❧ ❧

COMPLEX OMISSIONS
The omission of combinations of words that must be supplied by the listener.

The more words Shakespeare omits, the more work the listener has to do to unravel the meaning of a line or passage. In the examples below, the ear and the mind are asked to work overtime.

COMPLEX OMISSIONS IN SPEECHES

ARMADO: You that way; we this way.   LLL 5.2.931
  (Omitted: must go)
  *(Rewritten: You **must go** that way; we **must go** this way)*

STEPHANO: If you prove a mutineer — the next tree!   TMP 3.2.36
  (Omitted: you'll hang from)
  *(Rewritten: If you prove a mutineer, **you'll hang from** the next tree)*

LYSANDER: As you on him, Demetrius dote on you!   MND 1.1.225
  (Omitted: may)
  *(Rewritten: As you dote on Demetrius, **may** Demetrius dote on you)*

CHORUS: But passion lends them power, time means, to meet   ROM 2.pr.13
  (Carried over: lends them)
  *(Rewritten: But passion lends them power, and time **lends them** means, to meet)*

PROSPERO: What, I say,
My foot, my tutor?   TMP 1.2.470
  (Rewritten: Shall my subordinate become my tutor?)

LEONTES: Wishing clocks more swift?
Hours, minutes? Noon, midnight?   WT 1.2.289
  (Carried over: wishing)
  *(Rewritten: **Wishing** that hours were minutes? **Wishing** that noon was midnight?*)

⟪ ⟫ ⟪ ⟫ ⟪ ⟫

ANTONY: Haply you shall not see me more; or if,
A mangled shadow.

ANT 4.2.26

    (Rewritten: or if you do see me, you shall see no more than my mangled shadow)

HELENA: And, as he errs, doting on Hermia's eyes,
So I, admiring of his qualities.

MND 1.1.230

    (Rewritten: So do I err)

ARCHBISHOP: O thoughts of men accurst!
Past, and to come, seems best; things present, worst.

2H4 1.3.107

    (Rewritten: Things past and to come seem best, things present seem worse)

BASSIANUS: Many good morrows to your Majesty.
Madam, to you as many and as good.

TIT 2.2.11

    (To the emperor, a cordial greeting;
    To the empress, a greeting with no title, no verb, and no noun in it)

JOHN: Then talk no more of flight, it is no boot;
If son to Talbot, die at Talbot's foot.

1H6 4.6.52

    (Rewritten: If son to Talbot, I shall die at Talbot's foot)

BAPTISTA: Fie, doff this habit, shame to your estate,
An eyesore to our solemn festival.

SHR 3.2.100

    (Rewritten: which is a shame to your estate, and an eyesore to our solemn festival)

KING RICHARD: So Judas did to Christ: but he, in twelve,
Found truth in all but one; I, in twelve thousand, none.

R2 4.1.170

    (Carried over: found truth in)
    *(Rewritten: I, in twelve thousand, **found truth in** none)*

QUEEN MARGARET: A husband and a son thou ow'st to me;
And thou a kingdom; all of you, allegiance.

R3 1.3.169

    (Rewritten: And thou ow'st me a kingdom; and all of you owe me your allegiance)

POMPEY: Thou must know
'Tis not my profit that does lead mine honor;
Mine honor, it.   ANT 2.7.75
    (Rewritten: But rather it is mine honor that does lead my profit)

FALSTAFF: This is the English, not the Turkish court:
Not Amurath an Amurath succeeds,
But Harry Harry.   2H4 5.2.47
    (Rewritten: But King Henry the Fifth succeeds King Henry the Fourth)

CAESAR: Promise,
And in our name, what she requires. Add more
As thine invention offers.   ANT 3.12.27
    (Rewritten: Add more promises)

ANTONY: My very hairs do mutiny, for the white
Reprove the brown for rashness, and they them
For fear and doting.   ANT 3.11.13
    (Rewritten: And the brown hairs quarrel with the white hairs for fear and doting)

ANTONY: Henceforth,
The white hand of a lady fever thee;
Shake thou to look on't.   ANT 3.13.137
    (Omitted: May or let)
    *(Rewritten: **May** the white hand of a lady fever thee)*

CLEOPATRA: No more but e'en a woman, and commanded
By such poor passion as the maid that milks
And does the meanest chores.   ANT 4.15.73
    (Omitted: Now I am)
    *(Rewritten: **Now I am** no more than a woman)*

NORTHUMBERLAND: Ha? Again:
Said he young Harry Percy's spur was cold?
Of Hotspur, Coldspur?   2H4 1.1.48
    (Rewritten: Does he make of Hotspur, a Coldspur?)

❧ ❧ ❧

MARTIUS: He that trusts to you,
Where he should find you lions, finds you hares;
Where foxes, geese.   COR 1.1.170
    (Rewritten: Where he should find you foxes, finds you geese)

PROSPERO: You do yet taste
Some subtleties o' th' isle that will not let you
Believe things certain.   TMP 5.1.123
    (Rewritten: Believe things that are certain)

AUMERLE: For ever may my knees grow to the earth,
My tongue cleave to the roof within my mouth,
Unless a pardon ere I rise or speak.   R2 5.3.30
    (Omitted: thou grant'st)
    *(Rewritten: Unless **thou grant'st** a pardon)*

CLEOPATRA: Nay, pray you, seek no color for your going,
But bid farewell and go. When you sued staying,
Then was the time for words. No going then.   ANT 1.3.32
    (Rewritten: There were no words of going then)

MESSENGER: She creeps.
Her motion and her station are as one.
She shows a body rather than a life,
A statue than a breather.   ANT 3.3.18
    (Rewritten: She appears to be a statue, rather than one who breathes)

ANTONY: I, that with my sword
Quarter'd the world, and o'er green Neptune's back
With ships made cities, condemn myself to lack
The courage of a woman; less noble mind
Than she which by her death our Caesar tells
"I am conquerer of myself."   ANT 4.14.57
    (Carried over: condemn myself to)
    *(Rewritten: **condemn myself to** have a less noble mind)*

JAQUES: [*To Duke Senior*] You to your former honor I bequeath,
Your patience and your virtue well deserve it.
[*To Orlando*] You to a love that your true faith doth merit;

[*To Oliver*] You to your land, and love, and great allies;

[*To Silvius*] You to a long and well-deservèd bed;

[*To Touchstone*] And you to wrangling, for thy loving voyage

Is but for two months victuall'd.   AYL 5.4.186

> (*Carried over: I bequeath*)
>
> (*Rewritten:* ***I bequeath*** *you to a love that your true faith doth merit;*
>
> ***I bequeath*** *you to your land, and love, and great allies;*
>
> ***I bequeath*** *you to a long and well-deservèd bed*
>
> *And* ***I bequeath*** *you to wrangling, for thy loving voyage*
>
> *Is but for two months victuall'd*)

KING RICHARD: I'll give my jewels for a set of beads,

My gorgeous palace for a hermitage,

My gay apparel for an almsman's gown,

My figur'd goblets for a dish of wood,

My scepter for a palmer's walking staff,

My subjects for a pair of carvèd saints,

And my large kingdom for a little grave,

A little, little grave, an obscure grave   R2 3.3.147

> (*Carried over: I'll give*)
>
> (*Rewritten:* ***I'll give*** *my jewels for a set of beads,*
>
> ***I'll give*** *my gorgeous palace for a hermitage,*
>
> ***I'll give*** *my gay apparel for an almsman's gown,*
>
> ***I'll give*** *my figur'd goblets for a dish of wood,*
>
> ***I'll give*** *my scepter for a palmer's walking staff,*
>
> ***I'll give*** *my subjects for a pair of carvèd saints,*
>
> *And* ***I'll give*** *my large kingdom for a little grave*)

COMPLEX OMISSIONS IN DIALOGUE

In dialogue, a deliberate omission can speak louder than words—and get bigger laughs—as in this quick comeback:

PETRUCHIO: Pray, have you not a daughter

Called Katherina, fair and virtuous?

Baptista: I have a daughter, sir, called Katherina.   SHR 2.1.42

> (*Baptista deliberately omits fair and virtuous*)

UNFINISHED THOUGHTS
The omission of the end of a statement or thought; an uncompleted or unexpressed idea.

In everyday life, it's common to hear someone fail to finish a sentence. Sometimes the person stops himself before completing what he had to say. Sometimes another person interrupts him before he can finish his thought. Sometimes the thought is (rather rudely) finished for him. And sometimes the person *dies* before — well, perhaps that's not so common.

In any case, Shakespeare's characters, too — for all the same reasons — sometimes have trouble finishing a sentence.

SELF-INTERRUPTED THOUGHTS
Sometimes a character stops himself before finishing what he had to say.

Self-Interruption in Verse

LEAR: Fiery? The fiery Duke? Tell the hot Duke that —
No, but not yet. May be he is not well   LR 2.4.104

PLANTAGENET: Well, I will lock his counsel in my breast,
And what I do imagine — let that rest.   1H6 2.5.118

JULIET: I'll call them back to comfort me.
Nurse! — What should she do here?
My dismal scene I needs must act alone.   ROM 4.3.17

CRESSIDA: Hard to seem won; but I was won, my lord,
With the first glance that ever — pardon me;
If I confess too much you will play the tyrant.   TRO 3.2.117

HAMLET: Why she would hang on him
As if increase of appetite had grown
By what it fed on. And yet, within a month —
Let me not think on't; frailty, thy name is woman.   HAM 1.2.143

∞ ∞ ∞

ANTONIO: What might,
Worthy Sebastian, O what might — ? No more.
And yet methinks I see it in thy face
What thou shouldst be.   TMP 2.1.204

LEAR: No, you unnatural hags,
I will have such revenges on you both
That all the world shall — I will do such things —
What they are yet, I know not, but they shall be
The terrors of the earth!   LR 2.4.278

CLEOPATRA: Sir, you and I must part, but that's not it;
Sir, you and I have lov'd, but that's not it;
That you know well. Something it is I would —
O, my oblivion is a very Antony,
And I am all forgotten.   ANT 1.3.87

EGEON: The seas wax'd calm, and we discoverèd
Two ships from far, making amain to us:
Of Corinth that, of Epidarus this.
But ere they came — O, let me say no more!
Gather the sequel by that went before.   ERR 1.1.91

HAMLET: You that look pale and tremble at this chance,
That are but mutes or audience to this act,
Had I but time (as this fell sergeant, Death,
Is strict in his arrest), O, I could tell you —
But let it be.   HAM 5.2.334

IMOGEN: Then, true Pisanio,
Who long'st, like me, to see thy lord; who long'st —
O let me bate, but not like me — yet long'st,
But in a fainter kind; O, not like me,
For mine's beyond beyond   CYM 3.2.52

Self-Interruption in Prose

HAMLET: For if the sun breed maggots in a dead dog, being a good kissing carrion — Have you a daughter?

HAM 2.2.181

NURSE: Your love says, like an honest gentleman, and a courteous, and a kind, and a handsome, and, I warrant, a virtuous — Where is your mother?

ROM 2.5.55

POLONIUS: And then, sir, does he this, he does — what was I about to say? By the mass, I was about to say something. Where did I leave?

HAM 2.1.49 (Q2)

BOTTOM: Methought I was — there is no man can tell what. Methought I was — and methought I had — but man is but a patched fool if he will offer to say what methought I had.

MND 4.1.207

BEATRICE: What, bear her in hand until they come to take hands, and then, with public accusation, uncovered slander, unmitigated rancor — O God, that I were a man! I would eat his heart in the marketplace.

ADO 4.1.303

VIOLA: Most radiant, exquisite, and unmatchable beauty — I pray you tell me if this be the lady of the house, for I never saw her. I would be loath to cast away my speech, for, besides that it is excellently well penned, I have taken great pains to con it.

TN 1.5.170

THOUGHTS PROMPTED BY A SCENE PARTNER

Sometimes another character must urge a reticent speaker to finish his thought.

IAGO: Ha, I like not that.
OTHELLO: What dost thou say?
IAGO: Nothing, my lord; or if — I know not what.

OTH 3.3.35

GENTLEMAN: Help, help, O help!
EDGAR: What kind of help?

216 SHAKESPEARE'S WORDCRAFT

ALBANY: Speak, man.
EDGAR: What means this bloody knife?
GENTLEMAN: 'Tis hot, it smokes.
It came ev'n from the heart of — O, she's dead!   LR 5.3.223 (F)

OTHELLO: What hath he said?
IAGO: Faith, that he did — I know not what he did.
OTHELLO: What? What?
IAGO: Lie —
OTHELLO: With her?
IAGO: With her, on her; what you will.   OTH 4.1.31

SUFFOLK: I'll undertake to make thee Henry's queen,
To put a golden scepter in thy hand
And set a precious crown upon thy head,
If thou wilt condescend to be my —
MARGARET: What?
SUFFOLK: His love.   1H6 5.3.117

CLARENCE: Who sent you hither? Wherefore do you come?
SECOND MURDERER: To — to — to —
CLARENCE: To murder me?
BOTH: Ay, ay.
CLARENCE: You scarcely have the hearts to tell me so,
And therefore cannot have the hearts to do it.   R3 1.4.171

THOUGHTS INTERRUPTED BY A SCENE PARTNER

Sometimes another character obstructs the completion of a thought.

SHYLOCK: Three thousand ducats — 'tis a good round sum.
Three months from twelve — then let me see, the rate —
ANTONIO: Well, Shylock, shall we be beholding to you?   MV 1.3.103

SECOND MURDERER: We shall, my lord,
Perform what you command us.
FIRST MURDERER: Though our lives —
MACBETH: Your spirits shine through you.   MAC 3.1.125

LYSANDER: Our intent
Was to be gone from Athens, where we might,
Without the peril of the Athenian law —
EGEUS: Enough, enough, my lord; you have enough.
I beg the law, the law, upon his head.   MND 4.1.151

ROMEO: Lady, by yonder blessèd moon I vow,
That tips with silver all these fruit-tree tops —
JULIET: O, swear not by the moon, th' inconstant moon,
That monthly changes in her circled orb,
Lest that thy love prove likewise variable.   ROM 2.2.107 (Q2)

SHYLOCK: When Jacob graz'd his uncle Laban's sheep —
This Jacob from our holy Abram was,
As his wise mother wrought in his behalf,
The third possessor; ay, he was the third —
ANTONIO: And what of him? Did he take interest?   MV 1.3.71

PLAYER KING: Faith, I must leave thee love, and shortly too;
My operant powers their functions leave to do.
And thou shalt live in this fair world behind,
Honor'd, belov'd; and haply one as kind
For husband shalt thou —
PLAYER QUEEN: O, confound the rest!
Such love must needs be treason in my breast.   HAM 3.2.173 (Q2)

THOUGHTS COMPLETED BY A SCENE PARTNER

Sometimes a thought is (rather rudely) finished for a character.

LEAR: Now by Apollo —
KENT: Now by Apollo, King,
Thou swear'st thy gods in vain.   LR 1.1.160

AUSTRIA: Well, ruffian, I must pocket up these wrongs
Because —
BASTARD: Your breeches best may carry them.   JN 3.1.200

KING: Peace!
COSTARD: Be to me, and every man that dares not fight.
KING: No words!
COSTARD: Of other men's secrets, I beseech you.   LLL 1.1.226

MARCADE: I'm sorry, madam, for the news I bring
Is heavy in my tongue. The King your father —
PRINCESS: Dead, for my life.
MARCADE: Ev'n so: my tale is told.   LLL 5.2.718

MACBETH: The devil damn thee black, thou cream-faced loon!
Where got'st thou that goose look?
SERVANT: There is ten thousand —
MACBETH: Geese, villain?
SERVANT: Soldiers, sir.   MAC 5.3.11

BEROWNE: Your capacity
Is of that nature that to your huge store
Wise things seems foolish, and rich things but poor.
ROSALINE: This proves you wise and rich, for in my eye —
BEROWNE: I am a fool and full of poverty.
ROSALINE: But that you take what doth to you belong,
It were a fault to snatch words from my tongue.   LLL 5.2.376

VALENTINE: So it stead you, I will write
(Please you command) a thousand times as much;
And yet —
SYLVIA: A pretty period! Well, I guess the sequel;
And yet I will not name it — and yet I care not —
And yet take this again — and yet I thank you,
Meaning henceforth to trouble you no more.
SPEED: *[Aside]* And yet you will, and yet another "yet."   TGV 2.1.113

THOUGHTS LEFT UNFINISHED
And sometimes a character *dies* before he can finish his thought.

CLEOPATRA: What should I stay — [*Dies.*]
CHARMIAN: In this vile world? So, fare thee well.   ANT 5.2.313

HOTSPUR: O, I could prophesy,
But that the earthy and cold hand of death
Lies on my tongue. No, Percy, thou art dust,
And food for — [*Dies.*]
PRINCE: For worms, brave Percy. Fare thee well, great heart,   1H4 5.4.83

HUMILITY
To talk about not being able to talk about something.

Although humility has long gone out of fashion in modern political discourse, it was once a staple of public speaking. The tactic was simple but effective: begin by lowering the expectations of your audience with a heartfelt apology for your shortcomings.

Consider, for example, this remarkable statement made by Gerald R. Ford when he was unexpectedly elevated to vice president on December 12, 1973:

GERALD R. FORD: I'm a Ford, not a Lincoln.   (Bartlett 2002, 790)

Six score and seven years earlier, Frederick Douglass routinely began his speeches with humble apologies for his lack of eloquence, despite the fact that he was without doubt one of the most eloquent speakers in American history. Consider, for example, this reception speech he gave in Moorfields, England, on May 12, 1846:

FREDERICK DOUGLASS: I feel exceedingly glad of the opportunity now afforded me of presenting the claims of my brethren in bonds in the United States, to so many in London and from various parts of Britain, who have assembled here on this present occasion. I have nothing to commend me to your consideration in the way of learning, nothing in the way of education to entitle me to your attention; and you are aware that slavery is a very bad school for rearing teachers of morality and religion. Twenty-one years of my life have been spent in slavery — personal slavery — surrounded by degrading influences, such as can exist nowhere beyond the pale of slavery; and it will not be strange, if under such circumstances, I should betray, in what I have to say to you, a deficiency of that refinement which is seldom or ever found, except among persons that have experienced superior advantages to those which I have enjoyed. But I will take it for granted that you know something about the degrading influences of slavery, and that you will not expect great things from me this evening, but simply such facts as I may be able to advance immediately in connection with my own experience of slavery. (Foner and Taylor 1999, 31)

In the same way, Shakespeare's most articulate characters will sometimes speak of an inability to talk about something. At times, as with Cordelia before her father, they are truly tongue-tied. But sometimes, as with Antony before the mobs of Rome, it is pure tactic.

HUMILITY IN VERSE

HERMIA: I am amaz'd, and know not what to say.   MND 3.2.344

BASSANIO: Madam, you have bereft me of all words.   MV 3.2.175

BENEDICK: For my part, I am so attir'd in wonder,
I know not what to say.   ADO 4.1.144

SCROOP: Both young and old rebel,
And all goes worse than I have pow'r to tell.   R2 3.2.119

COMINIUS: I shall lack voice; the deeds of Coriolanus
Should not be utter'd feebly.   COR 2.2.82

CORDELIA: Unhappy that I am, I cannot heave
My heart into my mouth. I love your majesty
According to my bond, no more nor less.   LR 1.1.91

OTHELLO: Rude am I in my speech,
And little bless'd with the soft phrase of peace;
For since these arms of mine had seven years' pith,

Till now some nine moons wasted, they have us'd
Their dearest action in the tented field;
And little of this great world can I speak
More than pertains to feats of broil and battle,
And therefore little shall I grace my cause
In speaking for myself.   OTH 1.3.81

ANTONY: I come not, friends, to steal away your hearts.
I am no orator as Brutus is,
But, as you know me all, a plain blunt man
That love my friend, and that they know full well
That gave me public leave to speak of him.
For I have neither wit, nor words, nor worth,
Action, nor utt'rance, nor the power of speech
To stir men's blood. I only speak right on.
I tell you that which you yourselves do know,
Show you sweet Caesar's wounds, poor poor dumb mouths,
And bid them speak for me.   JC 3.2.216 (F2)

HUMILITY IN PROSE

FALSTAFF: Come, I cannot cog and say thou art this and that, like many
of these lisping hawthorn buds, that come like women in men's apparel
and smell like Bucklersbury in simple time. I cannot. But I love thee, none
but thee.   WIV 3.3.70

SWEARING
The omission of God's name in swearing.

The third commandment carved into those stone tablets Moses brought down with him from
Mount Sinai is unequivocal:

> Thou shalt not take the name of the Lord thy God in vain.
> (Exodus 20:7)

This is why some people say "doggone it" or "gosh darn it" rather than "God damn it!" Or
"jeez," "gee whiz," or "golly gee" rather than "Jesus Christ!"

To avoid breaking the third commandment, Shakespeare's characters, too, omit God's name when they swear. This is especially true after 1606, when the Act to Restrain Abuses of Players made it illegal to use the name of God either "jestingly or profanely" in performance and levied a stiff fine for all offences.

FALSTAFF: '**Sblood**, my lord, they are false.   1H4 2.4.443 (Q1)
   (meaning, by God's blood)

SIR ANDREW: '**Slid**, I'll after him again and beat him.   TN 3.4.391
   (meaning, by God's eyelid)

SIR ANDREW: '**Slight**, will you make an ass o' me?   TN 3.2.13
   (meaning, by God's light)

HAMLET: '**Swounds**, show me what thou't do.   HAM 5.1.274 (Q2)
   (meaning, by God's wounds)

BUCKINGHAM: **Zounds**! I'll entreat no more.   R3 3.7.219 (Q1)
   (meaning, by God's wounds)

MARTIUS: '**Sdeath**!
The rabble should have first unroof'd the city
Ere so prevail'd with me.   COR 1.1.217
   (meaning, by God's death)

THERSITES: '**Sfoot**, I'll learn to conjure and raise devils, but I'll see some
issue of my spiteful execrations.   TRO 2.3.5
   (meaning, by God's foot)

EDMUND: **Fut**, I should have been that I am, had the maidenliest star in
the firmament twinkled on my bastardizing.   LR 1.2.131 (Q1)
   (meaning, by Christ's foot)

CHAPTER 8

Order

In Ikebana, the Japanese art of flower arranging, it's not just the elements drawn together—the vase, stems, leaves, and branches—but how they are *arranged* that is the essence of the art. These organic arrangements follow many principles, rules that offer not only aesthetic beauty, but also express deep philosophical meaning.

Like Ikebana, Shakespeare's verbal art draws the elements of the English language together—the sounds, words, phrases, and sentences—into familiar constructions, carefully ordered arrangements that he skillfully assembles in pleasing patterns that follow certain rules and deeply express his characters' meaning.

"IF" CONSTRUCTIONS
A conditional statement beginning with, or including, the word "if."

There are so many instances of the word "if" in Shakespeare that the *Harvard Concordance*—the massive tome that lists every word Shakespeare used and where he used it—does not even attempt to list them.

The virtue of the word "if" is its unparalleled versatility. "If" can be a beginning, a fork in the road, or an end. "If" can defend the past, change the present, or predict the future. "If" can reveal the truth, heal the sick, chop off a limb, throw down the gauntlet, and tame a tempest. "If" can marry and divorce, give birth and sentence death, crown kings and destroy kingdoms.

Much power in "if."

"IF" TO BEGIN A PLAY

ORSINO: **If** music be the food of love, play on.   TN 1.1.1

"IF" TO BEGIN A SCENE

MIRANDA: **If** by your art, dearest father, you have
Put the wild waters in this roar, allay them.   TMP 1.2.1

"IF" AS AN EPILOGUE, TO END A PLAY

PUCK: **If** we shadows have offended,
Think but this and all is mended,
That you have but slumber'd here
While these visions did appear.   MND 5.1.423

"IF" AS A HYPOTHETICAL PROPOSITION

HAMLET: **If** his occulted guilt
Do not itself unkennel in one speech,
It is a damnèd ghost that we have seen   HAM 3.2.80

AGAMEMNON: **If** in his death the gods have us befriended,
Great Troy is ours, and our sharp wars are ended.   TRO 5.9.9

MACBETH: **If** chance will have me king, why, chance may crown me
Without my stir.   MAC 1.3.143

"IF" AS A PROPHECY

CARLISLE: And **if** you crown him, let me prophesy:
The blood of English shall manure the ground,
And future ages groan for this foul act.

R2 4.1.136

CARLISLE: O, **if** you raise this house against this house,
It will the woefullest division prove
That ever fell upon this cursèd earth!

R2 4.1.145

"IF" AS A THREAT

STEPHANO: Trinculo, **if** you trouble him any more in's tale, by this hand, I
will supplant some of your teeth.

TMP 3.2.48

"IF" AS A BARGAIN

AARON: Titus Andronicus, my lord the emperor
Sends thee this word, that, **if** thou love thy sons,
Let Marcus, Lucius, or thyself, old Titus,
Or any one of you, chop off your hand
And send it to the King: he for the same
Will send thee hither both thy sons alive,
And that shall be the ransom for their fault.

TIT 3.1.150

"IF" AS A VOW

LUCIUS: **If** Lucius live, he will requite your wrongs
And make proud Saturnine and his empress
Beg at the gates like Tarquin and his queen.

TIT 3.1.296

CLAUDIO: **If** I see anything tonight why I should not marry her tomorrow, in
the congregation where I should wed, there will I shame her.

ADO 3.2.123

"IF" AS A PROPOSAL

FERDINAND: O, **if** a virgin,
And your affection not gone forth, I'll make you
The Queen of Naples.

TMP 1.2.448

"IF" AS A WARNING

BOTTOM: **If** I do it, let the audience look to their eyes. I will move storms; I
will condole in some measure.

MND 1.2.26

"IF" AS A PREDICTION

ARIEL: Your charm so strongly works 'em
That **if** you now beheld them, your affections
Would become tender.

TMP 5.1.17

"IF" AS A CHALLENGE

BANQUO: **If** you can look into the seeds of time
And say which grain will grow and which will not,
Speak, then, to me, who neither beg nor fear
Your favors nor your hate.

MAC 1.3.58

"IF" AS A COMMAND

KING: **If** you are arm'd to do, as sworn to do,
Subscribe to your deeps oaths, and keep it too.

LLL 1.1.22

"IF" AS AN EXCUSE

BEROWNE: **If** I break faith, this word shall speak for me:
I am forsworn "on mere necessity."

LLL 1.1.153

"IF" AS A DEFENSE

CELIA: **If** she be a traitor, why so am I.

AYL 1.3.72

"IF" AS AN APPEAL TO THE GODS

LEAR: O heavens!
If you do love old men, **if** your sweet sway
Allow obedience, **if** you yourselves are old,
Make it your cause; send down, and take my part.

LR 2.4.189 (F)

"IF" AS A SURRENDER

LEAR: **If** you have poison for me, I will drink it.
I know you do not love me; for your sisters
Have, as I do remember, done me wrong.
You have some cause, they have not.

LR 4.7.71

"IF" AS A JUSTIFICATION FOR WAR

RICHMOND: Then **if** you fight against God's enemy,
God will in justice ward you as his soldiers;
If you do sweat to put a tyrant down,
You sleep in peace, the tyrant being slain;
If you do fight against your country's foes,
Your country's fat shall pay your pains the hire;
If you do fight in safeguard of your wives,
Your wives shall welcome home the conquerors;
If you do free your children from the sword,
Your children's children quits it in your age.

R3 5.3.253 (Q1)

⚜ ⚜ ⚜

"IF" AS A DEADLY FAUX PAS

HASTINGS: **If** they have done this deed, my noble lord —
RICHARD: **If**? Thou protector of this damnèd strumpet,
Talk'st thou to me of "**if**s"? Thou art a traitor.
Off with his head!

R3 3.4.73 (F)

"IF/IF" CONSTRUCTIONS

These if/if constructions offer two — and *only* two — possible choices to the listener.

OLIVIA: **If** you be not mad, be gone; **if** you have reason, be brief.

TN 1.5.199

CLEOPATRA: **If** you find him sad,
Say I am dancing; **if** in mirth, report
That I am sudden sick.

ANT 1.3.3

LEONATO: **If** they speak but truth of her,
These hands shall tear her; **if** they wrong her honor,
The proudest of them shall well hear of it.

ADO 4.1.190

IMOGEN: Ho! Who's here?
If any thing that's civil, speak; **if** savage,
Take or lend. Ho!

CYM 3.6.23

KING HENRY: **If** we are mark'd to die, we are enough
To do our country loss; and **if** to live,
The fewer men, the greater share of honor.

H5 4.3.20

MACBETH: **If** thou speak'st false,
Upon the next tree shalt thou hang alive
Till famine cling thee. **If** thy speech be sooth,
I care not if thou dost for me as much.

MAC 5.5.37

"IF/THEN" CONSTRUCTIONS

If/then constructions are like a one-two punch — a logical argument that insists with two fists: if this *first* condition is true, then this second condition must be the result.

LUCIANA: **If** you did wed my sister for her wealth,
Then for her wealth's sake use her with more kindness

ERR 3.2.5

BOLINGBROKE: **If** guilty dread have left thee so much strength
As to take up mine honor's pawn, **then** stoop.

R2 1.1.73

MACBETH: **If** it were done when 'tis done, **then** 'twere well
It were done quickly.

MAC 1.7.1

"IF/IF NOT" CONSTRUCTIONS

If/if not constructions usually mark a fork in the road, a glimpse of two possible journeys ahead, where one road looks good, and the other, bad.

MIRANDA: I am your wife, **if** you will marry me.
If not, I'll die your maid.

TMP 3.1.83

PROTEUS: **If** I can check my erring love, I will;
If not, to compass her I'll use my skill.

TGV 2.4.213

FALSTAFF: **If** your father will do me any honor, so; **if not**, let him kill the next Percy himself.

1H4 5.4.141

MALVOLIO: [*He throws down the ring*] **If** it be worth stooping for, there it lies, in your eye; **if not**, be it his that finds it.

TN 2.2.15

AARON: **If thou do this**, I'll show thee wondrous things
That highly may advantage thee to hear;
If thou wilt not, befall what will befall,
I'll speak no more — but vengeance rot you all.

TIT 5.1.55

"IF" IN THE FORM OF "AND"

Shakespeare frequently uses the word "and" to mean "if."

DOGBERRY: **And** there be any matter of weight chances, call up me.

ADO 3.3.85

BOYET: I'll give you Aquitaine and all that is his,
And you give him for my sake but one loving kiss.

LLL 2.1.249

OMITTED "IF"

It's possible for the word "if" to be omitted in the text, yet strongly implied by the context.

WILLOUGHBY: **Hold out my horse**, and I will first be there.   R2 2.1.300
    (Rewritten: If my horse holds out…)

DUCHESS OF YORK: **Hadst thou groan'd for him**
As I have done, thou wouldst be more pitiful.   R2 5.2.102
    (Rewritten: If thou hadst groaned for him…)

ELEANOR: **Were I a man**, a duke, and next of blood,
I would remove these tedious stumbling blocks,
And smooth my way upon their headless necks   2H6 1.2.63
    (Rewritten: If I were a man…)

"EITHER/OR" CONSTRUCTIONS

An arrangement that presents two clear options: either A or B.

On September 20, 2001, George W. Bush presented this "either/or" to the world:

GEORGE W. BUSH: Every nation in every region now has a decision to make. Either you are with us, or you are with the terrorists.
        (New York Times, September 21, 2001)

An either/or construction like this one, in a Shakespearean speech, offers a choice with no wiggle room, no gray area, no loopholes, no exceptions.

"EITHER/OR"

ANTIOCHUS: Your time's expir'd.
Either expound now, **or** receive your sentence.   PER 1.1.89

PRINCE: The land is burning, Percy stands on high,
And **either** we **or** they must lower lie.   1H4 3.3.203

EXETER: Remember, lords, your oaths to Henry sworn:
Either to quell the Dauphin utterly,
Or bring him in obedience to your yoke.

1H6 1.1.162

EGEUS: As she is mine, I may dispose of her,
Which shall be **either** to this gentleman,
Or to her death, according to our law
Immediately provided in that case.

MND 1.1.42

"EITHER" WITH TWO "OR"S

This variation is a bit more liberal than a strict "either/or," offering three possible choices: either A or B or C.

BENVOLIO: We talk here in the public haunt of men.
Either withdraw unto some private place,
Or reason coldly of your grievances,
Or else depart; here all eyes gaze on us.

ROM 3.1.50

ROMEO: Mercutio's soul
Is but a little way above our heads,
Staying for thine to keep him company.
Either thou **or** I, **or** both, must go with him.

ROM 3.1.126

"OR/OR"

In this variation, the first "or" functions exactly the same as the word "either."

FLORIZEL: **Or** I'll be thine, my fair,
Or not my father's.

WT 4.4.42

BRUTUS: **Or** let us stand to our authority,
Or let us lose it.

COR 3.1.207

KING HENRY: For my part, noble lords, I care not which;
Or Somerset **or** York, all's one to me.

2H6 1.3.101

IMPLIED "EITHER/OR"

This variation omits—but strongly implies—the word "either."

ANTONY: These strong Egyptian fetters I must break,
Or lose myself in dotage.

ANT 1.2.116

"NEITHER/NOR" CONSTRUCTIONS

An arrangement that eliminates two options: neither A nor B.

Where "either/or" forces a listener to choose between Door Number One and Door Number Two, "neither/nor" slams those two doors shut in the listener's face. Often this leaves no choice at all.

"NEITHER/NOR"

POLONIUS: **Neither** a borrower **nor** a lender be

HAM 1.3.75 (F)

TRINCULO: Here's **neither** bush **nor** shrub to bear off any weather at all.

TMP 2.2.18

PORTIA: I may **neither** choose who I would, **nor** refuse who I dislike

MV 1.2.23

ISABELLA: Yes, I do think that you might pardon him,
And **neither** heaven **nor** man grieve at the mercy.

MM 2.2.49

KING HENRY: To honor me as thy king and sovereign,
And **neither** by treason **nor** hostility
To seek to put me down and reign thyself.

3H6 1.1.198

"NEITHER" WITH MORE THAN ONE "NOR"

The unofficial motto of the Unites States Postal Service—attributed to the Greek historian Herodotus (485–425 B.C.)—delivers a first-class example of this order:

HERODOTUS: Neither snow, nor rain, nor heat, nor gloom of night stays these couriers from the swift completion of their appointed rounds.

(Bartlett 2002, 71)

Note how this variation slams shut more than two options: neither A nor B nor C, etcetera.

BEATRICE: The Count is **neither** sad, **nor** sick, **nor** merry, **nor** well

ADO 2.1.293

ANTONY: For I have **neither** wit, **nor** words, **nor** worth,
Action, **nor** utterance, **nor** the pow'r of speech
To stir men's blood; I only speak right on.

JC 3.2.221

FESTE: Well held out i' faith! No, I do not know you, **nor** I am not sent to
you by my lady to bid you come speak with her, **nor** your name is not
Master Cesario, **nor** this is not my nose, **neither**.

TN 4.1.5

"NOR/NOR"

In this variation, the first "nor" means the same as "neither."

LEONTES: **Nor** night, **nor** day, no rest.

WT 2.3.1

YORK: **Nor** friends **nor** foes, to me welcome you are.

R2 2.3.170

PRINCESS: **Nor** God **nor** I delights in perjur'd men.

LLL 5.2.346

SIMILES

A comparison of two unlike things, most often by using the word "like" or "as."

There are so many modern expressions built upon this device, we take them for granted. Here are just a few, using "like":

Eat like a bird	Crazy like a fox	Fits like a glove
Sleep like a log	Sticks out like a sore thumb	Avoid it like the plague
Like a fish out of water	Like a bat out of hell	Like water off a duck's back

✽ ✽ ✽

All of these similes—old, tired clichés to our ears—were at one time so original and so evocative that they spread like wildfire and became part of common usage.

Most of Shakespeare's four-hundred-year-old similes, however, still sound strikingly fresh to us:

"LIKE" CONSTRUCTIONS

CELIA: I found him under a tree, **like** a dropped acorn.   AYL 3.2.235

KING HENRY: I see you stand **like** greyhounds in the slips,
Straining upon the start.   H5 3.1.31

TALBOT: My thoughts are whirlèd **like** a potter's wheel;
I know not where I am, nor what I do.   1H6 1.5.19

TALBOT: A witch, by fear, not force, **like** Hannibal,
Drives back our troops and conquers as she lists   1H6 1.5.21

NORTHUMBERLAND: Yea, this man's brow, **like** to a title-leaf,
Foretells the nature of a tragic volume.   2H4 1.1.60

FABIAN: You are now sailed into the north of my lady's opinion, where
you will hang **like** an icicle on a Dutchman's beard   TN 3.2.26

ANGUS: Now does he feel his title
Hang loose about him, **like** a giant's robe
Upon a dwarfish thief.   MAC 5.2.20

KING HENRY: I'll weep for thee;
For this revolt of thine, methinks, is **like**
Another fall of man.   H5 3.2.140

❧ ❧ ❧

MARINA: I am a maid,
My lord, that ne'er before invited eyes,
But have been gaz'd on **like** a comet.   PER 5.1.84

PUCELLE: Glory is **like** a circle in the water,
Which never ceaseth to enlarge itself
Till by broad spreading it disperse to nought.   1H6 1.2.133

WARWICK: The commons, **like** an angry hive of bees
That want their leader, scatter up and down,
And care not who they sting in his revenge.   2H6 3.2.125

KING RICHARD: Now is this golden crown **like** a deep well
That owns two buckets filling one another,
The emptier ever dancing in the air,
The other down, unseen, and full of water.   R2 4.1.184

CASSIUS: Why man, he doth bestride the narrow world
Like a Colossus, and we petty men
Walk under his huge legs and peep about
To find ourselves dishonorable graves.   JC 1.2.135

HASTINGS: He now doth lack
The very instruments of chastisment;
So that his power, **like** to a fangless lion,
May offer, but not hold.   2H4 4.1.214

QUEEN MARGARET: Hath this lovely face
Rul'd **like** a wand'ring planet over me,
And could it not enforce them to relent
That were unworthy to behold the same?   2H6 4.4.15

GARDENER: Go bind thou up yond dangling apricots
Which, **like** unruly children, make their sire
Stoop with oppression of their prodigal weight;

Give some supportance to the bending twigs.
Go thou, and, **like** an executioner,
Cut off the heads of too fast growing sprays
That look too lofty in our commonwealth:
All must be even in our government.

R2 3.4.29

"LIKE" IN COMPOUND WORDS

Sometimes a simile is hidden in a compound word that contains the word "like."

MACBETH: Then, prophet-**like**,
They hail'd him father to a line of kings.

MAC 3.1.58

PROTEUS: Yet, spaniel-**like**, the more she spurns my love,
The more it grows and fawneth on her still.

TGV 4.2.14

QUEEN: When down the weedy trophies and herself
Fell in the weeping brook. Her clothes spread wide,
And, mermaid-**like**, awhile they bore her up

HAM 4.7.174

QUEEN MARGARET: Why do you rate my lord of Suffolk thus?
Although the Duke was enemy to him,
Yet he most Christian-**like** laments his death.

2H6 3.2.56

"AS" CONSTRUCTIONS

These comparisons of unlike things are built upon the word "as."

ANTONIO: For all the rest,
They'll take suggestion **as** a cat laps milk

TMP 2.1.287

KING HENRY: Lay not thy hands upon me; forbear I say!
Their touch affrights me **as** a serpent's sting.

2H6 3.2.46

❦ ❦ ❦

GLOUCESTER: **As** flies to wanton boys, are we to th' gods;
They kill us for their sport.   LR 4.1.36

PORTIA: The quality of mercy is not strained.
It droppeth **as** the gentle rain from heaven
Upon the place beneath.   MV 4.1.184

CLEOPATRA: His face was **as** the heav'ns, and therein stuck
A sun and moon, which kept their course and lighted
The little O, the earth.   ANT 5.2.79

JULIET: So tedious is this day
As is the night before some festival
To an impatient child that hath new robes
And may not wear them.   ROM 3.2.28

TITUS: For now I stand **as** one upon a rock,
Environ'd with a wilderness of sea,
Who marks the waxing tide grow wave by wave,
Expecting ever when some envious surge
Will in his brinish bowels swallow him.   TIT 3.1.93

BOLINGBROKE: See, see, King Richard doth himself appear,
As doth the blushing discontented sun
From out the fiery portal of the east
When he perceives the envious clouds are bent
To dim his glory and to stain the track
Of his bright passage to the occident.   R2 3.3.62

YORK: **As** in a theater the eyes of men,
After a well-grac'd actor leaves the stage,
Are idly bent on him that enters next,
Thinking his prattle to be tedious,
Ev'n so, or with much more contempt, men's eyes
Did scowl on Richard.   R2 5.2.23

"AS/AS" CONSTRUCTIONS

Where the word "as" is used twice, a simile goes one step further, likening something to a particular *quality* of another unlike thing, as in these familiar expressions:

As hot as hell	As light as a feather	As stubborn as a mule
As busy as a beaver	As naked as a jaybird	As fit as a fiddle
As dull as dishwater	As proud as a peacock	As snug as a bug in a rug

Shakespeare — as flexible as a gymnast with his similes — uses the same formula:

FALSTAFF: Tut, never fear me. I am **as** vigilant **as** a cat to steal cream.　　1H4 4.2.58

HELENA: No, no, I am **as** ugly **as** a bear
For beasts that meet me run away for fear.　　MND 2.2.94

LEONTES: You smell this business with a sense **as** cold
As is a dead man's nose　　WT 2.1.151

LEWIS: Life is **as** tedious **as** a twice-told tale,
Vexing the dull ear of a drowsy man.　　JN 3.4.108

VIOLA: What I am, and what I would, are **as** secret **as** maidenhead: to
your ears, divinity; to any other's, profanation.　　TN 1.5.216

OTHER SIMILE WORDS

Although these lines use neither "like" nor "as," they do contain similes, for they compare one thing with another unlike thing.

PROTEUS: O, how this spring of love **resembleth**
The uncertain glory of an April day,
Which now shows all the beauty of the sun,
And by and by a cloud takes all away!　　TGV 1.3.84

SUFFOLK: Be not offended, nature's miracle,
Thou art allotted to be ta'en by me:

So doth the swan her downy cygnets save,
Keeping them pris'ner underneath her wings.   1H6 5.3.54

HAMLET: And indeed it goes so heavily with my disposition that this goodly frame, the earth, **seems** to me a sterile promontory; this most excellent canopy, the air, look you, this brave o'erhanging firmament, this majestical roof fretted with golden fire, why, it **appeareth** nothing to me but a foul and pestilent congregation of vapors.   HAM 2.2.297 (Q2)

METAPHOR
A comparison of two unlike things using a form of the verb "to be."

Cole Porter was at the top of his game when he wrote these lyrics:

You're the top! You're the Colosseum.
You're the top! You're the Louvre Museum.
                              (Kimball 1983, 119)

Note that the song doesn't say, "Shall I compare thee to the Colosseum?" or, "Thou dost remind me of the Louvre." No! It says, "You *are* the Colosseum; you *are* the Louvre." This is metaphor—a comparison of two unlike things by using a form of the verb "to be."

Mr. Porter uses a contracted form of "you are" to make his metaphors sing. But any form of the verb "to be" will do, as Shakespeare amply demonstrates:

"IS" CONSTRUCTIONS

ROMEO: But soft, what light through yonder window breaks?
It **is** the east, and Juliet **is** the sun.   ROM 2.2.2

SUFFOLK: No: let him die, in that he **is** a fox,
By nature prov'd an en'my to the flock   2H6 3.1.257

KING HENRY: Believe me lords, my tender years can tell
Civil dissension **is** a vip'rous worm
That gnaws the bowels of the commonwealth.   1H6 3.1.71

IAGO: O, beware, my lord, of jealousy!
It **is** the green-ey'd monster which doth mock
The meat it feeds on.   OTH 3.3.165

KING JOHN: Hubert, throw thine eye
On yon young boy. I'll tell thee what, my friend,
He **is** a very serpent in my way,
And wheresoe'er this foot of mine doth tread,
He lies before me. Dost thou understand me?   JN 3.3.59

"IS" CONTRACTED TO 'S

Sometimes a metaphor is less apparent to the listener because the verb "is" — the equivalent of an *equal sign* in mathematics — has been contracted.

HAMLET: Denmark**'s** a prison.   HAM 2.2.243 (F)

FOOL: Truth**'s** a dog must to kennel.   LR 1.4.111 (F)

JAQUES: All the world**'s** a stage,
And all the men and women merely players.   AYL 2.7.139

MACBETH: Life**'s** but a walking shadow, a poor player
That struts and frets his hour upon the stage,
And then is heard no more.   MAC 5.5.24

TIMON: I'll example you with thievery:
The sun**'s** a thief, and with his great attraction
Robs the vast sea. The moon**'s** an arrant thief,
And her pale fire she snatches from the sun.
The sea**'s** a thief, whose liquid surge resolves
The moon into salt tears. The earth**'s** a thief,
That feeds and breeds by a composture stol'n
From gen'ral excrement. Each thing**'s** a thief.   TIM 4.3.435

OTHER FORMS OF "TO BE"

"Are"

ROSALIND: No, no, Orlando, men **are** April when they woo, December
when they wed.   AYL 4.1.147

HELENA: Your eyes **are** lodestars, and your tongue's sweet air
More tunable than lark to shepherd's ear   MND 1.1.183

"Am"

HAMLET: Beggar that I **am**, I am even poor in thanks   HAM 2.2.272 (F)

HELENA: I **am** your spaniel, and Demetrius,
The more you beat me I will fawn on you.   MND 2.1.203

"Art"

ANTONY: Thou **art**
The armorer of my heart.   ANT 4.4.7

KING HENRY: O Westmerland, thou **art** a summer bird,
Which ever in the haunch of winter sings
The lifting up of day.   2H4 4.4.91

"Wast"

PROSPERO: O, a cherubin
Thou **wast** that did preserve me.   TMP 1.2.152

"Was"

> PROSPERO: Me, poor man, my library
> **Was** dukedom large enough.
>
> TMP 1.2.109

"Were"

> EDGAR: As I stood here below, methought his eyes
> **Were** two full moons
>
> LR 4.6.69

PARABLE
A short story, used as an extended metaphor.

Anybody who has ever listened to a grandparent spin a seemingly unrelated yarn to arrive at a salient point understands the power of parable. Here are two Shakespearean examples of these fables-in-brief, these allegories-in-miniature:

> LEONTES: There may be in a cup
> A spider steep'd, and one may drink, depart,
> And yet partake no venom (for his knowledge
> Is not infected); but if one present
> Th' abhorr'd ingredient to his eye, make known
> How he hath drunk, he cracks his gorge, his sides,
> With violent hefts. I have drunk and seen the spider.
>
> WT 2.1.39

> BASSANIO: In my schooldays, when I had lost one shaft,
> I shot his fellow of the selfsame flight
> The selfsame way with more advisèd watch
> To find the other forth; and by advent'ring both,
> I oft found both. I urge this childhood proof
> Because what follows is pure innocence.
> I owe you much, and like a willful youth,
> That which I owe is lost; but if you please
> To shoot another arrow that self way
> Which you did shoot the first, I do not doubt,
> As I will watch the aim, or to find both,

Or bring your latter hazard back again,
And thankfully rest debtor for the first. MV 1.1.140

PERSONIFICATION

An animal, inanimate object, or abstract idea represented as having human attributes.

Personification — a device that humanizes that which is not human — appears in Shakespeare in three different forms: an animal, object, or idea will be spoken *to*, spoken *of*, or heard *speaking* as if it were human.

SPOKEN TO

In these examples of personification, an animal, inanimate object, or abstract idea **is addressed** as if it were human:

MACBETH: **Time**, thou anticipat'st my dread exploits. MAC 4.1.144

IACHIMO: **Boldness** be my friend!
Arm me, **Audacity**, from head to foot! CYM 1.6.18

VIOLA: O **Time**, thou must untangle this, not I.
It is too hard a knot for me t'untie. TN 2.2.40

ARTHUR: The wall is high, and yet will I leap down.
Good **ground**, be pitiful and hurt me not! JN 4.3.1

JULIA: Be calm, good **wind**, blow not a word away,
Till I have found each letter in the letter TGV 1.2.115

KING RICHARD: Dear **earth**, I do salute thee with my hand,
Though rebels wound thee with their horses' hoofs R2 3.2.6

FORTINBRAS: O proud **death**,
What feast is toward in thine eternal cell
That thou so many princes at a shot
So bloodily hast struck? HAM 5.2.364

KING HENRY: O **sleep**, O gentle sleep,
Nature's soft nurse, how have I frighted thee,
That thou no more wilt weigh my eyelids down,
And steep my senses in forgetfulness?   2H4 3.1.5

YOUNG CLIFFORD: O **war**, thou son of hell,
Whom angry heav'ns do make their minister,
Throw in the frozen bosoms of our part
Hot coals of vengeance.   2H6 5.2.33

CORIOLANUS: A goodly city is this Antium. **City**,
'Tis I that made thy widows. Many an heir
Of these fair edifices fore my wars
Have I heard groan and drop. Then know me not,
Lest that thy wives with spits, and boys with stones,
In puny battle slay me.   COR 4.4.1

QUEEN ELIZABETH: Pity, you ancient **stones**, those tender babes,
Whom envy hath immur'd within your walls —
Rough cradle for such little pretty ones,
Rude ragged nurse, old sullen playfellow
For tender princes, use my babies well.
So foolish sorrow bids your stones farewell.   R3 4.1.98 (F)

SPOKEN OF

In these examples, an animal, inanimate object, or abstract idea is given human qualities and
emotions, and **talked about** as if it were human:

RICHARD: See how my **sword** weeps for the poor King's death.   3H6 5.6.63
    (A sword weeps with blood)

OLIVIA: The **clock** upbraids me with the waste of time.   TN 3.1.130
    (A clock scolds)

❦ ❦ ❦

CLEOPATRA: O my lord, my lord,
Forgive my fearful **sails**!   ANT 3.11.54
    (Sails as fearful)

QUEEN: One **woe** doth tread upon another's heel,
So fast they follow.   HAM 4.7.163 (Q2)
(Woes can walk)

AUTOLYCUS: Ha, ha, what a fool **Honesty** is! And **Trust**, his sworn
brother, a very simple gentleman.   WT 4.4.595
    (Trust and Honesty as foolish brothers)

OTHELLO: O balmy breath, that dost almost persuade
Justice to break her sword.   OTH 5.2.16
    (Justice carries a sword)

HORTENSIO: And tell me now, sweet friend, what happy **gale**
Blows you to Padua here from old Verona?   SHR 1.2.48
    (A gale as happy)

HORATIO: But look, the **morn** in russet mantle clad
Walks o'er the dew of yon high eastern hill.   HAM 1.1.166 (F)
    (The morning wears clothes and walks)

ROMEO: Night's candles are burnt out, and jocund **day**
Stands tiptoe on the misty mountain tops.   ROM 3.5.9
    (Day as a person on tiptoes)

KING JOHN: And none of you will bid the **winter** come
To thrust his icy fingers in my maw   JN 5.7.36
    (Winter as having cold fingers)

ANTONY: The next time I do fight
I'll make **Death** love me, for I will contend
Even with his pestilent scythe.   ANT 3.13.191
    (Death as a lover)

VERNON: If I, my lord, for my opinion bleed,
Opinion shall be surgeon to my hurt,
And keep me on the side where still I am.   1H6 2.4.52
    (Opinion as a doctor)

HERMIONE: But thus: if powers divine
Behold our human actions, as they do,
I doubt not then but innocence shall make
False **accusation** blush, and **tyranny**
Tremble at patience.   WT 3.2.28
    (Accusation blushes, tyranny trembles)

RICHARD: Grim-visag'd **war** hath smooth'd his wrinkled front:
And now, instead of mounting barbèd steeds
To fright the souls of fearful adversaries,
He capers nimbly in a lady's chamber,
To the lascivious pleasing of a lute.   R3 1.1.9
    (War as a courtier)

TALBOT: But, if you frown upon this proffer'd peace,
You tempt the fury of my three attendants,
Lean **Famine**, quart'ring **Steel**, and climbing **Fire**,
Who in a moment even with the earth
Shall lay your stately and air-braving towers
If you forsake the offer of their love.   1H6 4.2.9
    (Famine, Steel, Fire as alive)

CONSTANCE: **Grief** fills the room up of my absent child,
Lies in his bed, walks up and down with me,
Puts on his pretty looks, repeats his words,
Remembers me of all his gracious parts,
Stuffs out his vacant garments with his form;
Then, have I reason to be fond of grief?   JN 3.4.93
    (Grief as a person)

HEARD SPEAKING

In these examples, an abstract idea becomes a character in the play and addresses the audience, **speaking** as if it were human.

RUMOR: Open your ears; for which of you will stop
The vent of hearing when loud Rumor speaks?   2H4 pr.1
    (Rumor personified as a chorus)

TIME: I, that please some, try all, both joy and terror
Of good and bad, that makes and unfolds error,
Now take upon me, in the name of Time,
To use my wings.   WT 4.1.1
    (Time personified as a chorus)

PARALLEL LISTS

A list of subjects, verbs, or objects, followed by another such list or lists of the same length whose parts are presented in corresponding order.

Imagine someone were to tell you:

Buy bread, eggs, and oranges, to slice, scramble, and squeeze, for toast, omelets, and juice.

After some initial confusion, you would understand this request by taking the elements in the three lists in the order in which they appear, and reassembling the sentence—connecting each element with its proper partners:

Buy bread to slice for toast,

eggs to scramble for omelets,

and oranges to squeeze for juice.

Shakespeare characters sometimes use parallel lists such as these to express complex thoughts or feelings. The best-known example of this device appears in *Antony and Cleopatra*, where Enobarbus lists six nouns and holds them in his mind while he thinks up six appropriate verbs, which he lists in the same order:

ENOBARBUS: Hoo! Hearts, tongues, figures, scribes, bards, poets cannot
Think, speak, cast, write, sing, number, hoo!
His love to Antony.   ANT 3.2.16

❦ ❦ ❦

The fun for the listener is to assemble the two lists, attaching each noun to the proper verb in order to form complete thoughts. Rewritten in this manner, the line would read:

ENOBARBUS: Hoo! Hearts cannot think, tongues cannot speak, figures cannot cast, scribes cannot write, bards cannot sing, poets cannot number his love to Antony. Hoo!

Here are some other carefully synchronized parallel lists that appear in Shakespeare, followed by a rewrite that connects the parts with their appropriate partners:

PARALLEL LISTS IN SPEECHES

BANQUO: Speak then to me, who neither beg nor fear
Your favors nor your hate.   MAC 1.3.60
  (Rewritten: who neither begs your favors, nor fears your hate)

PUCK: Sometime a horse I'll be, sometime a hound,
A hog, a headless bear, sometime a fire,
And neigh and bark, and grunt, and roar, and burn,
Like horse, hound, hog, bear, fire, at every turn.   MND 3.1.108
  (Rewritten: Sometimes I'll be a horse and neigh; a hound and bark; a
  hog and grunt; a bear and roar; a fire and burn)

DAUPHIN: For peace itself should not so dull a kingdom,
Though war nor no known quarrel were in question,
But that defenses, musters, preparations,
Should be maintain'd, assembl'd, and collected,
As were a war in expectation.   H5 2.4.16
  (Rewritten: But that defenses should be maintained, musters should
  be assembled, and preparations be collected as were a war in ex-
  pectation)

DUCHESS OF GLOUCESTER: One vial full of Edward's sacred blood,
One flourishing branch of his most royal root,
Is crack'd, and all the precious liquor spilt,

Is hack'd down, and the summer leaves all faded,
By envy's hand, and murder's bloody axe.   R2 1.2.17
    (Rewritten: One vial full of Edward's sacred blood is cracked by envy's
    hand and all the liquor spilt; one flourishing branch of his most royal root is
    hacked down by murder's bloody axe, and the summer leaves all faded)

ADRIANA: The time was once when thou unurg'd wouldst vow
That never words were music to thine ear,
That never object pleasing in thine eye,
That never touch well welcome to thy hand,
That never meat sweet-savor'd in thy taste,
Unless I spake, or look'd, or touch'd, or carv'd to thee.   ERR 2.2.113
    (Rewritten:
    That never words were music to thine ear unless I spake to thee,
    That never object pleasing in thine eye unless I look'd to thee,
    That never touch well welcome to thy hand unless I touch'd to thee,
    That never meat sweet-savor'd in thy taste unless I carv'd to thee)

LEONTES: I chose
Camillo for the minister to poison
My friend Polixenes; which had been done,
But that the good mind of Camillo tardied
My swift command, though I with death and with
Reward did threaten and encourage him
Not doing it and being done.   WT 3.2.159
    (Rewritten: though I with death did threaten him not doing it, and with
    reward did encourage him it being done)

PARALLEL LISTS IN DIALOGUE

In dialogue, the ability to retain a list and verbally dissect the parts in corresponding order shows a scalpel-like mind at work. Here, for example, a sacred vow—conceived as a list by an overreaching Richard—is aborted word for word by a savvy Elizabeth:

KING RICHARD: Now, by my George, my Garter, and my crown —
QUEEN ELIZABETH: Profan'd, dishonor'd, and the third usurp'd.   R3 4.4.366

While here, four questions defensively posed by Berowne are picked off in a line — like decoy ducks in a shooting gallery — by Rosaline's rifle-fast wit:

> ROSALINE: Which of the vizards was it that you wore?
> BEROWNE: Where? When? What vizard? Why demand you this?
> ROSALINE: There, then, that vizard, that superfluous case,
> That hid the worse, and showed the better face.
>
> LLL 5.2.385

NEGATION
To assert something by denying its contrary.

On the subject of banishment, Socrates (469 – 399 B.C.) is famously quoted as saying:

> SOCRATES: I am not an Athenian or a Greek, but a citizen of the world.
>
> (Bartlett 2002, 72)

This is a fine example of negation, an arrangement that asserts the truth of a statement by flatly rejecting an opposing statement as false.

George W. Bush used the exact same device with great success during the 2000 presidential campaign when he told the American people:

> GEORGE W. BUSH: I'm a uniter, not a divider. (Apple 2000)

Shakespeare's characters will also use the same logical tactic, asserting the truth of a statement, the value of an idea, or the fitness of an action by rejecting, denying, or dismissing an opposing proposition.

> ANNE: To take is not to give.
>
> R3 1.2.202 (Q1)

> ANTONY: I come to bury Caesar, not to praise him.
>
> JC 3.2.74

> LYSANDER: Not Hermia, but Helena I love.
>
> MND 2.2.113

❧ ❧ ❧

GAUNT: Think not the King did banish thee,
But thou the King.   R2 1.3.279

BRUTUS: Let's carve him as a dish fit for the gods,
Not hew him as a carcass fit for hounds   JC 2.1.173

CASSIUS: The fault, dear Brutus, is not in our stars,
But in ourselves, that we are underlings.   JC 1.2.140

POSTHUMUS: I speak not out of weak surmises, but from proof as strong
as my grief and as certain as my revenge.   CYM 3.4.23

BRUTUS: If then that friend demand why Brutus rose against Caesar, this
is my answer: not that I loved Caesar less, but that I loved Rome more.   JC 3.2.20

ANTITHESIS
The juxtaposition of contrasting ideas in balanced phrases.

One of the most famous examples of antithesis is the first passage of Charles Dickens's 1859 story *A Tale of Two Cities*:

> It was the best of times, it was the worst of times, it was the age of wisdom, it was the age of foolishness, it was the epoch of belief, it was the epoch of incredulity, it was the season of Light, it was the season of Darkness, it was the spring of hope, it was the winter of despair, we had everything before us, we had nothing before us, we were all going direct to Heaven, we were all going direct the other way — in short, the period was so far like the present period, that some of its noisiest authorities insisted on its being received, for good or for evil, in the superlative degree of comparison only.
>
> (Dickens 1993, 1)

The passage is structured so that every phrase is perfectly balanced by a contrasting idea in the phrase that follows—like a pendulum swinging back and forth between two extremes.

Abraham Lincoln used antithesis in his Gettysburg Address on November 19, 1863. Here we see *two* elements balanced in opposition to each other in the same sentence:

ABRAHAM LINCOLN: The world will little note, nor long **remember**, what we **say** here, but it can never **forget** what they **did** here.

(Copeland, 1942, 315)

Neil Armstrong used antithesis when he set foot on the moon on July 20, 1969. At the same time, he also managed to balance *three* elements in opposition to one another in the same sentence:

NEIL ARMSTRONG: That's one **small step** for **a man**, one **giant leap** for **mankind**.   (Andrews 1993, 601)

Edward Kennedy used antithesis in his eulogy for Robert F. Kennedy on June 8, 1968. Note how Kennedy balances *four* pairs in opposition to one another in the same sentence:

EDWARD KENNEDY: As he said many times, in many parts of this nation, to those he touched and who sought to touch him: "**Some men see** things as they **are** and say **why**. **I dream** things that **never were** and say **why not**."   (Torricelli 1999, 276)

Shakespeare does all of the above, and more.

ANTITHESIS IN VERSE

One Pair of Opposites

CLAUDIO: I have hope to **live**, and am prepar'd to **die**.	MM 3.1.4
OLIVIA: Love **sought** is good, but given **unsought** is better.	TN 3.1.156
GAUNT: Things **sweet** to taste prove in digestion **sour**.	R2 1.3.236
EXTON: This **dead** king to the **living** King I'll bear.	R2 5.5.117
BUCKINGHAM: Why, then All-**Soul**s' Day is my **body**'s doomsday.	R3 5.1.12
MACBETH: This supernatural soliciting Cannot be **ill**, cannot be **good**.	MAC 1.3.130

ANGELO: As for you,
Say what you can, my **false** o'erweighs your **true**.   MM 2.4.169

QUEEN MARGARET: Come, make him stand upon this **molehill** here,
That reach'd at **mountains** with outstretchèd arms.   3H6 1.4.67

LEAR: How, how Cordelia? **Mend** your speech a little,
Lest you may **mar** your fortunes.   LR 1.1.94 (F)

TROILUS: Why should I war **without** the walls of Troy,
That find such cruel battle here **within**?   TRO 1.1.2

RICHARD: Now is the **winter** of our discontent
Made glorious **summer** by this son of York   R3 1.1.1

GRATIANO: Who **riseth** from a feast
With that keen appetite that he **sits down**?   MV 2.6.8

BRUTUS: The **evil** that men do lives after them;
The **good** is oft interrèd with their bones.   JC 3.2.75

JULIET: If he be marrièd,
My **grave** is like to be my **wedding bed**.   ROM 1.5.134

LADY MACBETH: Look like the innocent **flower**,
But be the **serpent** under it.   MAC 1.5.65

LADY MACBETH: **Naught**'s had, **all**'s spent,
Where our desire is got without content.   MAC 3.2.4

MACDUFF: Such **welcome** and **unwelcome** things at once
'Tis hard to reconcile.   MAC 4.3.138

HAMLET: The **funeral** bak'd meats
Did coldly furnish forth the **marriage** tables.   HAM 1.2.180

❧ ❧ ❧

KING RICHARD: By the apostle Paul, **shadows** tonight
Have struck more terror to the soul of Richard
Than can the **substance** of ten thousand soldiers

R3 5.3.216

CYMBELINE: O disloyal thing,
That shouldst repair my **youth**, thou heap'st
A year's **age** on me!

CYM 1.1.131

VIOLA: As I am **man**,
My state is desperate for my master's love.
As I am **woman** — now, alas the day! —
What thriftless sighs shall poor Olivia breathe!

TN 2.2.36

Two Pairs of Opposites

POLONIUS: Give **every** man thy **ear**, but **few** thy **voice**.

HAM 1.3.68

IAGO: You **rise** to **play**, and **go to bed** to **work**.

OTH 2.1.115

CAESAR: **Cowards** die **many times** before their deaths;
The valiant never taste of death but **once**.

JC 2.2.32

QUEEN MARGARET: This **sorrow** that I have by right is **yours**,
And all the **pleasures** you usurp are **mine**.

R3 1.3.171

ROMEO: Love goes **toward** love as schoolboys **from** their books,
But love **from** love, **toward** school with heavy looks.

ROM 2.2.156

FATHER: O boy, thy father **gave** thee life too **soon**,
And hath **bereft** thee of thy life too **late**.

3H6 2.5.92

GRATIANO: And let my **liver** rather **heat** with wine
Than my **heart cool** with mortifying groans.

MV 1.1.81

BASSANIO: To do a **great right**, do a **little wrong**,
And curb this cruel devil of his will.

MV 4.1.216

KING RICHARD: If I did **take** the kingdom from your **sons,**
To make amends I'll **give** it to your **daughter.**   R3 4.4.294

KING RICHARD: Your children were **vexation** to your **youth,**
But mine shall be a **comfort** to your **age.**   R3 4.4.305

MOWBRAY: For what I speak
My **body** shall make good upon this **earth,**
Or my divine **soul** answer it in **heaven.**   R2 1.1.36

POLONIUS: This above all: to thine own self be **true,**
And it must follow, as the **night** the **day,**
Thou canst not then be **false** to any man.   HAM 1.3.78

Three Pairs of Opposites

LAERTES: O heav'ns, is't possible a **young maid's wits**
Should be as mortal as an **old man's life**?   HAM 4.5.160 (F)

More than Three Pairs

Beyond three pairs, the ability of the human ear to comprehend reaches its zenith, and the balanced opposites tend to arrive in a linear sequence, one at a time—like sunrise and sunset.

QUEEN MARGARET: Decline all this, and see what now thou art:
For happy **wife,** a most distressèd **widow;**
For **joyful** mother, **one that wails** the name;
For one **being sued to,** one that humbly **sues;**
For **Queen,** a very **caitiff,** crown'd with care;
For she that **scorn'd at** me, now **scorn'd of** me;
For she being **fear'd of all,** now **fearing one;**
For she **commanding all, obey'd of none.**   R3 4.4.97 (F)

❧ ❧ ❧

ANTITHESIS IN PROSE

One Pair of Opposites

BENEDICK: In a **false** quarrel, there is no **true** valor.	ADO 5.1.120
HAMLET: The **less** they deserve, the **more** merit is in your bounty.	HAM 2.2.531
PANDARUS: Would I were as deep **under** the earth as I am **above**.	TRO 4.2.82
SHEPHERD: Thou met'st with things **dying**, I with things **new-born**.	WT 3.3.114
MESSENGER: He hath borne himself beyond the promise of his age doing, in the figure of a **lamb**, the feats of a **lion**.	ADO 1.1.13
CHIEF JUSTICE: **Pay** her the debt you owe her, and **unpay** the villainy you have done her	2H4 2.1.118

Two Pairs of Opposites

PORTIA: So is the will of a **living daughter** curbed by the will of a **dead father**.	MV 1.2.24
KING HENRY: Now fie upon my **false French**! By mine honor, in **true English**, I love thee, Kate.	H5 5.2.220
FALSTAFF: I **went to** her, Master Brook, as you see, like a poor old **man**, but I **came from** her, Master Brook, like a poor old **woman**.	WIV 5.1.15

Three Pairs of Opposites

ROBIN: I had rather, forsooth, **go before you** like a **man**, than **follow him** like a **dwarf**.	WIV 3.2.5

❧ ❧ ❧

More than Three Pairs

In prose—as in verse—beyond three pairs, the balanced opposites usually roll in like waves on the beach, one set at a time.

> DROMIO OF EPHESUS: When I am **cold**, he **heats** me with beating. When I am **warm**, he **cools** me with beating. I am **waked** with it when I **sleep**, **raised** with it when I **sit**, **driven out of doors** with it when I come home, **welcomed home** with it when I return.

ERR 4.4.32

> PORTER: Lechery, sir, it **provokes** and **unprovokes**. It provokes the **desire**, but takes away the **performance**. Therefore much drink may be said to be an equivocator with lechery. It **makes** him, and it **mars** him; it **sets him on**, and it **takes him off**; makes him **stand to** and **not stand to**; in conclusion, equivocates him in his sleep and, giving him the lie, leaves him.

MAC 2.3.29

ANTITHESIS IN DIALOGUE

In dialogue, an antithesis makes an unbeatable rebuttal—fighting back fire with water, fending off hate with love, filling up night with light.

One Pair in Dialogue

> FESTE: I think his soul is in **hell**, Madonna.
> OLIVIA: I know his soul is in **heaven**, fool.

TN 1.5.68

> DOCTOR: You see her eyes are **open**.
> GENTLEWOMAN: Ay, but their sense are **shut**.

MAC 5.1.24

> TALBOT: Shall all thy mother's hopes lie in one **tomb**?
> JOHN: Ay, rather than I'll shame my mother's **womb**.

1H6 4.5.34

> ANNE: O wonderful, when **devils** tell the truth!
> RICHARD: More wonderful, when **angels** are so angry.

R3 1.2.73

> POSTHUMUS: The stone's too **hard** to come by.
> IACHIMO: Not a whit,
> Your lady being so **easy**.

CYM 2.4.46

Two Pairs in Dialogue

HAMLET: **Come, come**, you **answer** with an idle tongue.
QUEEN: **Go, go**, you **question** with a wicked tongue.   HAM 3.4.11 (Q2)

JAQUES: The **worst fault** you have is to be in love.
ORLANDO: 'Tis a fault I would not change for your **best virtue**.   AYL 3.2.282

HORATIO: My lord, I came to see your **father's funeral**.
HAMLET: I prithee, do not mock me, fellow student.
I think it was to see my **mother's wedding**.   HAM 1.2.176 (Q2)

ASKING QUESTIONS
The posing of a question or questions for which one does not expect an answer.

This device is commonly referred to as a "rhetorical question." And who doesn't know what that is?

IN VERSE

LAERTES: Do you see this, O God?   HAM 4.5.202

CARLISLE: What subject can give sentence on his king?
And who sits here that is not Richard's subject?   R2 4.1.121

CLEOPATRA: O Charmian,
Where think'st thou he is now? Stands he, or sits he?
Or does he walk? Or is he on his horse?
O happy horse, to bear the weight of Antony.   ANT 1.5.18

LADY MACBETH: Was the hope drunk
Wherein you dressed yourself? Hath it slept since?
And wakes it now, to look so green and pale
At what it did so freely?   MAC 1.7.35

KING RICHARD: Is the chair empty? Is the sword unsway'd?
Is the King dead? The empire unpossess'd?
What heir of York is there alive but we?
And who is England's king but great York's heir?

R3 4.4.469

YORK: Seek you to seize and grip into your hands
The royalties and rights of banish'd Herford?
Is not Gaunt dead? And doth not Herford live?
Was not Gaunt just? And is not Harry true?
Did not the one deserve to have an heir?
Is not his heir a well-deserving son?

R2 2.1.189

IN PROSE

PANDARUS: Why, have you any discretion? Have you any eyes? Do you
know what a man is? Is not birth, beauty, good shape, discourse, manhood,
learning, gentleness, virtue, youth, liberality, and so forth, the spice and salt
that season a man?

TRO 1.2.251

CHIEF JUSTICE: Do you set down your name in the scroll of youth, that are
written down old with all the characters of age? Have you not a moist eye?
a dry hand? a yellow cheek? a white beard? a decreasing leg? an increasing
belly? Is not your voice broken? your wind short? your chin double? your
wit single? and every part of you blasted with antiquity? and will you call
yourself young? Fie, fie, fie, Sir John!

2H4 1.2.178

SHYLOCK: Hath not a Jew eyes? Hath not a Jew hands, organs,
dimensions, senses, affections, passions? Fed with the same food, hurt
with the same weapons, subject to the same diseases, healed by the same
means, warmed and cooled by the same winter and summer as a Christian
is? If you prick us, do we not bleed? If you tickle us, do we not laugh? If
you poison us, do we not die? And if you wrong us, shall we not revenge?

MV 3.1.59

ANSWERING QUESTIONS
Asking, and immediately answering, your own questions.

Do Shakespeare's characters ever ask and answer their own questions? Yes, absolutely they do. *When* do they do this? When talking to a friend or a foe; in public or in private; conversing with God, the audience, or themselves. *Why* do they do this? To explore an issue, solve a problem, make a decision, or score a point.

IN A SCENE
Here the questions posed, and the answers given, are *public*—a catechism for the enlightenment of others present.

In Verse

KING RICHARD: What must the King do now? Must he submit?
The King shall do it. Must he be depos'd?
The King shall be contented. Must he lose
The name of King? In God's name, let it go.   R2 3.3.143

KING RICHARD: God save the King! Will no man say "amen"?
Am I both priest and clerk? Well then, amen.
God save the King, although I be not he;
And yet, amen, if heav'n do think him me.   R2 4.1.172

KING HENRY: Show men dutiful?
Why, so did'st thou. Seem they grave and learnèd?
Why, so did'st thou. Come they of noble family?
Why, so did'st thou. Seem they religious?
Why, so did'st thou.   H5 2.2.127

KING RICHARD: Say, is my kingdom lost? Why, 'twas my care,
And what loss is it to be rid of care?
Strives Bolingbroke to be as great as we?
Greater he shall not be: if he serve God

We'll serve Him too, and be his fellow so.
Revolt our subjects? That we cannot mend.
They break their faith to God as well as us.

R2 3.2.95

EMILIA: What is it that they do
When they change us for others? Is it sport?
I think it is. And doth affection breed it?
I think I doth. Is't frailty that thus errs?
It is so too. And have we not affections,
Desires for sport, and frailty, as men have?
Then let them use us well; else let them know
The ills we do, their ills instruct us so.

OTH 4.3.96

In Prose

SHYLOCK: If a Jew wrong a Christian, what is his humility? Revenge! If a Christian wrong a Jew, what should his sufferance be by Christian example? Why, revenge!

MV 3.1.68

IN SOLILOQUY

Here the Q & A is held in *private*—part of a larger conversation with God, the audience, or themselves.

In Verse

RICHARD: Can I do this, and cannot get a crown?
Tut, were it farther off, I'll pluck it down.

3H6 3.2.194

JULIET: What if this mixture do not work at all?
Shall I be marry'd then tommorow morning?
No, no, this shall forbid it. Lie thou there.

ROM 4.3.21

❧ ❧ ❧

HAMLET: What is a man
If his chief good and market of his time
Be but to sleep and feed? A beast, no more.

HAM 4.4.33 (Q2)

MACBETH: Will all great Neptune's ocean wash this blood
Clean from my hand? No, this my hand will rather
The multitudinous seas incarnadine,
Making the green one red.

MAC 2.2.57

IMOGEN: Two beggars told me
I could not miss my way. Will poor folks lie,
That have afflictions on them, knowing 'tis
A punishment or trial? Yes; no wonder,
When rich ones scarce tell true.

CYM 3.6.8

KING HENRY: Gives not the hawthorn-bush a sweeter shade
To shepherds looking on their silly sheep,
Than doth a rich embroider'd canopy
To kings that fear their subjects' treachery?
O yes, it doth! a thousand-fold it doth!

3H6 2.5.42

WARWICK: Ah, who is nigh? Come to me, friend or foe,
And tell me who is victor, York or Warwick?
Why ask I that? My mangl'd body shows,
My blood, my want of strength, my sick heart shows,
That I must yield my body to the earth,
And by my fall, the conquest to my foe.

3H6 5.2.5

HAMLET: What would he do
Had he the motive and the cue for passion
That I have? He would drown the stage with tears,
And cleave the gen'ral ear with horrid speech,
Make mad the guilty and appall the free,
Confound the ignorant, and amaze indeed
The very faculties of eyes and ears.

HAM 2.2.560

KING RICHARD: What do I fear? Myself? There's none else by.
Richard loves Richard, that is, I and I.

Is there a murderer here? No. Yes, I am.
Then fly. What, from myself? Great reason. Why?
Lest I revenge. What, myself upon myself?
Alack, I love myself. Wherefore? For any good
That I myself have done unto myself?
Oh, no, alas, I rather hate myself
For hateful deeds committed by myself.

R3 5.3.182 (Q1)

KING: But, O what form of prayer
Can serve my turn? "Forgive me my foul murder?"
That cannot be, since I am still possess'd
Of those effects for which I did the murder:
My crown, mine own ambition, and my queen.
May one be pardon'd and retain th' offense?
In the corrupted currents of this world,
Offence's gilded hand may shove by justice,
And oft 'tis seen the wicked prize itself
Buys out the law. But 'tis not so above.
There is no shuffling; there the action lies
In his true nature, and we ourselves compell'd
Ev'n to the teeth and forehead of our faults,
To give in evidence. What then? What rests?
Try what repentance can. What can it not?
Yet what can it, when one cannot repent?
O wretched state! O bosom black as death!

HAM 3.3.51

In Prose

FALSTAFF: Well, 'tis no matter; honor pricks me on. Yea, but how if honor
prick me off when I come on? How then? Can honor set to a leg? No. Or
an arm? No. Or take away the grief of a wound? No. Honor hath no skill in
surgery, then? No. What is honor? A word. What is in that word, honor?
What is that honor? Air. A trim reckoning. Who hath it? He that died o'
Wednesday. Doth he feel it? No. Doth he hear it? No. 'Tis insensible, then?
Yea, to the dead. But will it not live with the living? No. Why? Detraction will
not suffer it. Therefore I'll none of it. Honor is a mere scutcheon. And so
ends my catechism.

1H4 5.1.129

CHAPTER 9

Disorder

Depicting disorder is a great challenge to an artist in any medium. Whether it be the cubism of Picasso's *Guernica*, the harmonic dissonance of Stravinsky's *Rite of Spring*, the shifting forms of Gehry's Guggenheim Museum in Bilbao, or the madness of the Marx Brothers in *A Night at the Opera*, beneath the chaos on the surface, the accomplished artist knows he must impose a strict structure.

Shakespeare's plays are also loaded with organized chaos, with planned anarchy, where one or more verbal elements are deliberately disjointed—out of sequence, out of place, illogical, ambiguous, contradictory.

PARENTHESIS
A word, phrase, or sentence inserted inside a complete sentence.

Shakespeare's characters (like most human beings) will often digress when speaking, inserting a word or phrase (or more!) inside a sentence to explore a secondary thought before returning to the main topic. A *parenthesis* in a speech is like a cul-de-sac—a scenic spur that leaves the main road, but returns to the point of departure to resume the journey.

In Shakespearean text—whether it be a list, a description, a reflection, a blessing, a confirmation, a qualification, or an instruction—parenthetical ideas usually appear set off between a pair of dashes—like this—or between a pair of parentheses (like this). Sometimes, however, a parenthesis is simply set off between two modest commas, like this, so vigilance is a must.

PARENTHESES IN VERSE

PORTIA: There's something tells me (but it is not love)
I would not lose you

MV 3.2.4

RICHARD: Upon my life, she finds — although I cannot —
Myself to be a marv'lous proper man.

R3 1.2.253

MENENIUS: If you'll bestow a small (of what you have little)
Patience awhile, you'st hear the belly's answer.

COR 1.1.125

FERDINAND: My prime request,
Which last I do pronounce, is — O you wonder —
If you be maid or no?

TMP 1.2.426

POLONIUS: I have a daughter (have whil'st she is mine)
Who, in her duty and obedience, mark,
Hath given me this.

HAM 2.2.106

IAGO: I know not that; but such a handkerchief —
I am sure it was your wife's — did I today
See Cassio wipe his beard with.

OTH 3.3.437

DESDEMONA: My love doth so approve him
That even his stubbornness, his checks, his frowns —
Prithee unpin me — have grace and favor in them.

OTH 4.3.19 (Q1)

HAMLET: Why she, even she —
O God! A beast that wants discourse of reason
Would have mourn'd longer — married with mine uncle,
My father's brother

HAM 1.2.149 (Q2)

BOLINGBROKE: Bushy and Green, I will not vex your souls,
(Since presently your souls must part your bodies)
With too much urging your pernicious lives,
For 'twere no charity.

R2 3.1.2

ANGELO: Yea, my gravity,
Wherein — let no man hear me — I take pride,
Could I with boot change for an idle plume
Which beats the air for vain.   MM 2.4.9

MELUN: But ev'n this night — whose black contagious breath
Already smokes about the burning crest
Of the old, feeble and day-weary'd sun —
Ev'n this ill night, your breathing shall expire   JN 5.4.33

PORTIA: But lest you should not understand me well —
And yet a maiden hath no tongue but thought —
I would detain you here some month or two
Before you venture for me.   MV 3.2.7

TIMON: Forgive my gen'ral and exceptless rashness,
You perpetual-sober gods. I do proclaim
One honest man — mistake me not, but one,
No more I pray — and he's a steward.   TIM 4.3.495

KING HENRY: Then shall our names,
Familiar in his mouth as household words —
Harry the King, Bedford and Exeter,
Warwick and Talbot, Salisbury and Gloucester —
Be in their flowing cups freshly remember'd.   H5 4.3.51

HAMLET: Now, whether it be
Bestial oblivion, or some craven scruple
Of thinking too precisely on th' event —
A thought which, quarter'd, hath but one part wisdom,
And ever three parts coward — I do not know
Why yet I live to say "this thing's to do"   HAM 4.4.40 (Q2)

LEONTES: There have been
(Or I am much deceiv'd) cuckolds ere now,
And many a man there is (e'vn at this present,

Now, while I speak this) holds his wife by th' arm
That little thinks she has been sluic'd in's absense,
And his pond fish'd by his next neighbor, by
Sir Smile, his neighbor.   WT 1.2.190

IACHIMO: Upon a time — unhappy was the clock
That struck the hour! — it was in Rome — accurst
The mansion where! — 'twas at a feast — O, would
Our viands had been poison'd, or at least
Those which I heav'd to head! — the good Posthumus —
What should I say? He was too good to be
Where ill men were, and was the best of all
Amongst the rar'st of good ones — sitting sadly,
Hearing us praise our loves of Italy
For beauty that made barren the swell'd boast
Of him that best could speak   CYM 5.5.153

PARENTHESES IN PROSE

LUCIO: The Duke — I say to thee again — would eat mutton on Fridays.   MM 3.2.181

BOTTOM: Masters, you ought to consider with yourselves, to bring in —
God shield us! — a lion among ladies, is a most dreadful thing.   MND 3.1.29

NURSE: 'Tis since the earthquake now eleven years, and she was
weaned — I never shall forget it — of all the days of the year, upon that day   ROM 1.3.23

NOUNS AND ADJECTIVES
To reverse the order of an adjective and its noun.

In English, the adjective typically comes *before* the noun it modifies: a red car, a big dog, a long walk. But sometimes Shakespeare will reverse the usual positions, so that the adjective *follows* the noun, such as: a car red, a dog big, a walk long. In verse, Shakespeare most often does this to empower the *noun* as the key word in a phrase while keeping the meter pulsating properly, as in: a vehicle vermillion, a canine monumental, a saunter time-consuming.

NOUNS AND ADJECTIVES IN VERSE

PRINCE EDWARD: I fear no **uncles dead**.   R3 3.1.146

YOUNG CLIFFORD: **Tears virginal**
Shall be to me even as the dew to fire   2H6 5.2.52

IACHIMO: On her left breast
A **mole cinque-spotted**   CYM 2.2.38

HAMLET: And my two schoolfellows,
Whom I will trust as I will **adders fang'd**,
They bear the mandate.   HAM 3.4.202 (Q2)

IMOGEN: The garments of Posthumus?
I know the shape of's leg; this is his hand,
His **foot Mercurial**, his Martial thigh   CYM 4.2.308

LEONTES: One grave shall be for both; upon them shall
The causes of their deaths appear (unto
Our **shame perpetual**).   WT 3.2.236

LENNOX: That a swift blessing
May soon return to this our suff'ring country
Under a **hand accurs'd**!   MAC 3.6.47

CASSIUS: How many ages hence
Shall this our lofty scene be acted over
In **states unborn** and **accents** yet **unknown**!   JC 3.1.111

BEROWNE: Taffeta phrases, silken **terms precise**,
Three-piled hyperboles, spruce affectation,
Figures pedantical — these summer flies have blown me
Full of maggot ostentation.   LLL 5.2.406

POLONIUS: Mad let us grant him then, and now remains
That we find out the cause of this effect,

Or rather say, the cause of this defect,
For this **effect defective** comes by cause.   HAM 2.2.100

RICHARD: Plots have I laid, **inductions dangerous**,
By drunken prophecies, libels, and dreams
To set my brother Clarence and the King
In deadly hate, the one against the other.   R3 1.1.32

NOUNS AND ADJECTIVES IN PROSE

In prose, Shakespeare sometimes uses this device for comic effects:

HOLOFERNES: A **soul feminine** saluteth us.   LLL 4.2.81

TOUCHSTONE: I will name you the degrees. The first, the **Retort Courteous**; the second, the **Quip Modest**; the third, the **Reply Churlish**; the fourth, the **Reproof Valiant**; the fifth, the **Countercheck Quarrelsome**; the sixth, the **Lie with Circumstance**; the seventh, the **Lie Direct**.   AYL 5.4.92

WORD ORDER

Any intended deviation from normal word order.

The typical word order used in English is subject — verb — object:

I ran home.   Rachel kissed me.   We loved Paris.

This word order is so strictly programmed in our minds that any deviation from it sounds odd to our ears:

Home ran I.   Rachel me kissed.   Paris we loved.

A cinematic example of atypical word order can be heard in the *Star Wars* films, in the character of Yoda. This example is from the 1980 film *The Empire Strikes Back*:

YODA: If once you start down the dark path, forever will it dominate your
destiny — consume you it will.   (Brackett 1980, 79)

Rewritten in the expected word order, Yoda's line might read:

YODA: If you start down the dark path once, it will dominate your destiny
forever. It will consume you.

Note how the rewrite makes the line clear, but pedestrian, demonstrating how Yoda's unusual word order contributes to character by producing an "ancient" quality that gives the Jedi Master profound wisdom and gravity.

It's important to remember that four hundred years ago there was much greater flexibility in word order than exists today, and that many of Shakespeare's inversions would not have sounded strange to an Elizabethan audience. Nevertheless, fair to say it would be, that when Shakespeare chooses for his lines a word order, he does so not only character to reveal, but also the *rhythm* of the verse to aid, or a *rhyme* to accommodate.

TO AID RHYTHM

YOUNG CLIFFORD: York not our old men spares   2H6 5.2.51
   (Rewritten: *York spares not our old men*)

GONERIL: My lord, entreat him by no means to stay.   LR 2.4.299
   (Rewritten: *by no means entreat him*)

MARIA: This, and these pearls, to me sent Longaville.   LLL 5.2.53
   (Rewritten: *Longaville sent this, and these pearls, to me*)

MOBRAY: My native English, now I must forgo   R2 1.3.160
   (Rewritten: *Now I must forgo my native English*)

PROSPERO: At this hour
Lies at my mercy all mine enemies.   TMP 4.1.262
   (Rewritten: *all my enemies lie at my mercy*)

MOWBRAY: If not, we ready are to try our fortunes
To the last man.   2H4 4.2.43
   (Rewritten: *we are ready*)

FERDINAND: This is a most majestic vision
And harmonious charmingly.   TMP 4.1.118
   (Rewritten: *and charmingly harmonious*)

POSTHUMUS: Me of my lawful pleasure she restrain'd
And pray'd me oft forbearance   CYM 2.5.9
    (Rewritten: she restrained me of my lawful pleasure)

OTHELLO: Yet I'll not shed her blood,
Nor scar that whiter skin of hers than snow   OTH 5.2.3
    (Rewritten: that skin of hers, whiter than snow)

GONERIL: This admiration, sir, is much o' th' savor
Of other your new pranks.   LR 1.4.237 (F)
    (Rewritten: of your other new pranks)

KING EDWARD: A pleasing cordial, princely Buckingham,
Is this thy vow unto my sickly heart.   R3 2.1.41
    (Rewritten: thy vow is a pleasing cordial unto my sickly heart)

CHORUS: The country cocks do crow, the clocks do toll,
And the third hour of drowsy morning name.   H5 4.pr.15
    (Rewritten: and name the third hour of drowsy morning)

PROSPERO: You demi-puppets that
By moonshine do the green sour ringlets make
Whereof the ewe not bites   TMP 5.1.36
    (Rewritten: that do make the green sour ringlets whereof the ewe bites not)

ARIEL: Jove's lightning, the precursors
O' th' dreadful thunderclaps, more momentary
And sight-outrunning were not.   TMP 1.2.201
    (Rewritten: were not more momentary and sight-outrunning)

THESEUS: I must employ you in some business
Against our nuptial, and confer with you
Of something nearly that concerns yourselves.   MND 1.1.124
    (Rewritten: something that concerns yourselves nearly)

❦ ❦ ❦

ANTONY: Triple-turn'd whore! 'Tis thou
Hast sold me to this novice, and my heart
Makes only wars on thee.   ANT 4.12.13
    (Rewritten: *Makes wars on thee only*)

MACBETH: If charnel-houses and our graves must send
Those that we bury back, our monuments
Shall be the maws of kites   MAC 3.4.70
    (Rewritten: *send back those that we bury*)

QUEEN: Good gentlemen, he hath much talk'd of you,
And sure I am two men there are not living
To whom he more adheres.   HAM 2.2.19 (F)
    (Rewritten: *And I am sure there are not two men living*)

BASTARD: Beyond the infinite and boundless reach
Of mercy, if thou didst this deed of death,
Art thou damn'd, Hubert.   JN 4.3.117
    (Rewritten: *Hubert, if thou didst this deed of death, thou art damned
    beyond the boundless reach of mercy*)

CORDELIA: O you kind gods,
Cure this great breach in his abusèd nature;
Th' untun'd and jarring senses, O wind up,
Of this child-changèd father!   LR 4.7.13 (F)
    (Rewritten: *O, wind up the untuned and jarring senses of this child-
    changèd father*)

PAULINA: We do not know
How he may soften at the sight o' th' child:
The silence often of pure innocence
Persuades, when speaking fails.   WT 2.2.37
    (Rewritten: *often the silence of pure innocence persuades*)

FLORIZEL: Dear, look up.
Though Fortune, visible an enemy,
Should chase us, with my father, pow'r no jot
Hath she to change our loves.   WT 5.1.215

(Rewritten: Though Fortune can be seen as our enemy, pursuing us
with my father, she has no power to change our loves)

ARIEL: Thee of thy son, Alonso,
They have bereft; and do pronounce by me
Ling'ring perdition, worse than any death
Can be at once, shall step by step attend you
And your ways; whose wraths to guard you from —
Which here, in this most des'late isle, else falls
Upon your heads — is nothing but heart's sorrow,
And a clear life ensuing.   TMP 3.3.75
    (Rewritten: Alonso, the powers have bereft thee of thy son,
    And do pronounce through me
    That here upon this desolate isle
    Lingering perdition,
    Worse than any death can be at once,
    Shall step by step attend you and your ways,
    And there is no way to guard yourself from their wraths
    Except through heart-felt repentance
    And an ensuing clear life)

TO ACCOMMODATE RHYME

To make a rhyme, the Bard sometimes elected
To place his words in order unexpected.

HELENA: Nor hath Love's mind of any **judgment taste**;
Wings and no eyes figure unheedy haste.   MND 1.1.236
    (Rewritten: any taste of judgment)

ESCALUS: Well, heav'n forgive him, and forgive us all;
Some rise by sin, **and some by virtue fall**.   MM 2.1.37
    (Rewritten: And some fall by virtue)

❧ ❧ ❧

MARINA: If fires be hot, knives sharp, or waters deep,
Untied I still my virgin knot will keep.   PER 4.2.146
     (Rewritten: I will still keep my virgin knot untied)

HYMEN: Whiles a wedlock hymn we sing,
Feed yourselves with questioning,
That reason wonder may diminish
How thus we met, and these things finish.   AYL 5.4.137
     (Rewritten: That reason may diminish wonder)

CART BEFORE THE HORSE
Putting first that which occurs, or should occur, later.

In Lewis Carroll's *Alice in Wonderland*, the Queen of Hearts refuses to puts first things first during Alice's trial:

"Let the jury consider their verdict," the King said, for about the twentieth time that day.

"No, no!" said the Queen. "Sentence first — verdict afterwards."
                             (Carroll 1962, 200)

Shakespeare's characters sometimes put the cart before the horse as well:

IN SPEECHES

ENOBARBUS: Th'Antoniad, the Egyptian admiral,
With all their sixty, **fly and turn the rudder**.   ANT 3.10.2
     (Reordered: turn the rudder and fly)

PROSPERO: The time 'twixt **six** and **now**
Must by us both be spent most preciously.   TMP 1.2.240
     (Reordered: now and six)

DOGBERRY: Masters, it is **proved** already that you are little better than
false knaves, and it will go near to be **thought** so shortly.   ADO 4.2.20

(Reordered: Masters, it is thought already that you are little better than false knaves, and it will go near to be proved so shortly)

KING: It likes us well,
And, at our more consider'd time, we'll **read**,
Answer, and **think** upon this business.   HAM 2.2.80
     (Reordered: we'll read, think, and answer)

SILVIUS: The common executioner,
Whose heart th' accustom'd sight of death makes hard,
Falls not the axe upon the humbled neck
But first begs pardon. Will you sterner be
Than he that **dies and lives** by bloody drops?   AYL 3.5.3
     (Reordered: lives and dies)

IN DIALOGUE

In dialogue, the speaker must sometimes penetrate the poor thinking of the listener, as when Costard goes off to do Berowne's errand before knowing what it is. Or the listener must accommodate the poor thinking of the speaker, as when Catesby is sent off by King Richard without a message to deliver.

BEROWNE: Stay, slave, I must employ thee.
As thou wilt win my favor, good my knave,
Do one thing for me that I shall entreat.
COSTARD: When would you have it done, sir?
BEROWNE: This afternoon.
COSTARD: Well, I will do it, sir. Fare you well.
BEROWNE: Thou knowest not what it is.
COSTARD: I shall know, sir, when I have done it.
BEROWNE: Why, villain, thou must know first.
COSTARD: I will come to your worship tomorrow morning.
BEROWNE: It must be done this afternoon.   LLL 3.1.151

KING RICHARD: Catesby, fly to the Duke.
CATESBY: I will, my lord, with all convenient haste.
KING RICHARD: Ratcliff, come hither. Post to Salisbury.
When thou com'st thither — [*To Catesby*] Dull, unmindful villain,

Why stay'st thou here, and go'st not to the Duke?
CATESBY: First, mighty liege, tell me your Highness' pleasure,
What from your Grace I shall deliver to him.   R3 4.4.442 (F)

DOGBERRY: Marry, sir, they have committed false report; moreover they
have spoken untruths; secondarily, they are slanders; sixth and lastly, they
have belied a lady; thirdly, they have verified unjust things; and to conclude,
they are lying knaves.
DON PEDRO: First, I ask thee what they have done; thirdly, I ask thee
what's their offense; sixth and lastly, why they are committed; and to
conclude, what you lay to their charge.
CLAUDIO: Rightly reasoned, and in his own division   ADO 5.1.215

DIVORCED PARTNERS
The exchanging of words from their appropriate partners to other less logical partners.

Would you deliberately wear sneakers with a tuxedo? Or wingtips with a tennis outfit?
Sometimes Shakespeare does this in his language, deliberately mismatching items that would
be properly paired elsewhere in the sentence:

KING HENRY: Our gayness and our gilt are all besmirch'd
With **rainy marching** in the **painful field**.   H5 4.3.110

Normally, "rainy" would go with "field," and "painful" would go with "marching" —like
this:

With **painful marching** in the **rainy field**.

But Shakespeare deliberately divorces these words from their suitable partners and couples
them to other, less logical partners, heightening the idea that the English forces are disordered
and ill-prepared to fight the French before the Battle of Agincourt.

Although this example occurs in a history play, Shakespeare uses this device most often in the
comedies:

BOTTOM: I **see** a **voice**! Now will I to the chink,
To spy an I can **hear** my Thisby's **face**.   MND 5.1.192

BOTTOM: Will it please you to **see** the **Epilogue**, or to **hear** a Bergomask **dance** between two of our company?

MND 5.1.353

SLENDER: All his **successors gone before him** hath done't, and all his **ancestors that come after him** may.

WIV 1.1.14

STEPHANO: **Every man shift for all the rest**, and **let no man take care for himself**; for all is but fortune.

TMP 5.1.256

BOTTOM: The **eye** of man hath not **heard**, the **ear** of man hath not **seen**, man's **hand** is not able to **taste**, his **tongue** to **conceive**, nor his **heart** to **report** what my dream was.

MND 4.1.211

DISORDERED LISTS

A list of subjects, verbs, or objects, followed by another list or lists of the same length whose parts are not presented in corresponding order.

In the previous chapter, we saw how Shakespeare's characters sometimes use parallel lists to express complex thoughts or feelings. This device—disordered lists—differs from parallel lists in that it does not deal out items in corresponding order. That is to say, the necessary cards are all there, but the deck has been shuffled. So, instead of:

Buy bread, eggs, and oranges, to slice, scramble, and squeeze, for toast, omelets, and juice.

which reassembled looks like this:

Buy bread to slice for toast,

eggs to scramble for omelets,

and oranges to squeeze for juice.

you might hear:

Buy bread, eggs, and oranges, to scramble, squeeze, and slice, for juice, toast, and omelets.

In other words, the lists have been jumbled so that the subjects, verbs, and objects are not arranged in analogous order, making the listeners' job of reassembling them in their minds that much more difficult.

Shakespeare usually employs this device to reveal the psychic splintering of a character under duress, such as Ophelia after the murder of her father, or Cleopatra after the death of her Antony.

DISORDERED LISTS IN SPEECHES

KING HENRY: Weep gentle man. I'll aid thee tear for tear;
And let our hearts and eyes, like civil war,
Be blind with tears, and break o'ercharg'd with grief. 3H6 2.5.76
> (Reordered: *And let our eyes and hearts*)
> (Rewritten: *And let our eyes and hearts, like civil war,*
> *Be blind with tears, and break o'ercharg'd with grief*)

OPHELIA: O, what a noble mind is here o'erthrown!
The courtier's, soldier's, scholar's, eye, tongue, sword HAM 3.1.150
> (Reordered: *The courtier's, soldier's, scholar's, tongue, sword, eye*)
> (Rewritten: *The courtier's tongue,*
> *The soldier's sword,*
> *The scholar's eye*)

CLEOPATRA: If knife, drugs, serpents, have
Edge, sting or operation, I am safe. ANT 4.15.25
> (Reordered: *If knife, serpents, drugs, have*
> *Edge, sting or operation, I am safe*)
> (Rewritten: *So long as knives haves edges, drugs have operation, and*
> *serpents have stings, I am safe*)

DISORDERED LISTS IN DIALOGUE

In dialogue, especially in a comedy, Shakespeare sometimes uses this device to serve up a dish of fresh quips, as with Launcelot's hopeless bungling of Lorenzo's dinner order:

❦ ❦ ❦

LORENZO: Wilt thou show the whole wealth of thy wit in an instant? I pray thee, understand a plain man in his plain meaning: go to thy fellows, bid them cover the table, serve in the meat, and we will come in to dinner.
LAUNCELOT: For the table, sir, it shall be served in; for the meat, sir, it shall be covered; for your coming in, why, let it be as humors and conceits shall govern.

MV 3.5.56

PARADOX
A statement or observation that appears to contradict itself, but reveals a larger truth.

Any good collection of quotations will contain hundreds of examples of paradox, for the device is pithy, clever, and memorable:

MIES VAN DER ROHE: Less is more.   (Giedion 1976, 617)

YOGI BERRA: The future ain't what it used to be.   (Berra 1998, 118)

BENJAMIN FRANKLIN: Success has ruined many a man. (Grothe 2004, 44)

DOLLY PARTON: You'd be surprised how much it costs to look this cheap.
(Grothe 2004, 13)

OSCAR WILDE: When the Gods wish to punish us they answer our prayers.
(Andrews 1993, 723)

Each of these statements appears false or illogical on the outside, but expresses an insightful truth just beneath the surface.

Shakespeare's characters, too, will often contradict themselves with enigmatic statements such as these:

CLOTEN: I love and hate her   CYM 3.5.70

FRIAR: Come, lady, die to live.   ADO 4.1.253

TROILUS: This is and is not Cressid.   TRO 5.2.146

DUKE: If thou art rich, thou'rt poor   MM 3.1.25

HAMLET: I must be cruel only to be kind.   HAM 3.4.178

MACBETH: So foul and fair a day I have not seen.   MAC 1.3.38

ORLANDO: I do desire we may be better strangers.   AYL 3.2.258

TOUCHSTONE: The truest poetry is the most feigning   AYL 3.3.20

PRINCE: Therefore, thou best of gold art worst of gold.   2H4 4.5.160

BASSANIO: Gratiano speaks an infinite deal of nothing   MV 1.1.114

PISANIO: Wherein I am false, I am honest; not true, to be true.   CYM 4.3.42

FOURTH CITIZEN: You have deserved nobly of your country, and you have
not deserved nobly.   COR 2.3.88

BEDFORD: Unbidden guests
Are often welcomest when they are gone.   1H6 2.2.55

ADAM: Your virtues, gentle master,
Are sanctified and holy traitors to you.   AYL 2.3.12

CLAUDIO: To sue to live, I find I seek to die,
And seeking death, find life.   MM 3.1.42

FRANCE: Fairest Cordelia, that art most rich being poor,
Most choice forsaken, and most lov'd despis'd   LR 1.1.250

DUKE: Merely thou art Death's fool:
For him thou labor'st by thy flight to shun,
And yet run'st toward him still.   MM 3.1.11

JULIET: My bounty is as boundless as the sea,
My love as deep. The more I give to thee
The more I have, for both are infinite.   ROM 2.2.133

AENEAS: By Venus' hand I swear,
No man alive can love in such a sort
The thing he means to kill, more excellently.   TRO 4.1.23

OTHELLO: By the world,
I think my wife be honest, and think she is not.
I think that thou art just, and think thou art not.
I'll have some proof!   OTH 3.3.383

PRINCE: When that this body did contain a spirit,
A kingdom for it was too small a bound;
But now two paces of the vilest earth
Is room enough.   1H4 5.4.89

OXYMORON

A combination of contradictory or incongruous words.

An oxymoron is essentially a paradox that has been compacted into a phrase—like a paradox in a small box. It is neither a statement nor an observation unto itself, but a phrase whose parts cancel each other out with impossibility. Oxymoronic phrases have become so plentiful in modern life that we barely take note of them. Here are just a few:

elevated subway	original reproduction	terribly good
pretty ugly	real phony	new tradition
passive aggression	recorded live	peacekeeper missiles
jumbo shrimp	plastic glasses	working vacation
peacekeeping force	authentic replica	questionable answer
fatal injury	freezer burn	

Like the M. C. Escher lithograph of two hands drawing each other, or the waterfall that feeds itself, an oxymoron cannot exist but in the human imagination, making it a favorite device of playwrights and poets such as Shakespeare:

IAGO: Divinity of hell!   OTH 2.3.350

CLAUDIO: But fare thee well, most foul, most fair! Farewell,
Thou pure impiety and impious purity.   ADO 4.1.103

PARIS: This is the most despiteful gentle greeting,
The noblest hateful love that e'er I heard of.   TRO 4.1.33

KING HENRY: Why, Harry, do I tell thee of my foes,
Which art my near'st and dearest enemy?   1H4 3.2.122

FALSTAFF: Well, said, courageous Feeble. Thou wilt be as valiant as the
wrathful dove, or most magnanimous mouse.   2H4 3.2.159

THESEUS: "A tedious brief scene of young Pyramus
And his love Thisby; very tragical mirth."
Merry and tragical? Tedious and brief?
That is hot ice and wondrous strange snow.   MND 5.1.56

JULIET: Beautiful tyrant! fiend angelical!
Dove-feather'd raven! wolvish-ravening lamb!
Despisèd substance of divinest show!
Just opposite to what thou justly seem'st,
A damnèd saint, an honorable villain!   ROM 3.2.75

KING: Therefore, our sometime sister, now our queen,
Th' imperial jointress to this warlike state,
Have we, as 'twere with a defeated joy,
With an auspicious and a dropping eye,
With mirth in fun'ral, and with dirge in marriage,
In equal scale weighing delight and dole,
Taken to wife.   HAM 1.2.8 (Q2)

❦ ❦ ❦

ROMEO: Here's much to do with hate, but more with love.
Why then, O brawling love, O loving hate,
O anything of nothing first create!
O heavy lightness, serious vanity,
Misshappen chaos of well-seeming forms!
Feather of lead, bright smoke, cold fire, sick health,
Still-waking sleep, that is not what it is!
This love feel I, that feel no love in this.

ROM 1.1.175

PUNS

The use of a word in such a way as to suggest two or more meanings.

If puns make you groan, you're not alone. Our culture generally frowns upon the pun as one of the lowest forms of humor. But it's important to remember that this was not the case in Shakespeare's time, when punning was a greatly appreciated form of wordplay. A pun takes advantage of the fact that a great many words in the English language have more than one meaning, or sound exactly alike though spelled differently. The punster deliberately uses this ambiguity to make a statement that has two or more possible interpretations. The listener is meant to hear both senses at once, and take pleasure in grappling with the tension between them.

SAME SPELLING

Of the two basic types of puns, the first type is created from words that share the *same spelling*, but have different meanings:

Drilling for oil is **boring**.

I used to go to an origami class, until it **folded**.

If you don't pay your exorcist, you'll get **repossessed**.

When the ancient wall-sculptors were finally finished, it was a great **relief**.

Although modern puns like these are meant to be jokes, Shakespeare's characters use puns in both comic and serious contexts:

MERCUTIO: Ask for me tomorrow, and you shall find me a **grave** man   ROM 3.1.98

HAMLET: Call me what instrument you will, though you can **fret** me, you
cannot play upon me.   HAM 3.2.371 (F)

COBBLER: I am indeed, sir, a surgeon to old shoes. When they are in
great danger, I **recover** them.   JC 1.1.23

KING HENRY: For all the **soil** of the achievement goes
With me into the earth.   2H4 4.5.189

RICHARD: Well, your imprisonment shall not be long:
I will deliver you, or else **lie** for you.   R3 1.1.114 (F)

CLAUDIO: Ay, but to die, and go we know not where,
To lie in cold obstruction, and to rot,
This sensible warm motion to become
A kneaded clod, and the **delighted** spirit
To bathe in fiery floods, or to reside
In thrilling region of thick-ribbèd ice   MM 3.1.117
      (de-lighted, as in extinguished)

DIFFERENT SPELLING

The second type of pun is created from words that use different spellings, but *sound alike*. This type of pun is also known as a *homophone*, which literally means "sound alike":

I wanted to buy half a rabbit, but the butcher didn't want to split **hares**.

Dungeons and Dragons is just a lot of **Saxon** violence.

At the bottom of the Bermuda triangle is a **wreck tangle**.

Here are a few Shakespearean examples of homophones, from both comic and serious moments in the plays:

❧ ❧ ❧

HAMLET: No, no, they do but jest, poison **in jest**   HAM 3.2.234
    (in jest sounds like ingest)

FALSTAFF: When night-dogs run, all sorts of deer are **chased**.   WIV 5.5.238
    (chased sounds like chaste)

GLOUCESTER: Brave **peers** of England, pillars of the state,
To you Duke Humphrey must unload his grief   2H6 1.1.75
    (peers sounds like piers)

COBBLER: A trade, sir, that I hope I may use with a safe conscience,
which is indeed, sir, a mender of bad **soles**.   JC 1.1.13
    (soles sounds like souls)

COUNTESS: [*Reading a letter*] "I have wedded her, not bedded her, and
sworn to make the **'not'** eternal."   AWW 3.2.21
    (not sounds like knot)

LADY MACBETH: If he do bleed,
I'll gild the faces of the grooms withal,
For it must seem their **guilt**.   MAC 2.2.52
    (guilt sounds like gilt)

HAMLET: But to my mind, though I am native here
And to the **manner** born, it is a custom
More honor'd in the breach than the observance.   HAM 1.4.14 (Q2)
    (manner sounds like manor)

LOST PUNS

These are examples of puns that have been lost to us due to changes in pronunciation that have occurred over the past four hundred years:

GAUNT: Call it a **travel** that thou tak'st for pleasure.   R2 1.3.262
    (travel used to sound like travail)

FESTE: Let her hang me. He that is well hanged in this world needs to fear
no **colors**.   TN 1.5.5
     (colors used to sound like collars)

SIWARD: Had I as many sons as I have **hairs**,
I would not wish them to a fairer death.   MAC 5.9.14
     (hairs used to sound like heirs)

CASSIUS: Now is it Rome indeed and **room** enough,
When there is in it but one only man.   JC 1.2.156
     (room used to sound like Rome)

FALSTAFF: If **reasons** were as plenty as blackberries, I would give no
man a **reason** upon compulsion, I.   1H4 2.4.239
     (reason used to sound like raisins)

SHYLOCK: But ships are but boards, sailors but men; there be land rats
and water rats, water thieves and land thieves — I mean **pirates**   MV 1.3.22
     (pirates used to sound like pi-rats)

BEATRICE: The Count is neither sad, nor sick, nor merry, nor well; but civil
count, **civil** as an orange, and something of that jealous complexion.   ADO 2.1.293
     (civil used to sound like Seville)

BAWDY PUNS

Cole Porter knew what he was doing when he wrote:

> Birds do it, bees do it,
> Even educated fleas do it,
> Let's do it, let's fall in love.
>   (Kimball 1983, 72)

These lyrics are delicious fun because they can be understood in two ways: one innocent and
the other sexual. That's why this device is sometimes referred to as a *double-entendre*, which is

mangled French for "two meanings." In a bawdy pun, the primary meaning must be innocent enough to get the joke past the censors, while the secondary meaning must be lewd enough to titillate the masses.

Shakespeare's plays are impregnated with bawdy puns, stuffed with double-meaning words, like these:

prick	die	tool
will	horn	circle
nothing	bear	stand
sword	conceive	burden
ring	thing	

And there are many more.

BENEDICK: I will live in thy heart, die in thy lap, and be buried in thy eyes   ADO 5.2.102

MERCUTIO: The bawdy hand of the dial is now upon the prick of noon.   ROM 2.4.112

CLOTEN: Come on, tune: if you can penetrate her with your fingering, so;
we'll try with tongue too   CYM 2.3.14

IAGO: Even now, now, very now, an old black ram
Is tupping your white ewe.   OTH 1.1.88

RICHARD: I see the lady hath a thing to grant,
Before the King will grant her humble suit.   3H6 3.2.12

GRATIANO: Well, while I live, I'll fear no other thing
So sore, as keeping safe Nerissa's ring.   MV 5.1.306

CRESSIDA: My lord, come you again into my chamber.
You smile and mock me, as if I meant naughtily.   TRO 4.2.36

PANDARUS: Whereupon I will show you a chamber with a bed; which bed, because it shall not speak of your pretty encounters, press it to death.

TRO 3.2.207

IAGO: I am one, sir, that comes to tell you your daughter and the Moor are now making the beast with two backs.

OTH 1.1.115

MALVOLIO: By my life, this is my lady's hand. These be her very C's, her U's and her T's; and thus makes she her great P's.

TN 2.5.86

IACHIMO: This secret
Will force him think I've pick'd the lock, and ta'en
The treasure of her honor.

CYM 2.2.40

JULIET: What's Montague? It is nor hand, nor foot,
Nor arm, nor face, nor any other part
Belonging to a man.

ROM 2.2.40

JULIET: O, I have bought the mansion of a love
But not possess'd it, and though I am sold,
Not yet enjoy'd.

ROM 3.2.26

THAISA: By Juno, that is queen of marriage,
All viands that I eat do seem unsavory,
Wishing him my meat.

PER 2.3.30

CELIA: You have simply misused our sex in your love-prate. We must have your doublet and hose plucked over your head, and show the world what the bird hath done to her own nest.

AYL 4.1.201

SHEPHERD: Though I am not bookish, yet I can read waiting gentlewoman in this scape. This has been some stair-work, some trunk-work, some behind-door-work: they were warmer that got this than the poor thing is here.

WT 3.3.72

HOSTESS: So he bade me lay more clothes on his feet: I put my hand into the bed and felt them, and they were as cold as any stone; then I felt to his knees, and they were as cold as any stone; and so upward and upward, and all was as cold as any stone.

H5 2.3.22

MERCUTIO: 'Twould anger him to
To raise a spirit in his mistress' circle
Of some strange nature, letting it there stand
Till she had laid it and conjured it down   ROM 2.1.23 (Q2)

QUEEN: Therewith fantastic garlands did she make
Of crowflow'rs, nettles, daisies, and long purples,
That lib'ral shepherds give a grosser name,
But our cold maids do "dead men's fingers" call them.   HAM 4.7.168 (Q2)

NURSE: I must another way,
To fetch a ladder by the which your love
Must climb a bird's nest soon when it is dark.
I am the drudge and toil in your delight,
But you shall bear the burden soon at night.   ROM 2.5.72

MERCUTIO: I conjure thee by Rosaline's bright eyes,
By her high forehead, and her scarlet lip,
By her fine foot, straight leg, and quivering thigh,
And the domains that there adjacent lie,
That in thy likeness thou appear to us.   ROM 2.1.17

ISABELLA: Were I under the terms of death,
Th' impression of keen whips I'd wear as rubies,
And strip myself to death as to a bed
That longing have been sick for, ere I'd yield
My body up to shame.   MM 2.4.100

BAWDY DIALOGUE

Here, the speaker makes a perfectly fitting, well-suited statement—only to have its pants pulled down by the listener.

ROMEO: O wilt thou leave me so unsatisfied?
JULIET: What satisfaction canst thou have tonight?   ROM 2.2.125

OVERDONE: But what's his offense?
POMPEY: Groping for trouts in a peculiar river.   MM 1.2.89

KING: This "maid" will not serve your turn, sir.

COSTARD: This maid will serve my turn, sir.

LLL 1.1.298

HERO: God give me joy to wear it! For my heart is exceeding heavy.

MARGARET: 'Twill be heavier soon — by the weight of a man.

ADO 3.4.24

BEATRICE: I am stuffed, cousin; I cannot smell.

MARGARET: A maid, and stuffed! There's goodly catching of cold.

ADO 3.4.64

SHYLOCK: My own flesh and blood to rebel!

SOLANIO: Out upon it, old carrion! Rebels it at these years?

MV 3.1.34

ROSALIND: I prithee take the cork out of thy mouth, that I may drink thy tidings.

CELIA: So you may put a man in your belly.

AYL 3.2.202

NERISSA: Why, shall we turn to men?

PORTIA: Fie, what a question's that,
If thou wert near a lewd interpreter!

MV 3.4.78

CHARMIAN: Well, if you were but an inch of fortune better than I, where would you choose it?

IRAS: Not in my husband's nose.

ANT 1.2.59

DON PEDRO: You have put him down, lady, you have put him down.

BEATRICE: So I would not he should do me, my lord, lest I should prove the mother of fools.

ADO 2.1.283

GRATIANO: We'll play with them the first boy for a thousand ducats.

NERISSA: What, and stake down?

GRATIANO: No, we shall ne'er win at that sport, and stake down.

MV 3.2.213

NURSE: And thou like a knave must stand by, and see every jack use me at his pleasure.

PETER: I see no body use you at his pleasure. If I had, I would soon have drawn. You know my tool is as soon out as another's if I see time and place. ROM 2.4.154 (Q1)

CLAUDIO: Now you talk of a sheet of paper, I remember a pretty jest your daughter told us of.

LEONATO: O, when she had writ it, and was reading it over, she found "Benedick" and "Beatrice" between the sheet?

ADO 2.3.134

NATHANIEL: Sir, I praise the Lord for you, and so may my parishioners, for their sons are well tutored by you, and their daughters profit very greatly under you.

HOLOFERNES: *Mehercle*, if their sons be ingenious, they shall want no instruction; if their daughters be capable, I will put it to them.

LLL 4.2.73

SAMPSON: When I have fought with the men, I will be civil with the maids. I will cut off their heads.

GREGORY: The heads of the maids?

SAMPSON: Ay, the heads of the maids, or their maidenheads, take it in what sense thou wilt.

ROM 1.1.22

GUILDENSTERN: On Fortune's cap, we are not the very button.

HAMLET: Nor the soles of her shoe?

ROSENCRANTZ: Neither, my lord.

HAMLET: Then you live about her waist, or in the middle of her favors?

GUILDENSTERN: Faith, her privates we.

HAMLET: In the secret parts of Fortune? O, most true, she is a strumpet.

HAM 2.2.229

PETRUCHIO: Who knows not where a wasp does wear his sting? In his tail.

KATHERINA: In his tongue.

PETRUCHIO: Whose tongue?

KATHERINA: Yours, if you talk of tales, and so farewell.

PETRUCHIO: What, with my tongue in your tail? Nay, come again, good Kate, I am a gentleman.

SHR 2.1.213

FALSTAFF: Setting thy womanhood aside, thou art a beast to say otherwise.

HOSTESS: Say, what beast, thou knave, thou?

FALSTAFF: What beast? Why, an otter.

PRINCE: An otter, Sir John? Why an otter?

FALSTAFF: Why? She's neither fish nor flesh; a man knows not where to have her.

HOSTESS: Thou art an unjust man in saying so. Thou or any man knows where to have me, thou knave, thou.

1H4 3.3.122

HAMLET: Lady, shall I lie in your lap?
OPHELIA: No, my lord.
HAMLET: I mean, my head upon your lap?
OPHELIA: Ay, my lord.
HAMLET: Do you think I meant country matters?
OPHELIA: I think nothing, my lord.
HAMLET: That's a fair thought to lie between maids' legs.
OPHELIA: What is, my lord?
HAMLET: Nothing.

HAM 3.2.112 (F)

MISCOMMUNICATIONS

A response or dialogue based on a misunderstanding of a statement or question.

This old joke shows what happens when a listener hears a meaning not intended by a speaker:

QUESTION: Can you tell me how to get to Carnegie Hall?
ANSWER: Practice.

As does this exchange from the 1935 Marx Brothers' film *A Night at the Opera*:

GROUCHO: That's—that's in every contract. That's—that's what they call a sanity clause.
CHICO: Oh, no. You can't fool me. There ain't no Sanity Clause!
(Anobile 1971, 206)

What we have here is a failure to communicate.

Whether it be defective listening, willful ignorance, or plain thick-headedness, Shakespeare uses the same kind of logical blunder to foster misunderstandings and disagreements between characters.

COSTARD: Pray you, which is the head lady?
PRINCESS: That shalt know her, fellow, by the rest that have no heads.

LLL 4.1.43

BRACKENBURY: What wouldst thou, fellow, and how cam'st thou hither?
FIRST MURDERER: I would speak with Clarence, and I came hither on my legs.

R3 1.4.85 (F)

CASSIO: Dost thou hear, mine honest friend?
CLOWN: No, I hear not your honest friend; I hear you.

OTH 3.1.21

SIR ANDREW: Begin, fool: it begins, "Hold thy peace."
FESTE: I shall never begin if I hold my peace.

TN 2.3.68

ARMADO: By the North Pole, I do challenge thee.
COSTARD: I will not fight with a pole like a northern man. I'll slash; I'll do it by the sword.

LLL 5.2.693

PROVOST: Come hither, sirrah. Can you cut off a man's head?
POMPEY: If the man be a bachelor, sir, I can; but if he be a married man, he's his wife's head, and I can never cut off a woman's head.

MM 4.2.1

SPEED: How now, Signior Launce? What news with your mastership?
LAUNCE: With my master's ship? Why, it is at sea.
SPEED: Well, your old vice still: mistake the word.

TGV 3.1.281

FRIAR: You come hither, my lord, to marry this lady?
CLAUDIO: No.
LEONATO: To be married *to* her. Friar, you come to marry her.

ADO 4.1.4

KING EDWARD: You'd think it strange if I should marry her.
GEORGE: To who, my lord?
KING EDWARD: Why, Clarence, to myself.

3H6 3.2.111

DESDEMONA: Do you know, sirrah, where Lieutenant Cassio lies?
CLOWN: I dare not say he lies anywhere.
DESDEMONA: Why, man?
CLOWN: He's a soldier, and for me to say a soldier lies, 'tis stabbing.

OTH 3.4.1

SPEED: But, Launce, how sayst thou, that my master is become a notable lover?
LAUNCE: I never knew him otherwise.

SPEED: Than how?

LAUNCE: A notable lubber, as thou reportest him to be.

TGV 2.5.41

SPEED: What news then in your paper?

LAUNCE: The blackest news that ever thou heard'st.

SPEED: Why, man? How black?

LAUNCE: Why, as black as ink.

TGV 3.1.285

LADY PERCY: But hear you, my lord.

HOTSPUR: What sayst thou, my lady?

LADY PERCY: What is it carries you away?

HOTSPUR: Why, my horse, my love, my horse.

LADY PERCY: Out, you mad-headed ape!

1H4 2.3.73

PETRUCHIO: Villain, I say knock me here soundly.

GRUMIO: Knock you here, sir? Why, sir, what am I, sir, that I should knock you here, sir?

PETRUCHIO: Villain, I say, knock me at this gate,
And rap me well, or I'll knock your knave's pate.

SHR 1.2.8

VIOLA: Save thee, friend, and thy music. Dost thou live by thy tabor?

FESTE: No, sir, I do live by the church.

VIOLA: Art thou a churchman?

FESTE: No such matter, sir. I do live by the church, for I do live at my house, and my house doth stand by the church.

TN 3.1.1

SPEED: What an ass thou art! I understand thee not.

LAUNCE: What a block art thou, that thou canst not! My staff understands me.

SPEED: What thou say'st?

LAUNCE: Ay, and what I do too. Look thee, I'll but lean, and my staff understands me.

SPEED: It stands under thee, indeed.

TGV 2.5.24

LONGAVILLE: I beseech you a word. What is she in the white?

BOYET: A woman sometimes, and you saw her in the light.

LONGAVILLE: Perchance light in the light. I desire her name.

BOYET: She hath but one for herself; to desire that were a shame.
LONGAVILLE: Pray you, sir, whose daughter?
BOYET: Her mother's I have heard.
LONGAVILLE: God's blessing on your beard!   LLL 2.1.197

FIRST GRAVEDIGGER: There is no ancient gentlemen but gardeners, ditchers, and gravemakers. They hold up Adam's profession.
SECOND GRAVEDIGGER: Was he a gentleman?
FIRST GRAVEDIGGER: He was the first that ever bore arms.
SECOND GRAVEDIGGER: Why, he had none.
FIRST GRAVEDIGGER: What, art a heathen? How dost thou understand the scripture? The scripture says Adam digged. Could he dig without arms?   HAM 5.1.29 (F)

SHEPHERD: Come, boy, I am past more children, but thy sons and daughters will be all gentlemen born.
CLOWN: You are well met, sir. You denied to fight with me this other day, because I was no gentleman born. See you these clothes? Say you see them not, and think me still no gentleman born! You were best say these robes are not gentleman born. Give me the lie, do; and try whether I am not now a gentleman born.
AUTOLYCUS: I know you are now, sir, a gentleman born.
CLOWN: Ay, and have been so any time these four hours.   WT 5.2.126

PANDARUS: What music is this?
SERVANT: I do but partly know, sir: it is music in parts.
PANDARUS: Know you the musicians?
SERVANT: Wholly, sir.
PANDARUS: Who play they to?
SERVANT: To the hearers, sir.
PANDARUS: At whose pleasure, friend?
SERVANT: At mine, sir, and theirs that love music.
PANDARUS: "Command," I mean, friend.
SERVANT: Who shall I command, sir?
PANDARUS: Friend, we understand not one another: I am too courtly and thou too cunning.
                                                                    TRO 3.1.17

HAMLET: Whose grave's this, sir?

FIRST GRAVEDIGGER: Mine, sir.

> [*Sings*] O, a pit of clay for to be made
> For such a guest is meet.

HAMLET: I think it be thine indeed, for thou liest in it.

FIRST GRAVEDIGGER: You lie out on't, sir, and therefore 'tis not yours. For my part, I do not lie in't, and yet it is mine.

HAMLET: Thou dost lie in't, to be in't, and say 'tis thine. 'Tis for the dead, not for the quick; therefore thou liest.

FIRST GRAVEDIGGER: 'Tis a quick lie, sir; 'twill away again from me to you.

HAMLET: What man dost thou dig it for?

FIRST GRAVEDIGGER: For no man, sir.

HAMLET: What woman then?

FIRST GRAVEDIGGER: For none neither.

HAMLET: Who is to be buried in't?

FIRST GRAVEDIGGER: One that was a woman, sir, but, rest her soul, she's dead.

HAMLET: How absolute the knave is! HAM 5.1.117 (F)

Bibliography

Abbot, E. A. 1870. *A Shakespearian Grammar: An Attempt to Illustrate Some of the Differences Between Elizabethan and Modern English.* London: Macmillan.

Adamson, S., L. Hunter, L. Magnusson, A. Thompson, and K. Wales, eds. 2001. *Reading Shakespeare's Dramatic Language: A Guide.* London: Arden Shakespeare.

Allen, Michael J. B. and Kenneth Muir, eds. 1981. *Shakespeare's Plays in Quarto.* Berkeley and Los Angeles: University of California Press.

Allen, Woody. 1982. *Four Films of Woody Allen.* New York: Random House.

Andrews, Robert. 1993. *The Columbia Dictionary of Quotations.* New York: Columbia University.

Anobile, Richard J. 1971. *Why a Duck?* New York: Darien House.

Apple, J. W. 2000. "The 2000 Campaign: New Analysis; Iowa as Definer for Bush." *New York Times* (25 January).

Bartlett, John and Justin Kaplan, eds. 2002. *Bartlett's Familiar Quotations.* 17th ed. Boston: Little, Brown & Company.

Berra, Yogi. 1998. *The Yogi Book: I Really Didn't Say Everything I Said.* New York: Workman Publishing.

Bevington, David, ed. 1997. *The Complete Works of William Shakespeare.* NewYork: Addison Wesley Longman.

Brackett, Lee and Lawrence Kasdan. 1980. *Star Wars: The Empire Strikes Back: The Illustrated Screenplay.* New York: Ballantine Publishing Group.

Brown, Leslie, ed. 1993. *The New Shorter Oxford English Dictionary.* Oxford: Oxford University Press.

Bush, George W. 2001. "A Nation Challenged: President Bush's Address on Terrorism Before a Joint Meeting of Congress." *New York Times*: (21 September).

Cannadine, David, ed. 1989. *Blood, Toil, Tears, and Sweat: The Speeches of Winston Churchill.* Boston: Houghton Mifflin.

Carroll, Lewis. 1962. *Alice's Adventures in Wonderland.* London: Macmillan.

Cohen, Robert. 1991. *Acting in Shakespeare.* Mountain View, California: Mayfield Publishing.

Copeland, Lewis, ed. 1942. *The World's Great Speeches.* New York: Book League of America.

Crystal, David and Ben Crystal. 2002. *Shakespeare's Words.* London: Penguin Books.

Dickens, Charles. 1998. *The Pickwick Papers.* New York: Alfred A. Knopf.

Dickens, Charles. 1993. *A Tale of Two Cities.* New York: Barnes & Noble Books.

Ernst, Bruno. 1976. *The Magic Mirror of M. C. Escher.* New York: Ballantine Books.

Espy, Willard R. 1983. *The Garden of Eloquence.* New York: Harper & Row.

Evans, G. Blakemore. 1974. *The Riverside Shakespeare.* Boston: Houghton Mifflin.

Foner, Philip S. and Yuval Taylor. 1999. *Frederick Douglass: Selected Speeches and Writings.* Chicago: Lawrence Hill Books.

Giedion, Sigfried. 1976. *Space, Time and Architecture.* Cambridge: Harvard University Press.

Godley, A. D. 1961. *Herodotus.* Vol. 4, bks. 8–9. Cambridge: Harvard University Press.

Grothe, Mardy. 1999. *Never Let a Fool Kiss You or a Kiss Fool You.* New York: Viking.

Grothe, Mardy. 2004. *Oxymoronica.* New York: Harper Collins.

Harbage, Alfred, ed. 1969. *William Shakespeare: The Complete Works.* New York: Viking Press.

Harrison, James A. 1965. *The Complete Works of Edgar Allan Poe.* New York: AMS Press.

Hinman, Charlotte. 1968. *The Norton Facsimile: The First Folio of Shakespeare.* New York: W. W. Norton.

Hollander, John. 1981. *Rhyme's Reason.* New Haven: Yale University Press.

Houston, John Porter. 1988. *Shakespearean Sentences: A Study in Style and Syntax.* Baton Rouge: Louisiana State University Press.

Joseph, Bertram. 1987. *Acting Shakespeare.* New York: Theatre Arts Books.

Joseph, Sister Miriam. 1947. *Shakespeare's Use of the Arts of Language.* New York: Columbia University Press.

Kimball, Robert, ed. 1983. *The Complete Lyrics of Cole Porter.* New York: Alfred A. Knopf.

Kliman, Bernice W. and Paul Bertram, eds. 1991. *The Three-Text Hamlet: Parallel Texts of the First and Second Quartos and First Folio.* New York: AMS Press.

Knowles, Elizabeth, ed. 2004. *The Oxford Dictionary of Quotations.* 6th ed. Oxford: Oxford University Press.

Knowles, Elizabeth, ed., with Julia Elliott. 1998. *The Oxford Dictionary of New Words.* Oxford: Oxford University Press.

Kökeritz, Helge. 1953. *Shakespeare's Pronunciation.* New Haven: Yale University Press.

Lanham, Richard A. 1991. *A Handlist of Rhetorical Terms.* Berkeley and Los Angeles: University of California Press.

MacArthur, Brian, ed. 1992. *The Penguin Book of Twentieth Century Speeches.* London: Viking.

Magnusson, Magnus, ed. 1990. *Cambridge Biographical Dictionary.* Cambridge: Cambridge University Press.

Mahood, M. M. 1968. *Shakespeare's Wordplay*. London: Methuen & Company.

McArthur, Tom, ed. 1992. *The Oxford Companion to the English Language*. Oxford: Oxford University Press.

McDonald, Russ. 2001. *Shakespeare and the Arts of Language*. Oxford: Oxford University Press.

McFedries, Paul. 2004. *Word Spy: The Word Lover's Guide to Modern Culture.* New York: Broadway Books.

McQuain, Jeffrey and Stanley Malless. 1998. *Coined by Shakespeare*. Springfield, Massachusetts: Merriam-Webster.

Mish, Frederic C., ed. 2003. *Merriam-Webster's Collegiate Dictionary*. 11th ed. Springfield, Massachusetts: Merriam-Webster.

Morgan, Appleton. 1892. *The Bankside Shakespeare*. Vol. 20, *The Third Part of Henry the Sixth*. New York: Shakespeare Society of New York.

Moston, Doug, ed. 1998. *Mr. William Shakespeare's Comedies, Histories, and Tragedies: A Facsimile of the First Folio, 1623*. New York: Routledge.

Ness, Frederick W. 1969. *The Use of Rhyme in Shakespeare's Plays*. Hamden, Connecticut: Archon Books.

Partridge, Eric. 1990. *Shakespeare's Bawdy*. London: Routledge.

Peacham, Henry. 1954. *The Garden of Eloquence 1593: A Facsimile Reproduction*. Gainesville, Florida: Scholars' Facsimiles & Reprints.

Pei, Mario and Salvatore Ramondino. 1974. *Dictionary of Foreign Terms*. New York: Dell Publishing.

Perrine, Laurence. 1956. *Sound and Sense: An Introduction to Poetry*. New York: Harcourt, Brace & World.

Peterson, Houston, ed. 1954. *A Treasury of the World's Great Speeches*. New York: Simon & Schuster.

Proudfoot, Richard, A. Thompson, and D. S. Kastan, eds. 2002. *The Arden Shakespeare Complete Works*. London: Arden Shakespeare.

Quinn, Arthur. 1982. *Figures of Speech*. Layton, Utah: Gibbs M. Smith.

Ratcliffe, Susan. 2000. *The Oxford Dictionary of Quotations by Subject*. Oxford: Oxford University Press.

Roach, Peter. 1991. *English Phonetics and Phonology: A Practical Course*. Cambridge: Cambridge University Press.

Roberts, Philip Davies. 1986. *How Poetry Works*. Harmondsworth, England: Penguin Books.

Safire, William. 1992. *Lend Me Your Ears: Great Speeches in History*. New York: W. W. Norton.

Schäfer, Jürgen. 1980. *Documentation in the O.E.D.: Shakespeare and Nashe as Test Cases.* Oxford: Clarendon Press.

Schmidt, Alexander. 1971. *Shakespeare Lexicon and Quotation Dictionary.* New York: Dover Publications.

Shapiro, Karl and Robert Beum. 1965. *A Prosody Handbook.* New York: Harper & Row.

Sheridan, Richard Brinsley. 1968. *The Rivals.* London: Oxford University Press.

Smidt, Kristian, ed. 1969. *The Tragedy of King Richard the Third: Parallel Texts of the First Quarto and the First Folio with Variants of the Early Quartos.* Oslo, Norway: Universitetsforlaget.

Sonnino, Lee A. 1968. *A Handbook to Sixteenth-Century Rhetoric.* London: Routledge & Kegan Paul.

Spain, Delbert. 1988. *Shakespeare Sounded Soundly.* Santa Barbara: Capra Press.

Spevack, Marvin. 1973. *The Harvard Concordance to Shakespeare.* Hildesheim, Germany: Georg Olms Verlag.

Stanislavski, Constantin. 1989. *Building a Character.* Trans. Elizabeth Reynolds Hapgood. New York: Routledge/Theater Arts Books.

Taylor, Warren. 1972. *Tudor Figures of Rhetoric.* Whitewater, Wisconsin: Language Press.

Thomas, Charles W. 1892. *The Bankside Shakespeare.* Vol. 19, *The Second Part of Henry the Sixth.* New York: Shakespeare Society of New York.

Torricelli, Robert and Andrew Carroll. 1999. *In Our Own Words: Extraordinary Speeches of the American Century.* New York: Kodansha America.

Warren, Michael. 1989. *The Parallel King Lear, 1608--1623.* Berkeley and Los Angeles: University of California Press.

Weidhorn, Manfred. 1987. *Churchill's Rhetoric and Political Discourse.* Lanham, Maryland: University of Virginia.

Weisberg, Jacob, ed. 2004. *Bushisms: The First Term in His Own Special Words.* New York: Simon & Schuster.

Wells, J. C. and Greta Colson. 1990. *Practical Phonetics.* London: Pitman Publishing

Wells, Stanley, G. Taylor, J. Jowett, and W. Montgomery. 1986. *William Shakespeare: The Complete Works.* Oxford: Clarendon Press.

Wright, George T. 1988. *Shakespeare's Metrical Art.* Berkeley and Los Angeles: University of California Press.

Index of Shakespearean Quotations